Bey
TITHES
&OFFERINGS

Michael L. Webb
Mitchell T. Webb

Editor
Sharon Y. Brown

On Time Publishing
PO Box 1417
Tacoma, WA 98401-1417
Website: www.OnTimePub.com
Email: otp@OnTimePub.com

Order Information: Check your local bookstore. If not available, then call
BookWorld Companies at the following numbers:

United States and Canada	800-444-2524
All other locations	941-758-8094

Beyond Tithes & Offerings

by

Michael L. Webb
Mitchell T. Webb

Published by On Time Publishing.

Unless otherwise indicated, all Scriptures are taken from the New International Version of the Bible.

Verses marked KJV are taken from the King James Version of the Bible.

Verses marked NMV are taken from the New Money Version of the Bible. (Note: The NMV is not a published Bible to our knowledge.)

Cover designed by BookWorld Companies, Sarasota, Florida.

Printed and bound by Malloy Lithographing, Ann Arbor, Michigan. Uncoated free sheet, acid free, 85% recycled fiber (10% of which is post consumer).

Library of Congress Catalog Card Number: 97-92718
ISBN: 0-9660977-7-7

Dedicated to the poor among us.

Acknowledgments

We are here before the higher court of justice and mercy to respond to the charge of writing a book that is dedicated to the poor among us. In the jury we have our consciences bearing witness to the truth, either to condemn us or to defend us. For our opening statement, we would first like to thank God for the motive, means, and opportunity leading up to the charge against us:

We are eternally grateful to Jesus Christ, our Savior, who gave us the command to love our neighbor, thus giving us the motive to write this book. We are eternally grateful to the Holy Spirit whose enabling power and provision gave us the means by which to write this book. We are eternally grateful to our Father in Heaven through whose sovereignty we were afforded the opportunity to write this book.

We are also eternally grateful to the following people who are here as eyewitnesses to the writing of this book:

We thank Rhonda R. Webb (Michael's wife) and Tracy Webb (Mitchell's wife) for their remarkable patience and support during the entire research and writing process. We also thank them for the many sacrifices they made during this time. Our wives were a great source of strength and never-ending encouragement. Whenever we needed a sounding board, they were always there, ready and willing to listen. This book is definitely theirs as much as it is ours.

We thank our mother, Vickie L. Webb, for her unwavering faith. We do not know what we would have done without her constant support, encouragement, and prayers. She provided valuable feedback which helped make the book what it is.

Finally, we thank our editor, Sharon Y. Brown, for her prayers and tireless effort in taking our manuscript to a higher level. Her many constructive suggestions and keen insight contributed heavily to the completion of this book.

How do we plea to the charge of writing a book dedicated to the poor among us? Because of the many contributions made by the eyewitnesses, we are able to enter a plea of guilty!

May God have mercy on us!

Table of Contents
Brief Version

Table of Contents
Chapter Contents

Introduction

Mitchell has a friend whom he has known for several years. This friend has been homeless, in and out of hospitals, on and off drugs and alcohol, is HIV-positive, has overcome a few bouts of pneumonia, and at times is plagued with thoughts of suicide. Further, before they were married, Mitchell's wife, Tracy, was a single mother raising a son. At one point, she needed assistance with her utilities.

These are just two personal examples of people needing help. To see others in need, one needs only to look around at the harsh realities of today: low income families; minimum wage occupations; widespread hunger; children having babies, having to work too young, or being undernourished; unemployment; the elderly and rising medical costs; various sicknesses and diseases; disaster victims and refugees; and the homeless.

How are such problems solved today? Who are the caretakers? The problems are overwhelming and lead many to believe that it is the responsibility of each government to resolve. Solutions in the United States, whether good or bad, include Medicaid, food stamps, Red Cross, child and family services, Social Security, welfare, private charities and other federally funded programs. Regardless of the number of programs or charitable organizations that exist, the poor will always be among us (Deut. 15:11; Matt. 26:11) and in need of basic human necessities.

The problems listed above should, foremost, be the responsibility of the Christian community (Matt. 22:37-40; Rom. 15:25-26; Gal. 2:10; Jas. 2:15-16). Despite Tracy's membership and monetary support of her local church, she was told that her church did not help people with monetary needs. She was actually told to seek another church nearby for that kind of help! And although Mitchell's friend received some assistance from the local church, the church was not able to supply all of his needs.

Christians should help with activities that actually provide for people. Furthermore, the Christian community should put itself in a position to help those in need *in the name of Jesus*. Instead of taking direction from others, Christians should take the lead, organize, and make things happen. This is not to imply that God's people should not help through participation in government or secular programs, but their primary outreach ministry should come from within, as members of the body of Christ.

Regrettably, new covenant teachings are overlooked for old covenant practices, thus limiting both Christian responsibility and freedom due to the church's regulated rules for giving. Christians traditionally give monetary tithes and offerings to the local church. As a result of the rules and obligations of monetary tithing placed upon Christians, some find that they are in the unfortunate position of not being able to fulfill their desire to support those in need.

Ironically, Christians are taught to let the Spirit guide their walk in Christ, yet they are given rules to guide them when it comes to their giving. Goodness and kindness are identifying traits of the fruit of the Spirit. Galatians 5:22-23 makes it clear that the fruit of the Spirit cannot be regulated because against such there is no law. Consequently, the old covenant tithing ritual should not be used to govern Spirit-led giving. Today, it is not possible to fully walk in the Spirit in the area of giving, while following modified rules and regulations of old covenant tithing.

ISSUES ADDRESSED

All too often tithing Christians accuse other Christians of not obeying the whole Bible simply because they do not give tithes and offerings to a local church. Accusations are made, sometimes with love and sometimes with hostility, such as, "Do you believe the whole Bible, or just the parts you want to believe?" Or, "You will be cursed for robbing God of his tithe." What some people fail to realize is that tithes and offerings, as defined in the Bible, have nothing to do with Christian giving. Neither do old covenant practices have anything to do with the call of Christians to love one another. Tithes and offerings have a purpose for those under the law. According to the Bible, however, supporting one another is handled in a completely different way under the new covenant.

The issues addressed in this book do not discourage the church from securing financial support from Christians to support those in need (Acts 2:41-45; 4:32-35; 1 Cor. 16:1-2; 2 Cor. 8:1-11). Indeed, the church requires money to support itself and its outreach ministries, and should encourage its local members to provide accordingly. The issues of interest, however, are those involving the *method* used to collect the money - through monetary tithes and offerings - and its impact on corporate and individual responsibility.

Several areas of interest are covered in relation to true Christian economics. (Christian economics, responsibility, and stewardship, are used interchangeably throughout this book.) More specifically, the issues addressed in this book that adversely affect the responsibility of Christian giving include:

- Christians performing their giving in the 'name' of tithes, offerings and firstfruits
- Fear of a curse as motivation for giving
- Standard based giving of a 10 percent minimum
- The idea that a person's 'righteousness' surpasses that of the Pharisees by out-giving those who are under the law
- Financial legalism and its effect on what should be liberal, voluntary, and Spirit-led giving

GOALS

Based on the issues covered, the authors' goal is that the reader will learn and apply biblical truths surrounding the responsibility of Christian giving. More specifically, it is the authors' intention that every reader will realize: 1) the true calling of Christians, 2) that tithing is not for Christians, 3) that Christians are free from the old covenant laws and therefore are free to give, 4) that Christians should call their giving what it is, and 5) that Christians need to return to the ways of the early church.

The True Calling of Christians

Many people in today's church believe that tithing is the only way to give to the local church and that giving to the local church is the only way to determine their own level of godliness or faith. In fact, some pastors teach that a person's spiritual growth is determined by simply looking at whether or not monetary tithes are given. This ideology distorts the meaning of Christian responsibility. In addition, it prevents church support on a much larger scale since material blessings of all kinds should be shared with one another (1 Jn. 3:16-17).

The true calling of Christians is, in fact, to focus on giving to those in need. "The second is this: 'Love your neighbor as yourself.' There is no commandment greater than these" (Mk. 12:31). "The entire law is summed up in a single command: 'Love your neighbor as yourself' " (Gal. 5:14). "Carry each other's burdens, and in this way you will fulfill the law of Christ" (Gal. 6:2).

This book covers the call to love thy neighbor as it relates to Christian responsibility under the new covenant. In particular, it shows that the priority is, in fact, to give out of one's abundance, to those in need. When giving to the needy, one is actually giving unto Jesus (Matt. 25:35-40).

To Tithe or Not to Tithe

Although the church needs financial support, it should not be at the expense of the needy or sound doctrine. Unfortunately, the problem of careless biblical interpretation has led to traditional giving based on isolated portions of the tithing ritual. Christians in the Bible did not give tithes and offerings (and for those that disagree, this very idea provided additional motivation for writing this book). Furthermore, in the Book of Acts, although Christians did not tithe, there were no needy persons among them. This book explains how to work towards this goal today, and ends the assumption that 'not giving tithes' automatically means 'giving less than 10 percent.' This book points out that some Christians who are not tithers provide much more financial support to the church, and to one another, than people who claim to tithe.

When non-tithing Christians respond to the will of God in meeting the needs of fellow Christians - as well as others - they are actually giving to the church. Not giving to the *local* church every paycheck should not be confused with not giving to the *living* church.

The Freedom to Give

It is necessary to change the mindset concerning the present stipulations put on when and why to give, since these stipulations alter and overshadow the true meaning and motivations of giving (2 Tim. 2:15). The priority of Christian giving today revolves around supporting the local church rather than supporting the needy. This limits the spontaneity of the cheerful giver, and holds the Spirit of Christ within some Christians captive to superficial and unbiblical practices. In order to unleash the charitable heart of the Spirit-led Christian, this book uncovers the hidden truths behind tithing and the consequences of biblical misinterpretation. Once these truths are revealed, the limitations of tithing will be lifted and the grace of giving will be realized.

This book continues by showing that Christians are free from the rules of monetary tithes and offerings. Searching God's word reveals that Christians did not tithe anything in the Bible, and therefore, should not be mandated to tithe anything in today's churches. This book shows how giving is done freely, liberally, and without strings or human standards attached, thus, allowing Christians to mature spiritually. Although done freely, giving is not performed in chaos or without some form of order. In fact, Christian giving is handled responsibly.

This book provides support for non-tithing Christians who believe grace giving is 'mandatory to support the real church,' as opposed to monetary tithes and offerings being 'mandatory to support the four-walled church' (the institutionalized form of church that most Christians attend on a weekly basis). The giving that Christians do for the local church should be the 'desire' of the one giving the gift (2 Cor. 9:7) and not a 'requirement' of the one receiving the gift based on some measurable standard.

Call Your Giving What It Is

The Bible does not refer to Christian giving as a form of tithing, therefore, Christians should not refer to their financial support as tithing either. Instead, the Bible refers to Christian donations as acts of grace or simply, giving (2 Cor. 8:1-7).

If Christians call their giving something other than what it is, someone may apply stipulations where none belong. For example, suppose Christians call their giving something like 'driving' instead. This would seem harmless if everyone knew that 'driving' only meant 'giving.' However, someone will come along and demand Christians to obey speed limits and get regular tune-ups because of their 'driving' habits. The problem here is obvious, in that speed limits and tune-ups relate to driving, but they do not relate to the act of giving. Therefore, Christian giving should *not* be done in the name of 'driving,' otherwise, additional, non-related rules will be applied to their giving.

Similarly, if the Christian community calls its financial support to the church 'tithing,' someone can and will place additional rules on its giving. As a result, some of the rules and regulations associated with tithing are attached to what should be an act of grace. This is what is happening in today's church. For instance, people who want to give as they have decided in their heart to give are now told they will be cursed for not giving 10 percent of their income to the local church - all because their monetary gifts are called 'tithes.'

Applying old covenant rules and regulations to what should be Spirit-led acts, such as giving to the church, is what concerns the authors and furthers the need for writing this book. In order to end the confusion surrounding Christian giving, Christians must first stop calling their giving by the name of tithing and call it what it is - grace giving.

A Return to the Early Church

There is a need to return to the charity work of the early church. In the Book of Acts, for example, Christians held charity events, selling some of their possessions from time to time, and giving the money to anyone in need. When money was collected, it was dispersed accordingly. All of the believers were one in heart and mind, and they shared everything they had. As a result, there were no needy persons among them. Our churches today need to learn from the Christians in the Book of Acts how to work towards the goal of having no needy people among us!

Christians must reverse the trend of traditional giving. They must move towards that of loving thy neighbor if they are to reach the level of grace prevalent throughout the early church. Contrary to the traditional viewpoints of progress in today's society, Christianity is in a position that in order to move forward, it must first move backwards - back to the charity work of the early church.

BEFORE GETTING STARTED

In order to understand certain parts of this book, a distinction must be made among the phrases 'tithes and offerings,' 'supporting the local church,' and 'supporting the needy (our neighbor).' When the book refers to 'supporting the local church,' or 'supporting the needy,' it means doing so in a manner outside of tithes and offerings. For example, this support could be a fund raiser, a food or clothing drive, or a monetary gift or donation. When 'tithes and offerings' are mentioned in this book, it is in keeping with the definitions found in Chapters 3 and 4.

When reading that Christians should not tithe, do not assume that it means to stop giving to the Lord or supporting the local church. These two concepts are completely unrelated. The relationship between tithing and giving to support the tabernacle, the Levites, the church, and our neighbor in need, are all explained in this book. For emphasis, it should be clear from the beginning that supporting the local church is a good work and should continue, but through grace giving, as led by the Holy Spirit, and with the correct priorities in place.

When reading this book, think about whether or not Christians, as a whole, are grieving the Holy Spirit by their actions - or lack thereof. In addition, focus on what the Bible says is pleasing to God. Equally important, keep in mind our fellow brothers and sisters in need. With these particulars in mind, true Christian giving can be seen clearly for what it is, and for what it requires - the support of one another through responsible giving.

1

What Christians Are Taught

Welcome. Let us introduce the well-known Rev. Dr. Pastor Tithe from Tither's Temple. He is here today to teach every one of us all about tithing. The title of his message is, "A Return to Tithing." The Reverend can be long-winded at times, so hang in there.

TODAY'S MESSAGE: A RETURN TO TITHING

"Good morning, saints! Isn't it great to be alive today? Under grace and not under the law? To know that Christ died for our sins? To know that we have an advocate with the Father pleading our case, Jesus Christ, since we accepted Him as our Lord and Savior?

"This morning's message is on a topic in which a vast majority of Christians elect not to participate. I believe that if Christians practice this biblical principle that the Christian community, including the local church, would alleviate the financial difficulties it faces today. I am talking about tithing. That's right, tithing.

"Did you know that many Christians do not tithe? This is why I am led by the Spirit to preach about tithing. I am not talking about tithing because we need the money. However, I must preach about Christian stewardship in relation to finances so that you can act in obedience unto the Lord. The truth must be revealed because if you do not tithe as instructed by the Lord, you are literally closing your only opportunity to that blessing you have been waiting for. These blessings include the job promotion you have been seeking or a physical healing you may need.

"Let us pray. Father, I pray that you prepare the hearts and minds of those listening to your word this day. I pray that those present today will not harden their hearts to what you are trying to convey with this message. For those who do not believe tithing is for today's believer, I pray that you extend your hand and touch their hearts. Reach into their spirit and show them that tithing is not only for today's believer, but it is just the minimum you require from them. Show them through this message, that in order to become a true giver, they first need to release their tithe. Father, I pray that you will have your way today as your word goes forth. In Jesus' name we pray. Amen.

"I am going to jump right into today's message by saying that God tells his people specifically what to tithe, the way to tithe, and where to tithe. First, the definition of a tithe is 10 percent of one's income - of his/her increase. It is that simple. I know this may be a revelation to some, but $1.00 out of $500.00 is not 10 percent. It is not a tithe. This would not even be considered tipping God, which is what most Christians do today. You cannot get into the realm of offerings until you first release your tithe unto the Lord. Keep Leviticus 27:30 in mind concerning the tithe. It clearly states that the tithe is holy unto the Lord.

"For those of you who do not believe tithing is for today's believer and say it is strictly Old Testament law, let me inform you that tithing came before the law. Genesis 14:20 clearly states that Abraham gave tithes of all to Melchizedek - a priest during Abraham's day. This illustrates that tithing was practiced before the law. Cain and Abel also gave tithes and offerings before the law was established. Genesis 4:4 shows that Abel gave the firstlings of his flock and of the fat thereof. In addition, Proverbs 3:9-10 says to honor the Lord with your wealth, with the firstfruits of all your increase. Then will your barns be filled with plenty. If you do not tithe, how do you expect God to fill your barns with plenty?

"Not only did tithes and offerings start before the law, they also continued after the law. Jesus had a clear opportunity to refute tithing when talking to the Pharisees in Matthew 23:23. Jesus states, 'Woe to you, teachers of the law and Pharisees, you hypocrites! You give a tenth of your spices - mint, dill and cummin. But you have neglected the more important matters of the law - justice, mercy and faithfulness. You should have practiced the latter, without neglecting the former.' If tithing is not appropriate for today, don't you think Jesus would have said so right here? But, He says the opposite by saying that we should not neglect tithes.

"Turn with me to Hebrews 7. Here it states that Jesus' priesthood is on the order of Melchizedek. In verse 4, we are to consider how great this man, Melchizedek, was, unto whom Abraham gave the tenth of the spoils. In verse 5 we see that the Levites even had a commandment to collect the tithes from the people. And verse 15 restates that the priesthood of Jesus is on the order of Melchizedek. Now, if these Old Testament priests received tithes from the people, how much more so should Jesus receive tithes from Christians? After all, all of the priests in the past literally died, while Jesus' priesthood lives forever. Please understand that this is not Old Testament teaching, this is New Testament teaching!

"Once you have released your tithe unto the Lord, you can enter into the realm of offerings. An offering is a generous, spontaneous, freewill gift led by the Holy Spirit. Notice in 2 Corinthians 9:7 that, 'Each man should give what he has decided in his heart to give, not reluctantly or under compulsion, for God loves a cheerful giver.' When you give a tithe or offering, you should do so cheerfully. If you are not cheerful when you give, then you are better off not giving at all!

"Remember, God does not need your money. However, when you do not give - and do not give cheerfully - you are only hurting yourself in the area of blessings. These blessings only result from your obedience to the Lord in tithes and offerings. So don't act as if tithes and offerings are the worst part of church service!

"Next, where is the tithe supposed to go? Malachi 3:10 states, 'Bring the whole tithe into the storehouse, that there may be food in my house.' Tithers are responsible for bringing the tithes to the storehouse. This is the local church where you receive your spiritual food or meat. The tithe supports the ministers of the word and furthers the spreading of the gospel. Your offering, however, is Holy Spirit designated. If the Spirit moves you to give to a television ministry or to a missionary fund, then do so voluntarily. That is your offering above and beyond your tithe. But if you do not tithe first, then God will not respect your offering, just as God did not respect Cain's offering in Genesis chapter 4.

"When you tithe, Malachi 3:11 says the Lord will rebuke the devourer for your sake. Here are some signs that the devourer has a foothold in your life: insecurity, fear, anxiety, insomnia, bitterness, and several other situations which time will not permit us to get into today.

"Have you ever known someone who had a lot of money, but has problems sleeping; how about fear of the future; or fear of a possible stock market crash? How many of you are in a relationship where money is the root of all arguments? What about those kids God blessed you with? Do you ever wonder why they are always out of hand? Once again, these are just a few of the signs that the devourer has a foothold in your life. This is clearly a result of not trusting God in the area of finances.

"Withholding tithes and offerings activates biblical principles in your lives. Malachi 3:8-9 states, 'Will a man rob God? Yet you rob me. 'But you ask, 'How do we rob you?' In tithes and offerings. You are under a curse - the whole nation of you - because you are robbing me.' When you keep the tithe for yourself, then this biblical principle is set into motion. The Bible is talking about potential curses for the believer - a biblical principle concerning the non-tither. When you do not tithe, the devourer has no one to stop him from creating havoc in your life. The Lord's hands are tied due to your disobedience. You must start tithing so He can rebuke the devourer for your sake.

"On the other hand, when you release your tithes and offerings unto the Lord, you will be blessed. Malachi 3:10 says the windows of heaven will open up and you will not have room enough to receive the blessings. This is the biblical principle which I choose to activate in my life. The Bible also states in

2 Corinthians 9:6 that if you sow sparingly you shall reap sparingly, but if you sow bountifully you shall reap bountifully. These biblical principles apply to all Christians.

"You cannot say, 'Yes, Lord, I will obey,' in only selected areas of your life and expect everything to be okay. You have to obey all of His commandments. Deuteronomy 8:11 says, 'Be careful that you do not forget the LORD your God, failing to observe his commands, his laws and his decrees that I am giving you this day.' Proverbs 3:1-2 continues with, 'My son, do not forget my teaching, but keep my commands in your heart, for they will prolong your life many years and bring you prosperity.' The key for long life is right here - obey the Lord's commandments at all times.

"Jesus Himself says in Luke 6:46, 'Why do you call me, 'Lord, Lord,' and do not do what I say?' Not only should Christians do what He says, but we need to trust in Him with all our hearts. Proverbs 3:5-6 states, 'Trust in the LORD with all your heart and lean not on your own understanding; in all your ways acknowledge him, and he will make your paths straight.' If you want long life, peace, and the devourer rebuked, then you need to obey the word of God in all areas of your life - including the area of tithes and offerings.

"We as believers need to return to tithing. This will get us back in a right standing with the Lord, get our house back in order, and get a lot of churches out of debt. Turn with me to the book of Nehemiah to see what happened there. In chapter 13:10-12, notice that the Levites and the singers - the ones responsible for the work - lacked necessities because they had not received the proper portions due to them. However, the rulers were gathered together and set in their place. After the tithe was reinstituted, the people started to give again, and the Levites' and the other workers' needs were met. Here it is, in black and white. Church, we need to be set in our place! We need to return to Bible basics and start taking care of the church by giving our tithes and offerings.

"This is not Pastor Tithe talking here. This is the Bible. You can read it for yourself. How many of you believe the whole counsel of God's word? How many of you think I should teach the whole counsel of God's word? Acts 20:27 says, 'For I have not hesitated to proclaim to you the whole will of God.'

I also need to declare unto you today all of God's word. If you believe in God's word and God says do it, that takes care of it. There should not be any debate over what God requires of his people. Do not take my word for it. It's in the Bible.

"Deuteronomy 11:26-28 sums it up. It says God has set forth before you this day a blessing and a curse. A blessing if you obey the commandments of the Lord, and a curse if you do not. I do not know about you, but I want a blessing. Therefore, I am going to obey the commandments of the Lord.

"If you are not a tither, you need to start giving unto the Lord today. Tithing is the minimum God requires from you. It is a great start, but you should strive to become a liberal giver. Luke 6:38 says to give and it shall be given unto you. If you do not give, then you should not expect a return on your non-investment into the kingdom of God. If you do not put money into a bank, do you expect it to earn interest? Of course not. The same applies to giving to the Lord. If you give a little, you will receive a little. If you give a lot, you will receive a lot. If you give nothing, then you will receive nothing.

"As we close out this message today, I would like for everyone to bow your heads and close your eyes. I would like all of the tithers to stand to your feet. To all those who were tithers before hearing God's word this morning, I want to thank the Lord for your obedience in this area. Now, I would like all of you who have decided to start tithing today, or have decided to recommit yourself to tithing today, to also stand to your feet. By standing to your feet, you are telling the Lord, 'I am trusting your word today.' Those of you who are still sitting, I ask that you pray to the Lord concerning whether or not you should give unto Him. Pray whether or not you should be obedient to the Lord in this area of your life. You may also want to read God's word and ask the Lord to speak to your heart, and to show you that this is a necessary good work.

"Let us pray."

Does this message sound familiar? This is what many Christians are taught today. Most tithing Christians are sincere in their efforts to support the church and its activities. However, many Christians are rebuked for giving less than 10 percent, even when this is all that they can afford to give.

These believers in particular are hurt because they are labeled as disobedient although they give from their heart and according to their means.

Following is a list of Bible passages and interpretations used to promote the traditional teachings of monetary tithes and offerings. This is a compilation of what other authors, teachers and pastors, teach concerning tithes and offerings. Next is a section of stand alone statements used by some to emphasize their points. The purpose for listing all the Bible verses and statements is to demonstrate that the authors of this book are exposed to the same teachings as their brothers and sisters in Christ.

RELATED BIBLE PASSAGES

The many Bible passages that some Christians use to validate the monetary tithe and offering practice of today are gathered together in this section. This compilation of passages consists of what the authors have been taught by others regarding tithes and offerings, followed by many misleading interpretations. Although some of the passages and interpretations may sound correct, it is their application to monetary tithing that is incorrect. The passages and related interpretations are not the views of the authors of this book.

Genesis 4:3-4
In the course of time Cain brought some of the fruits of the soil as an offering to the LORD.

But Abel brought fat portions from some of the firstborn of his flock. The LORD looked with favor on Abel and his offering,
- Tithes and offerings began with Cain and Abel.
- Abel brought a portion unto the Lord as if he were tithing.
- Cain's offering was not accepted by the Lord because he did not first release his tithe unto the Lord.

Genesis 14:20

"And blessed be God Most High, who delivered your enemies into your hand." Then Abram gave him a tenth of everything.

- Abraham was a tither.
- Tithing started before the law and should continue.

Genesis 28:20-22

Then Jacob made a vow, saying, "If God will be with me and will watch over me on this journey I am taking and will give me food to eat and clothes to wear

so that I return safely to my father's house, then the LORD will be my God

and this stone that I have set up as a pillar will be God's house, and of all that you give me I will give you a tenth."

- Jacob gave tithes before the law, therefore, Christians should also tithe.

Leviticus 27:30-32

"'A tithe of everything from the land, whether grain from the soil or fruit from the trees, belongs to the LORD; it is holy to the LORD.

If a man redeems any of his tithe, he must add a fifth of the value to it.

The entire tithe of the herd and flock - every tenth animal that passes under the shepherd's rod - will be holy to the LORD.'"

- Ten percent of a person's income is the minimum that should be given unto the Lord.
- Do not redeem or keep the tithe for yourself.
- To keep the tithe instead of offering it to the Lord requires the repayment of the whole amount including a fifth part of its value as a penalty (interest).
- The tithe is a bill owed to God and He expects His payment on time.

Deuteronomy 8:11

Be careful that you do not forget the LORD your God, failing to observe his commands, his laws and his decrees that I am giving you this day.

- God's people need to observe his commands at all times - including tithes and offerings.

Deuteronomy 8:18 KJV

But thou shalt remember the LORD thy God: for it is he that giveth thee power to get wealth, that he may establish his covenant which he sware unto thy fathers, as it is this day.

- Having money is not bad.
- It takes money to establish God's covenant.
- Money is the seed that furthers the kingdom of God.
- God has the right to tell his people how to spend money since he gives everyone the ability to obtain it .

Deuteronomy 11:26-28

See, I am setting before you today a blessing and a curse -

the blessing if you obey the commands of the LORD your God that I am giving you today;

the curse if you disobey the commands of the LORD your God and turn from the way that I command you today by following other gods, which you have not known.

- A curse comes to those who disobey the commands of the Lord - including the area of tithes and offerings.

Deuteronomy 26:1-10

When you have entered the land the LORD your God is giving you as an inheritance and have taken possession of it and settled in it,

take some of the firstfruits of all that you produce from the soil of the land the LORD your God is giving you and put them in a basket. Then go to the place the LORD your God will choose as a dwelling for his Name

and say to the priest in office at the time, ...

...

Then you shall declare before the LORD your God: ...

- When Christians give their tithes, they should tell the story of how God has blessed them.

Deuteronomy 26:14

I have not eaten any of the sacred portion while I was in mourning, nor have I removed any of it while I was unclean, nor have I offered any of it to the dead. I have obeyed the LORD my God; I have done everything you commanded me.

- Do not to eat (keep) the sacred portion (tithe).

1 Samuel 15:22

But Samuel replied: "Does the LORD delight in burnt offerings and sacrifices as much as in obeying the voice of the LORD? To obey is better than sacrifice, and to heed is better than the fat of rams."

- Giving tithes and offerings is a sacrifice for some people, but obedience is better than sacrifice.

Nehemiah 13:10-12

I also learned that the portions assigned to the Levites had not been given to them, and that all the Levites and singers responsible for the service had gone back to their own fields.

So I rebuked the officials and asked them, "Why is the house of God neglected?" Then I called them together and stationed them at their posts.

All Judah brought the tithes of grain, new wine and oil into the storerooms.

- The workers of the church must have their needs met.
- How can the church buy what it needs without money?

Proverbs 3:1-2

My son, do not forget my teaching, but keep my commands in your heart,

for they will prolong your life many years and bring you prosperity.

- Christians need to obey God's commandments, and this includes tithing.

Proverbs 3:5-6
Trust in the LORD with all your heart and lean not on your own understanding;

in all your ways acknowledge him, and he will make your paths straight.
- Do not try to understand God with your own understanding.
- Obey God in all areas of life - including finances and the required tenth that belongs to God.
- If Jesus is not Lord of all, He is not Lord at all.

Proverbs 3:9-10
Honor the LORD with your wealth, with the firstfruits of all your crops;

then your barns will be filled to overflowing, and your vats will brim over with new wine.
- Honor the Lord with your substance or wealth, which is your money.
- The Lord should be given the firstfruits - the first 10 percent - of your income before taxes.
- Pay God first and then pay other bills later.

Proverbs 11:24
One man gives freely, yet gains even more; another withholds unduly, but comes to poverty.
- Do not withhold tithes or offerings from the Lord.

Hosea 4:6
my people are destroyed from lack of knowledge. "Because you have rejected knowledge, I also reject you as my priests; because you have ignored the law of your God, I also will ignore your children."
- Financial troubles may be caused by not adhering to biblical principles regarding finances.
- I (some pastor) want to free you from wrong thinking.

Haggai 1:5-6
Now this is what the LORD Almighty says: "Give careful thought to your ways.

You have planted much, but have harvested little. You eat, but never have enough. You drink, but never have your fill. You put on clothes, but are not warm. You earn wages, only to put them in a purse with holes in it."

- Does it seem as if every time payday comes around that there are holes in your pockets? This is one way the devourer causes havoc in a person's life.

Malachi 3:8-11

"Will a man rob God? Yet you rob me. "But you ask, 'How do we rob you?' "In tithes and offerings.

You are under a curse - the whole nation of you - because you are robbing me.

Bring the whole tithe into the storehouse, that there may be food in my house. Test me in this," says the LORD Almighty, "and see if I will not throw open the floodgates of heaven and pour out so much blessing that you will not have room enough for it.

I will prevent pests from devouring your crops, and the vines in your fields will not cast their fruit," says the LORD Almighty.

- Here is a clear example of believers robbing God.
- God will charge people with embezzlement for robbing him of that which belongs to him.
- This shows that believers can be cursed.
- The word 'food' (meat in KJV) is not so much physical food, but spiritual food - the meat of revelation.
- All tithes go to the storehouse - the local church where you are fed spiritual food.
- Food from Burger King should not be paid for at McDonalds! The tithe should be paid where the spiritual food is received.
- You need to take care of the teacher's physical needs as well as allowing the spiritual meat to go forth.
- Test the Lord to see if He will do what He says.
- The windows of heaven are only open to tithers.
- Lack of tithing may be why the devourer is having his way in some people's lives.
- When people do not tithe, God's hands are tied, and he cannot rebuke the devourer.

Matthew 5:17

"Do not think that I have come to abolish the Law or the Prophets; I have not come to abolish them but to fulfill them."

- The Bible never said Christians were free from the law.
- The law is the word of God, not just the law of Moses.
- God's word in its entirety is an instruction manual.
- The are so many things in the Old Testament that are still worth living by (i.e., circumcision and washing of hands).

Matthew 6:21

For where your treasure is, there your heart will be also.

- What kingdom a person is investing in can be determined by examining his checkbook.
- Money is a measuring device by which one can measure spiritual growth.

Matthew 22:21

... Then he said to them, "Give to Caesar what is Caesar's, and to God what is God's."

- Pay the government what is owed to the government, and pay God what is owed to God.

Matthew 23:23

"Woe to you, teachers of the law and Pharisees, you hypocrites! You give a tenth of your spices - mint, dill and cummin. But you have neglected the more important matters of the law - justice, mercy and faithfulness. You should have practiced the latter, without neglecting the former."

- Jesus did not tell the Pharisees that they were released from their obligation to tithe when he had the opportunity to do so. Therefore, tithing is still required today.
- Christian giving must surpass that of the Pharisees, therefore, Christians must give at least 10 percent.

Mark 12:42-44

But a poor widow came and put in two very small copper coins, worth only a fraction of a penny.

Calling his disciples to him, Jesus said, "I tell you the truth, this poor widow has put more into the treasury than all the others.

They all gave out of their wealth; but she, out of her poverty, put in everything - all she had to live on."

- If a poor widow can give all that she has, then Christians can give the required tenth.

Luke 6:38

"Give, and it will be given to you. A good measure, pressed down, shaken together and running over, will be poured into your lap. For with the measure you use, it will be measured to you."

- This is not a tithing verse since tithing is understood in the New Testament. Therefore, this verse is an offering verse, which is above and beyond a tithe.

Luke 6:46

"Why do you call me, 'Lord, Lord,' and do not do what I say?"

- Do not say, "Yes, Lord," in one area of your life and not in other areas and expect everything to be okay.
- Those who belong to the Lord should be tithers.

Luke 16:10-12

"Whoever can be trusted with very little can also be trusted with much, and whoever is dishonest with very little will also be dishonest with much.

So if you have not been trustworthy in handling worldly wealth, who will trust you with true riches?

And if you have not been trustworthy with someone else's property, who will give you property of your own?"

- Those who cannot be trusted to give God his 10 percent cannot be trusted with a higher paying job.
- People who do not tithe while working at a low paying occupation will not tithe at a higher paying one.

Luke 21:33

Heaven and earth will pass away, but my words will never pass away.

- Jesus did not come to abolish the Law, therefore, tithing is still in effect.

Acts 2:44-45; 4:32-35

All the believers were together and had everything in common.

Selling their possessions and goods, they gave to anyone as he had need.

...

All the believers were one in heart and mind. No one claimed that any of his possessions was his own, but they shared everything they had.

With great power the apostles continued to testify to the resurrection of the Lord Jesus, and much grace was upon them all.

There were no needy persons among them. For from time to time those who owned lands or houses sold them, brought the money from the sales

and put it at the apostles' feet, and it was distributed to anyone as he had need.

- In the early church, all believers not only tithed, but they gave all they could.

Acts 5:1-5

Now a man named Ananias, together with his wife Sapphira, also sold a piece of property.

With his wife's full knowledge he kept back part of the money for himself, but brought the rest and put it at the apostles' feet.

Then Peter said, "Ananias, how is it that Satan has so filled your heart that you have lied to the Holy Spirit and have kept for yourself some of the money you received for the land?

Didn't it belong to you before it was sold? And after it was sold, wasn't the money at your disposal? What made you think of doing such a thing? You have not lied to men but to God."

When Ananias heard this, he fell down and died. And great fear seized all who heard what had happened.
- Keeping that which belongs to the Lord is not only deceiving man, but also lying or tempting the Spirit.
- The couple was not destroyed for what they gave, but for what they withheld. God's people should not withhold their tithe.

Acts 20:27
For I have not hesitated to proclaim to you the whole will of God.
- Should Christians believe the whole Bible, or just parts of the Bible?
- Christians should be taught the whole counsel of God's word.

Acts 20:35
"In everything I did, I showed you that by this kind of hard work we must help the weak, remembering the words the Lord Jesus himself said: 'It is more blessed to give than to receive.'"
- Christians should tithe because it is simply a form of giving.

Romans 10:15
And how can they preach unless they are sent? As it is written, "How beautiful are the feet of those who bring good news!"
- Tithes and offerings are essential for those who preach the gospel - allowing them to go places they are called to preach.
- Spreading the gospel takes money.
- Those who want to share Christ with others will give a lot of money.

1 Corinthians 9:13-14
Don't you know that those who work in the temple get their food from the temple, and those who serve at the altar share in what is offered on the altar?

In the same way, the Lord has commanded that those who preach the gospel should receive their living from the gospel.

- If Christians do not tithe, then how would people in ministry receive support? How would they receive their living from the gospel?

1 Corinthians 10:26
for, "The earth is the Lord's, and everything in it."

- God does not want money - he wants everyone's heart.
- Tithing it is an act of obedience.

2 Corinthians 8:2-4
Out of the most severe trial, their overflowing joy and their extreme poverty welled up in rich generosity.

For I testify that they gave as much as they were able, and even beyond their ability. Entirely on their own,

they urgently pleaded with us for the privilege of sharing in this service to the saints.

- Give even if it hurts financially.
- Those in extreme poverty are still required to give the Lord His 10 percent.

2 Corinthians 9:6-7
Remember this: Whoever sows sparingly will also reap sparingly, and whoever sows generously will also reap generously.

Each man should give what he has decided in his heart to give, not reluctantly or under compulsion, for God loves a cheerful giver.

- These verses have nothing to do with tithing, but are offering verses.
- The tithe is already established, therefore, it does not need mentioning in the New Testament.

Galatians 3:17-18
What I mean is this: The law, introduced 430 years later, does not set aside the covenant previously established by God and thus do away with the promise.

For if the inheritance depends on the law, then it no longer depends on a promise; but God in his grace gave it to Abraham through a promise.
- What Abraham established 430 years before the law, the law cannot set aside. Therefore, tithing cannot be set aside by the law.

1 Timothy 3:15
if I am delayed, you will know how people ought to conduct themselves in God's household, which is the church of the living God, the pillar and foundation of the truth.
- The storehouse mentioned in Malachi 3:10 is the same as the church today - it is God's house.

1 Timothy 5:17
The elders who direct the affairs of the church well are worthy of double honor, especially those whose work is preaching and teaching.
- If Christians do not tithe, then how would preachers and teachers receive double pay?

Hebrews 7:1-28, 8:1-13
... In the one case, the tenth is collected by men who die; but in the other case, by him who is declared to be living.

... And what we have said is even more clear if another priest like Melchizedek appears,

one who has become a priest not on the basis of a regulation as to his ancestry but on the basis of the power of an indestructible life.

For it is declared: "You are a priest forever, in the order of Melchizedek."

... Now there have been many of those priests, since death prevented them from continuing in office;

but because Jesus lives forever, he has a permanent priesthood.

... The point of what we are saying is this: We do have such a high priest, who sat down at the right hand of the throne of the Majesty in heaven,

and who serves in the sanctuary, the true tabernacle set up by the Lord, not by man...
- The priesthood of Jesus is similar to Melchizedek's.
- Even men who died received tithes from the people. How much more so should Jesus receive the tithe today who lives forever?

Hebrews 13:8
Jesus Christ is the same yesterday and today and forever.
- Since Jesus is the same, His word for everybody is the same, which includes tithes and offerings.

James 1:8
he is a double-minded man, unstable in all he does.
- How can someone call himself a Christian and not tithe?

Revelation 3:15-16
I know your deeds, that you are neither cold nor hot. I wish you were either one or the other!

So, because you are lukewarm - neither hot nor cold - I am about to spit you out of my mouth.
- God will not accept average. Christians need to go all out for the Lord, which includes giving tithes and offerings.

SUPPORTING STATEMENTS

Below are some 'stand alone' statements used by many Christians to support the monetary tithe and offering. As with the Bible passages listed above, the statements are the compilation of remarks by tithing Christians. They are not the views of the authors of this book.

- God expected Adam and Eve to tithe.
- The tithe is a tax to God for living on Earth.

- There was darkness for four hundred years between the books of Malachi and Matthew because an entire nation had robbed God of his tithes and offerings.
- It is assumed that the tithe belongs to the Lord. This is why it is not spoken of much in the New Testament.
- Rich people became wealthy because of their obedience in the area of tithing. Therefore, all of the disciples must have tithed since they were wealthy.
- The tithe of your income represents time, work, energy, and talent.
- You can also tithe your time and talents unto the Lord.
- How many people are on God's side, on God's team?
- Some pastors have been mandated from God to teach on the subject of tithing.
- Christians should stop tipping God - like people do at restaurants.
- I tithe more than 10 percent of my income.
- Christians are not true givers until they give above and beyond the tithe.
- Christians cannot enter the realm of offerings until they first release the tithe unto the Lord.
- Offerings are free will, Holy Spirit designated gifts. These include support for building funds, benevolence funds, visiting evangelists, etc., and must come after the tithe has been given.
- God's people are all called to tithe. God wants the tithe.
- If tithing is not for today, then Christians should give more because grace goes beyond the law.
- People who do not tithe do not understand what it means to live under grace.
- Tithing is a principle of spiritual law and it will work for anyone including the unjust.
- Money is used today when tithing because business has changed from a bartering society to a monetary society.
- God instructed every believer to tithe before the law, during the law, and after the law.
- There are over 700 verses in the Bible regarding giving, receiving, and prospering. Therefore, it must be an important subject.

- God tells his people specifically what to tithe, the way to tithe, and where to tithe.
- The first 10 percent of income should be tithed. The second 10 percent should be an offering. Then each person should pay himself, at the least, the third 10 percent.
- The tithe is not given to the poor.
- Sowing the tithe in the wrong place will produce death.
- Whether or not Christians tithe, they are activating biblical principles in their lives.
- If someone is experiencing havoc in his life, it may be due to not tithing.
- Not tithing is disobedience.
- Tithing less than 10 percent means the heart is unregenerated, uncircumcised, and filthy.
- If it seems as if prayers are hitting the ceiling and coming back, it could be due to a lack of tithing.
- The reason preachers always talk about money is because they are trying to release Christians from the god of this world - money (mammon).
- Can a person on welfare rob God? Can a single parent rob God? Yes.
- Christians cannot afford not to tithe.
- I would rather live on the street than not pay God his tithe.
- Tithe is for protection. Offering is for progression.
- The more financial adversity God's people are in, the more they should tithe to get out of that situation.
- When Christians tithe, they are planting a seed into a ministry. When under physical or spiritual attack, they should double their seed (tithe) and prove the devil is a liar.
- Have you tried tithing?
- In order to get off welfare, people must start tithing.
- How are people's finances doing now as a result of not tithing?
- If your way of achieving financial success is not working, then try God's way.
- Christians can have much more if they quit holding on to the 10 percent they should be tithing.

- There must be a standard for giving, and that standard is the tithe.
- Christians need to read the Greek and the Hebrew texts to fully understand the requirement to tithe. The English translation does not explain it well enough.
- Whether or not Christians should tithe is as obvious as whether or not they should tell the truth.
- People who do not give at least 10 percent of their income really want the money for something else - like a new car, extended vacations, or finer clothes.
- If God's word says do it, then that takes care of it.
- Do not take my word for it, it's in the Bible.

The most common arguments in favor of the monetary tithe were presented in this chapter. Numerous passages in the Bible are cited by tithers that have nothing to do with Christian giving. However, this may not be evident right away. The authors encourage reading the message by Rev. Dr. Pastor Tithe - or even this entire chapter - for a second time after completing this book. By the time one has read this book and has searched the word of God, the confusion behind combining acts of Christian giving with the old covenant tithe and offering rituals will be cleared up.

Malachi 3:8-10

"Will a man rob God? Yet you rob me. "But you ask, 'How do we rob you?' "In tithes and offerings.

You are under a curse - the whole nation of you - because you are robbing me.

Bring the whole tithe into the storehouse, that there may be food in my house. Test me in this," says the Lord Almighty, "and see if I will not throw open the floodgate of heaven and pour out so much blessing that you will not have room enough for it."

2

Money and Occupations

Ask Christians why they tithe money and one of many answers include, "The financial situation has changed." What? How many times has someone used this response when explaining why Christians should tithe money? A typical response from the authors would be, "How have the items required for tithing changed?" This kind of conversation makes it necessary to study 'money and occupations in the Bible.'

Many Christians are taught that the way society conducts business has changed over the years - from a bartering society to a monetary society. A bartering society is one in which crops, livestock, and hand made materials, are exchanged for other goods and services. On the other hand, a monetary society is one in which money is used to purchase goods and services. As a result of this so-called change, some say the tithes and offerings required by the Lord have also changed. Consequently, the general consensus is that the only legitimate tithe or offering today is monetary in nature and not as originally described in the Old Testament (discussed in Chapters 3 and 4).

The variations in occupations have increased over time. Many people work in offices or have manual labor jobs other than tilling the ground or raising livestock. A closer look at the Bible reveals that even in biblical times, not all people had occupations related to farming. Nevertheless, Christians are instructed to give 10 percent of their monetary income to the local church, since most people today do not have a farm. They claim the first 10 percent of their income as their firstfruit or their increase.

Research shows that the Bible does not uphold this drastic shift in society. To infer that bartering, as described above, was the *only* form of commerce in the Bible is simply not supported. It is also not true that exchanging money for goods and services is the *only* way of doing business today. This generic classification of business and receiving compensation both during the law and afterwards is cleared up by simply reading the Bible.

Although bartering was performed during biblical times (Job 41:6; Ezek. 27:12-25), this chapter's primary focus is on money exchanges and occupations. This chapter illustrates, first, that goods and services were not always purchased via bartering. Second, there are many occupations in the Bible not related to farming. Third, money was used quite often to pay wages as well as taxes. Furthermore, this chapter shows that money was established and used before the law, incorporated into the written law, and used throughout the Old Testament as a part of everyday living.

The terms tithes, offerings, and firstfruit, are discussed in subsequent chapters. Those chapters, coupled with the present chapter, will allow comparisons to be made between the practice of tithing during biblical times and how tithing is practiced today. Ultimately, Christians will see that when the Lord claimed what is holy unto Him as a tithe, or declared what should be offered as the firstfruit to the priest, He did not include money.

THE MONEY STANDARD

Money has been around since the time of Abraham and possibly much earlier. This section defines a few terms relating to money today. These terms are used throughout this chapter when illustrating that money was indeed used during typical situations in the Bible.

Money: Money is a commodity (something bought or sold) such as gold, silver, or other metals legally established as an exchangeable equivalent of all other commodities; official currency or coins; or assets and property that may be converted into actual currency. Such commodities are used as a measure of their comparative values on the market in exchange for goods, services, or other items defined as commodities.

Standard: The commodity or commodities used to back a monetary system.

Gold/Silver Standard: A monetary standard where the basic unit of currency is equal in value to, and exchangeable for, a specified amount of gold/silver.

Weights: Method of determining consistent amounts of mass.

Barter: To trade goods or services without the exchange of money.

Early in the Old Testament, the weight of certain metals, such as silver and gold, was used in exchange for goods and services. Later in the Old Testament and during the New Testament, coined metals were used as money for the exchange of goods and services. This does not mean that bartering was eventually abolished during biblical times - only that coined money was established and used. Most countries today have some form of coined and paper currency used in exchange for goods and services, in addition to a bartering system.

Pre-Coined Money Era

Before coins were created with specific weights and identifying marks on them, the Old Testament indicates that the weight of certain metals - mainly silver - was used as a (monetary) weight standard in exchange for goods and services. The main unit of currency in Old Testament times was the shekel, which is a unit of weight or measure. There were different standards of weights and measures used, including a heavy standard and a light standard. For the sake of discussion, the word 'standard' refers in general to any standard. The standard was not an exact science during that time, and it even changed from time to time, and from country to country.

The approximate equivalent of the weights of the shekel and today's weight standard are put into the following table. A shekel is equivalent to the weight of 20 gerahs. A gerah is 16 barley grains. (Ex. 30:13; Lev. 27:25; Num. 3:47; 18:16). As seen in the table, one mina equals 60 shekels (Ezek. 45:12) and one talent equals 60 minas.

	Weight (SI)	Weight (U.S.)
1 Talent	60 kg	132 lbs
1 Mina	1 kg	2.2 lbs
1 Shekel	16.667 g	.59 oz

Scales and Balances

There are several places in Scripture indicating that scales were used to weigh metals and other items. The Law of Moses, for example, commands Jews not to use dishonest standards, but instead, to use honest scales and honest weights. (See also Deut. 25:13-15; Job 6:2-3; 31:6; Psa. 62:9; Prov. 11:1; 16:11; 20:10, 23; Isa. 40:12; 46:6; and Jer. 32:10).

Leviticus 19:35-36

Do not use dishonest standards when measuring length, weight or quantity.

Use honest scales and honest weights, an honest ephah and an honest hin. I am the LORD your God, who brought you out of Egypt.

Historians who have studied Old Testament money standards believe that scales or balances consisted of two metal pans suspended from a hand-held beam. Discoveries of

Egyptian items, as well as fragments of bronze beams, chains, and pans found from ancient sites in Palestine, strongly indicate the use of scales or balances.

The Weight Standard

In order for money to be an exchangeable equivalent for other commodities in today's society, there must be a standard in place. Likewise, the Old Testament also had a set standard both prior to the law and during the law. A reference to a pre-law standard is seen in Genesis.

Genesis 23:16
..., according to the weight current among the merchants.

Merchants in biblical times traveled from place to place conducting business. In this verse, Abraham was purchasing a piece of land, paying a price of four hundred shekels of silver *according to the* standard *weight current among the merchants.* On the other hand, according to the written law, the standard weight for metals was *set according to the sanctuary shekel* (See also Ex. 30:13, 24; 38:24-26; Lev. 5:15; Num. 7:13-86; 18:16).

Leviticus 27:25
Every value is to be set according to the sanctuary shekel, ...

In addition, 2 Samuel 14:26 shows that the weight standard for the shekel was set by the royal standard. No matter which era in history is studied, there existed a standard for the weight of precious metals.

Coined Money Era

In the United States today, coined money (i.e., penny, nickel, dime and quarter) is used for certain transactions. There are also several coined metals used as money throughout the Bible. Old Testament historians believe coins made trade simpler and more efficient. Merchants found that they no longer had to weigh the shekel because a royal stamp verified its weight. Below are a few examples of coined money used throughout biblical times.

Daric: One of the first biblical signs of coined money with a description on it was the 'daric' or 'dram.' The daric was at one time the principal gold coin and weighed 8.4 grams. See 1 Chronicles 29:7 and Ezra 8:27 for references of the daric.

Denarius: The principal coin used by the Roman empire was a silver coin called the 'denarius.' It was used to pay taxes (Matt. 22:19), and also appears to be equivalent to one day's wages for work (Matt. 20:2).

Mite: Another coin is the familiar widow's 'mite' (Mark 12:42) and was a small brass coin worth about 1/5 of a cent ('cent' is a United States coin worth 1/100 of a dollar).

MONEY EXCHANGES IN THE BIBLE

Some Christians believe they should give 10 percent of their money as a tithe because they claim that business transactions have changed from a bartering society to a monetary society. To demonstrate the problem behind the 'bartering only society' school of thought, commerce in the Bible involving the exchange of money for goods and services is discussed in this section.

Illustrations that monetary transactions were used throughout the entire Bible are provided. They are sectioned out as follows according to their appearance in the Bible: pre-law; included in the writing of the law; throughout the remaining Old Testament books; during Jesus' ministry on Earth; and after the earthly ministry of Jesus.

Before the Written Law

One of the well-known figures of the Old Testament is Abraham, and many already know that he was wealthy (Gen. 13:2). Part of his wealth consisted of precious metals, as well as livestock and servants (Gen. 24:34-35).

In the following passage, Abraham used money (shekels of silver) to purchase some land so he could bury his wife, Sarah. Since coined money was not yet established, notice that the silver was weighed. The weight determined how much silver to use for the purchase, and the standard at the time was *the weight current among the merchants.*

Genesis 23:15-16

"Listen to me, my lord; the land is worth four hundred shekels of silver, but what is that between me and you? Bury your dead."

Abraham agreed to Ephron's terms and weighed out for him the price he had named in the hearing of the Hittites: four hundred shekels of silver, according to the weight current among the merchants.

Other pre-law monetary exchanges for goods and services are also in the book of Genesis. Jacob purchased some land for one hundred pieces of silver (Gen. 33:19), and Genesis chapter 20 illustrates a case where Abraham and his wife used money to handle a particular situation (Gen. 20:16). In addition, Joseph was sold by his brothers to the Ishmaelites for twenty shekels of silver (Gen. 37:28). Finally, Joseph's brothers went to Egypt to buy food with silver during a famine (Gen. 42).

Included in the Written Law

Money was also used throughout the law. For example, God's people gave money to support the tabernacle (Ex. 30:14-16; 38:24-31). There are many other examples that illustrate money's place within the written law, thus indicating that money was indeed a part of everyday life. Exodus 35 provides such an example.

Exodus 35:5, 21-22

*From what you have, take an offering for the LORD.
Everyone who is willing is to bring to the LORD an offering
of gold, silver and bronze;*

...

*and everyone who was willing and whose heart
moved him came and brought an offering to the LORD for
the work on the Tent of Meeting, for all its service, and for
the sacred garments.*

*All who were willing, men and women alike, came and
brought gold jewelry of all kinds: brooches, earrings, rings
and ornaments. They all presented their gold as a wave
offering to the LORD.*

Under the law, money was sometimes used as part of a
penalty. For example, in Deuteronomy 22:28-29 it states that
if a man met a virgin who was not pledged to be married, raped
her and they were discovered, in addition to marrying her, he
was to pay the girl's father fifty shekels of silver. Leviticus 5:15
is another example of a monetary penalty. In sinning against
any of the Lord's holy items, the guilty person was not only to
bring a ram for the sin offering, but he was also required to pay
a certain amount in silver.

Throughout the Remaining Old Testament

Bartering was performed throughout the Old Testament as
illustrated in Job 41:6 and Ezekiel 27:12-25. The focus of this
chapter is on money, therefore, this subsection only demonstrates that money was used to purchase goods and services.
One of many examples is in 2 Samuel 24:21-24, when King
David wanted to buy something from Araunah, but Araunah
was reluctant to sell it to him. Araunah wanted to simply give
it to David, but David insisted on paying for it.

2 Samuel 24:24

*But the king replied to Araunah, "No, I insist on paying
you for it. I will not sacrifice to the LORD my God burnt*

offerings that cost me nothing." So David bought the threshing floor and the oxen and paid fifty shekels of silver for them.

This verse shows that in order to provide the correct burnt offering, one could 'buy' it, but was not allowed to offer actual money as a replacement for it. This concept is covered thoroughly in Chapters 3 and 4.

There are several other verses of Scripture wherein money was used to buy commodities. Solomon had horses and a chariot imported from Egypt. Each horse cost 150 shekels of silver and the chariot cost 600 shekels of silver (1 Ki. 10:28-29; 2 Chr. 1:16-17). In 2 Kings 7:1, flour sold for a shekel.

Purchasing land, like Abraham did before the law, was also paid for in shekels of silver or gold in later times. In 1 Chronicles 21:25, a piece of land cost David 600 shekels of gold, and in 1 Kings 16:24, Omri bought the hill of Samaria for two talents of silver. Notice the similarity of Jeremiah's land acquisition below with that of buying property or a house in today's society.

Jeremiah 32:9-11

so I bought the field at Anathoth from my cousin Hanamel and weighed out for him seventeen shekels of silver.

I signed and sealed the deed, had it witnessed, and weighed out the silver on the scales.

I took the deed of purchase - the sealed copy containing the terms and conditions, as well as the unsealed copy -

Jeremiah used money to pay for land, and money today is used to pay for land and houses. Jeremiah signed and sealed a deed, and home owners today also sign a Deed of Trust. His deed contained terms and conditions, and today's deeds also contain terms and conditions. It appears that real estate purchases have not changed over the past few thousand years!

Everyone probably knows that silver and gold, when invested, yield a profit over time. In addition, Psalms 15:5 talks about lending money without interest. Proverbs 3:13-14 states, "Blessed is the man who finds wisdom, the man who gains understanding, for she is more profitable than silver and yields better returns than gold." This passage from Proverbs would not make sense if money, profit, and interest, were not already understood in biblical times. This further substantiates the commonplace of money throughout the Old Testament.

During Jesus' Ministry on Earth

The use of money continued during the time of Jesus' ministry in the flesh. Some of the many examples include the widow who gave an offering of two small copper coins (Mk. 12:42-44); Jesus sending his disciples out two by two, instructing them not to take any money with them on their journey (Mk. 6:7-10); and Jesus declaring in Matthew 6:24, "You cannot serve both God and Money."

Parables also show that money was a part of society as evidenced by the first four books of the New Testament. Examples from the book of Matthew are provided here. One parable is told in Matthew 18:23-34, wherein a servant owed a king ten thousand talents. Another parable, in Matthew 25:15-18, involves servants who received varying amounts of talents. One received five talents, another received two, and a third received one. In both parables, the talents spoken of refer to money because the person who received one talent "hid his master's money" (Matt. 25:18). Whereas he could have at least put the money into a bank and earned interest (Matt. 25:27).

The authors are not implying that the word 'talent' cannot be used symbolically. The word talent is, in fact, used symbolically by some to mean special abilities such as singing. But in order to understand these parables, one must know the actual meaning of the word talent in order for the parables to make sense.

Money was so prevalent during the time of Jesus' ministry in the flesh that there were even money changers. The book of Mark shows that money changers were present in the temple areas when Jesus overturned the tables and benches.

Mark 11:15-17

On reaching Jerusalem, Jesus entered the temple area and began driving out those who were buying and selling there. He overturned the tables of the moneychangers and the benches of those selling doves,

and would not allow anyone to carry merchandise through the temple courts.

And as he taught them, he said, "Is it not written: " 'My house will be called a house of prayer for all nations' ? But you have made it 'a den of robbers.' "

Money changers were equivalent to bankers (see Matt. 25:27) and exchanged certain forms of currency for local shekels, adding a fee of four to eight percent. Some also believe moneychangers played a role in transactions involving sacrificial animals. The passage above shows an example of corruption in the temple areas - *"You have made it 'a den of robbers.' "*

Just as it does today, the greed of money encouraged lies, murders, and other evil works. A well-known example of money used to this end was the betrayal of Jesus. As a part of God's plan of reconciliation, money played a critical role in the crucifixion of Jesus.

Jesus and His disciples used money as illustrated in John 13:29, wherein Judas was in charge of the money. Judas, like the other disciples, was one of the closest people to Jesus. He was privy to the teachings and fellowship of Jesus that the average person was not. Yet, his love for money was stronger than his love for Jesus.

During the end of Jesus' ministry on Earth, the chief priests and elders were eager to get their hands on Jesus to kill Him. They conspired with Judas to capture Jesus for thirty silver coins. (For individuals who are into prophecies, look up Zechariah 11:12-13. Some say the price of thirty pieces of silver was actually prophesied in that passage.)

Matthew 26:14-15

Then one of the Twelve - the one called Judas Iscariot - went to the chief priests

*and asked, "What are you willing to give me if I hand
him over to you?" So they counted out for him thirty silver
coins.*

Sometime later, Judas found the opportunity to hand
Jesus over to the authorities. What Judas did is an example
of exchanging money for goods - in this case, Jesus.
Subsequently, in Matthew chapter 27, the deadly results of the
greed for money is evident. Judas returned the thirty silver
coins to the chief priests and the elders and committed suicide
by hanging himself (Matt. 27:3-7). Although they used the
money to kill Jesus, these highly religious people - chief priests
and elders - said it was against the law to put blood money
into the treasury. So they bought land for a burial place
instead.

After Jesus' Ministry on Earth

These priests and elders were not finished yet. They
accomplished one thing so far with the power that money has
over people - the death and burial of Jesus. However, they did
not anticipate Jesus rising from the dead. Observe the
conspiracy of the priests and elders to dispute the resurrection
of Jesus.

Matthew 28:12-13
*When the chief priests had met with the elders and
devised a plan, they gave the soldiers a large sum of
money,*
*telling them, "You are to say, 'His disciples came
during the night and stole him away while we were
asleep.' "*

The chief priests and elders gave the soldiers a *large sum of
money* to lie about what actually happened. It is obvious that
the priests and elders knew the value of money even back
then.

After the resurrection of Jesus, monetary transactions in
the Bible continued, and even mirror today's society. Acts
chapter 8 shows an example of trying to purchase a gift of God.

One day Peter and John placed their hands on some people so they might receive the Holy Spirit. Simon saw what happened and offered to pay Peter and John for the gift so that he, too, could lay hands on people and have them receive the Spirit.

Acts 8:17-20
Then Peter and John placed their hands on them, and they received the Holy Spirit.
When Simon saw that the Spirit was given at the laying on of the apostles' hands, he offered them money
and said, "Give me also this ability so that everyone on whom I lay my hands may receive the Holy Spirit."
Peter answered: "May your money perish with you, because you thought you could buy the gift of God with money!

People also begged for money in Bible days just like some are forced to do today. In Acts 3:1-6, Peter and John were about to enter the temple courts when a crippled man asked them for money. Some say the poor were required to position themselves at certain locations in order that others may have the opportunity to give to them. Therefore, this man was placed at the entrance of the temple courts every day to receive money.

Money was also used for good works. An example of this occurs in the Book of Acts where provisions for the needy were allocated from the sales of land and houses (Acts 4:34-35). "There were no needy persons among them. From time to time those who owned lands or houses sold them, brought the money from the sales and put it at the apostles' feet, and it was distributed to anyone as he had need." This type of giving displayed in the early church is covered in Chapter 9.

MONEY USED TO PAY TAXES

Taxes have been collected throughout the Bible and have been in the form of produce, livestock, and money. Depending on the translation of the Bible, the word 'tax' appears differently, either as tribute, levy, or duty. Numbers 31:26-41 provides an example of a tribute unto the Lord that included items other than money. The focus of this section, however, is to provide Bible verses illustrating that money was commonly used to pay taxes.

A tax is defined as a contribution for government support, or as a fee assessed to members of an organization to meet its expenses. Both kinds of taxes were used throughout the Bible and examples of each are provided. Money was used when appropriate to pay taxes and, at times, money, was the only option for payment.

Old Testament Taxes

There are several places throughout the Old Testament where money was used to pay taxes. The first example shows the children of Israel being taxed to support the tabernacle.

Exodus 30:14-16

"All who cross over, those twenty years old or more, are to give an offering to the LORD.

The rich are not to give more than a half shekel and the poor are not to give less when you make the offering to the LORD to atone for your lives.

Receive the atonement money from the Israelites and use it for the service of the Tent of Meeting. It will be a memorial for the Israelites before the LORD, making atonement for your lives."

This tax is defined as a fee put on its members to support an organization. Some teach this as being the temple tax of Matthew 17:24-27 and is discussed in the next subsection (See also 2 Chr. 24:6-9).

The next example illustrates the use of a monetary tax on land needed to support a government - similar to property taxes of today.

2 Kings 23:33, 35

Pharaoh Neco put him in chains at Riblah in the land of Hamath so that he might not reign in Jerusalem, and he imposed on Judah a levy of a hundred talents of silver and a talent of gold.

...

Jehoiakim paid Pharaoh Neco the silver and gold he demanded. In order to do so, he taxed the land and exacted the silver and gold from the people of the land according to their assessments.

Notice here, like in the previous example, that the levy imposed on the people involved money - *a hundred talents of silver and a talent of gold* (see also 2 Chr. 36:3).

Ezra 4:12-13 shows that a king was about to lose his revenues since the children of Israel were going back to Jerusalem to rebuild the city. The king was informed that if this happened, he would no longer receive taxes, tribute, or duty. (See also Ezra 7:24). In addition, some people can probably relate to Nehemiah 5:4, wherein some people, "had to borrow money to pay the king's tax."

Today, if taxes are not paid on time, then everyone can expect a collection agency to try to acquire it. This also happened in the Old Testament. Daniel 11:20 reads, "His successor will send out a tax collector to maintain the royal splendor." There were tax collectors then, and there are tax collectors now. Some things just do not change when money is involved!

New Testament Taxes

Tax collectors continued their line of work in the New Testament (Matt. 5:46; 9:10-11; 21:31-32; Mk. 2:15; Lk. 18:10-14), and they were often in the company of Jesus. Matthew chapter 17 contains a well-known example of paying tax collectors with money. Some believe Matthew chapter 17 is referring to the atonement money of Exodus 30:11-16 and Exodus 38:24-26. Notice that coined money was used to pay this tax.

Matthew 17:24-27

*After Jesus and his disciples arrived in Capernaum,
the collectors of the two-drachma tax came to Peter and
asked, "Doesn't your teacher pay the temple tax?"*

"Yes, he does," he replied. ...

...

*..., go to the lake and throw out your line. Take the
first fish you catch; open its mouth and you will find a
four-drachma coin. Take it and give it to them for my tax
and yours."*

Another well-known example of a monetary tax is in
Matthew 22 addressing whether or not to pay taxes to Caesar.
Notice again that coined money was used to pay this tax.

Matthew 22:17-21

*Tell us then, what is your opinion? Is it right to pay
taxes to Caesar or not?"*

*But Jesus, knowing their evil intent, said, "You
hypocrites, why are you trying to trap me?*

*Show me the coin used for paying the tax." They
brought him a denarius,*

*and he asked them, "Whose portrait is this? And
whose inscription?"*

*"Caesar's," they replied. Then he said to them, "Give
to Caesar what is Caesar's, and to God what is God's."*

Many people tend to focus on verse 21, *"Give to Caesar
what is Caesar's, and to God what is God's."* What Christians
usually miss in this example, as well as in the previous
example, is that money was used. In this example, Jesus says,
"Show me the coin used for paying the tax." The previous tax
was for the temple, which is similar to a fee used to support an
organization. This tax, on the other hand, was for Caesar and
is similar to a government tax.

In most societies, money is used to obtain the finer things
in life, as well as basic necessities. Because of the benefits of
having money, it is also used by the church for tithing today.
In verse 21 above, however, Caesar claimed ownership of the
denarius by having his inscription and portrait put on it.

Today's currency is also owned by someone as indicated by the markings on it. So if Jesus was here in the flesh and took a look at the money used today, He would probably tell the church what He said in the passage above. "Give to the owner what is the owner's, and to God what is God's."

BIBLICAL OCCUPATIONS

Proverbs 3:9 (KJV) is a very familiar verse of Scripture: "Honour the LORD with thy substance, and with the firstfruits of all thine increase." Many are taught that the money earned from their occupations is their firstfruit since there has been a change in occupations from biblical times to now; most people do not raise crops or livestock.

The focus of this section is to verify whether or not this occupational change in society has really taken place - and if so, when. Before listing the various jobs and occupations of biblical times, a couple of definitions are given.

Job: An action or task that needs completing. Also, something that is done regularly for payment.

Occupation: An activity serving as one's profession.

A person's occupation may consist of one or more jobs or tasks. Many people, however, interchange the words 'job' and 'occupation.'

The Requirement of Work

The Bible shows that work is normal and expected. The origin of work goes all the way back to Genesis before the fall - before Adam and Eve ate the forbidden fruit.

Genesis 2:15
The LORD God took the man and put him in the Garden of Eden to work it and take care of it.

Man was put in the Garden *to work it and take care of it*. This was carried on even after eating the forbidden fruit (Gen. 3:23). Cain and Abel continued this form of work in Genesis chapter 4. Abel was a shepherd and Cain worked the soil. Notice that the original occupation was to take care of the different plants and crops inside the garden first, then outside the garden. Cain followed suit while Abel functioned in the second occupation on record - a shepherd.

As the population increased, so did the number of varying occupations. This is evident in Genesis 11:1-5, where some men decided to build a city with a tower that reaches to heaven.

Genesis 11:3-5

They said to each other, "Come, let's make bricks and bake them thoroughly." They used brick instead of stone, and tar for mortar.

Then they said, "Come, let us build ourselves a city, with a tower that reaches to the heavens, so that we may make a name for ourselves and not be scattered over the face of the whole earth."

But the LORD came down to see the city and the tower that the men were building.

These verses indicate that not all occupations were related to farming. If all people worked as farmers or shepherds, then how could they build this tower? Instead, they learned how to make bricks and use tar for mortar in order to build this tower. In the New Testament, work is also commanded for people who are idle.

2 Thessalonians 3:10-12

For even when we were with you, we gave you this rule: "If a man will not work, he shall not eat."

We hear that some among you are idle. They are not busy; they are busybodies.

Such people we command and urge in the Lord Jesus Christ to settle down and earn the bread they eat.

List of Occupations

Several occupations located throughout the Bible are listed here and are those outside of farming or being a shepherd.

Arts and Crafts: Ex. 31:3-5; 35:31-35; 2 Ki. 16:10

Baker: Gen. 40:1-2; Jer. 37:21; Hos. 7:4

Builder: 2 Ki. 12:11; 22:6; Ezra 3:10; Matt. 21:42; Heb. 3:3; 1 Pet. 2:7

Carpenter: 2 Sam. 5:11; 2 Ki. 12:11; 2 Chr. 24:12; Ezra 3:7; Isa. 44:13; Matt. 13:55; Mk. 6:3

Cook: 1 Sam. 8:13; 9:23-24

Doorkeeper: 2 Ki. 22:4; 25:18; 1 Chr. 15:23-24; Jer. 35:4

Fisherman: Isa. 19:8; Jer. 16:16; Ezek. 47:10; Matt. 4:18; 13:48; Lk. 5:2

Foreman: Ruth 2:5-6; 1 Ki. 5:16; 2 Chr. 2:2, 18; Matt. 20:8

Fortune Teller: Deut. 13:1-3; Acts 16:16

Goldsmith: Neh. 3:8, 31-32; Isa. 40:19; 41:7; 46:6; Jer. 10:9, 14; 51:17

Hunter: Gen. 10:9; 25:27; Jer. 16:16

Innkeeper: Lk. 10:35

Mason - Stonemason: 2 Sam. 5:11; 2 Ki. 12:12; 1 Chr. 22:15; 2 Chr. 24:12

Merchant - Trader: Gen. 23:16; 37:28; 1 Ki. 10:15; Neh. 13:20; Ezek. 27:3, 22-23; Matt. 13:45

Musician: 1 Ki. 10:12; 1 Chr. 6:33; 9:33; 2 Chr. 5:12

Perfume Maker: Ex. 30:25, 33, 35; 37:29; 1 Sam. 8:13; Neh. 3:8

Prostitute: Gen. 38:15-24; Lev. 21:14; Josh. 6:17, 25; Judg. 11:1; 16:1; Jer. 3:1; Joel 3:3; Matt. 21:31-32; Lk. 15:30; 1 Cor. 6:15-16; Jas. 2:25

Scribe - Teacher of the law: 1 Chr. 2:55; 1 Chr. 24:6; 27:32; Neh. 8:1; 13:13; Jer. 36:26; Matt. 2:4; Mk. 2:6; Acts 4:5

Silversmith: Judg. 17:4; Prov. 25:4; Acts 19:24

Spinning - Weaving: Ex. 28:3; 35:25-26; 2 Ki. 23:7; Prov. 31:19; Acts 9:39

Stonecutter: 1 Ki. 5:15; 2 Ki. 12:12; 1 Chr. 22:15

Supervisor: 2 Chr. 31:13; 34:17
Tanner: Num. 31:20; Acts 9:43; 10:6, 32
Tax Collector: Dan. 11:20; Matt. 10:3; Lk. 5:27

Most Christians agree that Old Testament tithes and firstfruits consist of produce and livestock. Can Christians assume that people with the occupations listed above received crops and livestock as wages so they could participate in giving tithes and firstfruits? If not, then did these workers also have farming related jobs as second occupations so they could participate in these rituals?

If people do not raise crops or livestock themselves, then they cannot partake in giving of the firstfruit since they do not have the legitimate substance. There is no biblical indication that the firstfruit can be purchased. Likewise, the workers of the occupations above cannot tithe the required items for the same reason. The required items for tithing are listed in Chapter 4, "Tithing Defined," and the required items of the firstfruit are listed in Chapter 5, "Firstfruit Defined."

From the list of occupations above, it is apparent there were many occupations throughout the Bible as far back as Genesis. The idea of occupations changing over time does not seem valid, since all of the occupations listed above exist in today's society. However, there may actually be a greater variety of occupations today due to technological advances.

COMPENSATION IN THE BIBLE

Now that the various occupations have been listed, it is time to investigate monetary compensation. Not all people were paid with money. For example, Jacob worked a total of fourteen years and his wages included two women - Leah and Rachel (Gen. 29:15-30). He also received sheep and goats for his labor (Gen. 30:32). The focus of this section is, however, on the role of money in paying wages.

One of the main questions answered by this book is, "If people in the Old Testament were paid monetary wages, were they required to tithe from their money like Christians are told they are required to do today?" Chapter 4, "Tithing Defined," provides this answer. However, this section brings focus on the fact that people were, indeed, paid monetary wages regularly.

Old Testament Wages

There are several instances where money was used to pay wages in the Old Testament. Notice in Second Kings that the workers who repaired the temple were paid with money.

2 Kings 22:4-7
"Go up to Hilkiah the high priest and have him get ready the money that has been brought into the temple of the LORD, which the doorkeepers have collected from the people.

Have them entrust it to the men appointed to supervise the work on the temple. And have these men pay the workers who repair the temple of the LORD -

the carpenters, the builders and the masons. Also have them purchase timber and dressed stone to repair the temple.

But they need not account for the money entrusted to them, because they are acting faithfully."

The people here that received monetary wages include carpenters, builders and masons. There were probably other crafts involved since the temple had many different aspects to it like that of modern day buildings. See also 2 Chronicles 34:8-13, 2 Kings 12:13-15 and Ezra 3:6-7.

Another good example is in First Samuel, where money was paid to sharpen tools.

1 Samuel 13:19-21
Not a blacksmith could be found in the whole land of Israel, because the Philistines had said, "Otherwise the Hebrews will make swords or spears!"

So all Israel went down to the Philistines to have their plowshares, mattocks, axes and sickles sharpened.

*The price was two thirds of a shekel for sharpening
plowshares and mattocks, and a third of a shekel for
sharpening forks and axes and for repointing goads.*

Further examples of monetary payments in the Old
Testament include the seduction of Delilah and the hiring of
mercenaries or 'hit-men.' First, Judges 16:4-6 is an account of
Delilah receiving eleven hundred shekels of silver by each ruler
of the Philistines! What did she do to earn this? All she did
was obtain the secret to Samson's strength so they could
overpower him. Second, Judges 9:3-5 is an account of men
that were hired to partake in the murdering of seventy people
- all of whom were brothers (see also 2 Sam. 10:6 and Jer.
46:21).

New Testament Wages

A couple of parables that Jesus told are used to illustrate
the use of monetary wages during His time on Earth. Someone
may argue that parables are simply stories, but this is not the
case. Many parables contained common events of the day to
explain spiritual events or to symbolically describe other actual
events. If workers did not earn money from their labor, then
parables containing such examples would be confusing.

Matthew 20:1-2
*"For the kingdom of heaven is like a landowner who
went out early in the morning to hire men to work in his
vineyard.*
*He agreed to pay them a denarius for the day and
sent them into his vineyard."*

If it was not common to pay laborers money for a day's
work, then should one also assume it was not common for a
landowner to go out early in the morning to hire workers? It
would be confusing to have a parable contain realistic events
followed by unrealistic events. In any case, the denarius - a
Roman silver coin - was used in this parable to compensate the
workers.

The Good Samaritan is another parable. When the Samaritan found a man beaten and robbed, he took this man to an inn. Not only did the Samaritan bandage this man's wounds, but he took care of the man's expenses with money.

Luke 10:34-35
He went to him and bandaged his wounds, pouring on oil and wine. Then he put the man on his own donkey, took him to an inn and took care of him.

The next day he took out two silver coins and gave them to the innkeeper. 'Look after him,' he said, 'and when I return, I will reimburse you for any extra expense you may have.'

The Samaritan used two silver coins in exchange for a service. Again, if it was not common for an innkeeper to accept money, then this parable would confuse the people to whom Jesus was talking. A similar passage dealing with money is the parable of the workers in the vineyard in Matthew 20:8-10.

Yet another illustration of monetary wages is found in the Book of Acts. A great deal of money was made in this occupation and it is still being performed today. See also James 4:13.

Acts 16:16
Once when we were going to the place of prayer, we were met by a slave girl who had a spirit by which she predicted the future. She earned a great deal of money for her owners by fortune-telling.

Has society changed from a bartering system to a monetary system? The Bible clearly indicates that this is not the case. The Bible also reveals that a monetary standard has existed since the time of Abraham, and that money was used in exchange for goods and services. The Bible shows that money exchanges for goods and services took place before the law, was an integral part in the writing of the law, and continued throughout the Old and New Testaments.

Have jobs and occupations changed over time? Once again, the Bible clearly indicates that this is not the case. The Bible demonstrates that not all people had work relating to that of a farmer. There were varying occupations, and many of them were compensated through monetary wages, as is the case today.

Money has always been an integral part of societies throughout the world and throughout time. All biblical references from this study indicate business as usual.

2 Kings 22:4-7

"Go up to Hilkiah the high priest and have him get ready the money that has been brought into the temple of the LORD, which the doorkeepers have collected from the people.

Have them entrust it to the men appointed to supervise the work on the temple. And have these men pay the workers who repair the temple of the LORD

- the carpenters, the builders and the masons. Also have them purchase timber and dressed stone to repair the temple.

But they need not account for the money entrusted to them, because they are acting faithfully"

3

Offerings Defined

Many believers are taught and often pass along a new way to give offerings. They are taught to give 'money above and beyond their monetary tithe' in order to become true givers; this additional money is called an 'offering.' Many believers are also convinced that they can be cursed if this method of giving is not performed. This is clearly what happens when Christians call their gifts to the church something other than acts of grace.

This chapter, as well as the following two chapters, provide definitions that illustrate why the modern day practice of tithes and *offerings* should be questioned. As mentioned in the Introduction Chapter, the intention is not to question whether or not Christians should support the church. The church requires financial support. However, the method used to obtain this support should be in line with sound doctrine. The goal is to steer Christians away from traditional monetary offerings and to point them to Spirit-led giving, or grace giving.

This chapter focuses on giving when it is called an offering. The term offering is defined in accordance with old covenant rules and regulations. The offerings of tithes and firstfruits are discussed in detail in the following chapters, "Tithing Defined" and "Firstfruit Defined," respectively. These definitions should discourage Christians from declaring their giving as an 'offering above and beyond the tithe.' In order to understand biblical offerings, however, several other terms are also defined in this chapter, and include, tabernacle, temple, altar, and sacrifice. These definitions will aid in understanding the various old covenant laws associated with offerings.

Please note that depending on the version of the Bible used, different words appear in different versions. For example, the heave offering described in the King James Version actually uses the word 'heave,' whereas the New International Version uses words such a 'gift' and 'present' in some verses.

EARTHLY SANCTUARIES

The Tabernacle

The tabernacle was a portable sanctuary used by the Israelites during the wilderness period. As the word 'portable' suggests, the tabernacle was not a permanent building. When the Israelites traveled in the desert, the Levites were responsible for taking down and rebuilding the tabernacle.

Numbers 1:51
Whenever the tabernacle is to move, the Levites are to take it down, and whenever the tabernacle is to be set up, the Levites shall do it. Anyone else who goes near it shall be put to death.

Chapters 25 through 30 of Exodus give the directions on how to make a tabernacle, while chapters 35 through 40 tell of actually building the tabernacle, i.e., following the directions. One can easily see how the tabernacle was a portable structure since the walls consisted of different types of curtains, which were made of materials such as blue and purple yarn, goat hair, and ram skins (Ex. 26:1, 7, 14).

The tabernacle also had furniture designated for certain areas and included the ark of the testimony, the mercy seat, and the table of showbread (Ex. 25). The ark was put in the most holy place, or more commonly called, the Holy of Holies, which is also within the innermost part of the tabernacle (Ex. 26:33-34).

The Temple

Temples were built some time later and were not portable like tabernacles. One of the first temples in the Old Testament is described in First Kings 6 through 8, and was known as Solomon's Temple. The walls and ceiling were made of stone and wood in contrast to the curtains of the tabernacle.

1 Kings 7:9-11
All these structures, from the outside to the great courtyard and from foundation to eaves, were made of blocks of high-grade stone cut to size and trimmed with a saw on their inner and outer faces.

The foundations were laid with large stones of good quality, some measuring ten cubits and some eight.

Above were high-grade stones, cut to size, and cedar beams.

Solomon's Temple was similar to the tabernacle in that it also had a Holy Place and a Holy of Holies that housed the ark of the covenant (1 Ki. 8:5-11). This temple, however, was to be a permanent house of the Lord.

1 Kings 8:13
I have indeed built a magnificent temple for you, a place for you to dwell forever.

Further studies will reveal that this temple was destroyed during the reign of king Nebuchadnezzar of Babylon (2 Ki. 25:8-17) and rebuilt around 520 BC. The Temple is an important part of the religious life of the Jewish people as is clearly evident in its use described in the four gospels - Matthew, Mark, Luke, and John.

THE ALTAR

A simple definition of an altar is any elevated place or structure upon which sacrifices are offered or incense burned.

Throughout the Bible, tabernacles and temples always have altars as indicated in the descriptions of these structures. Additional altars, however, can reside outside of the confines of the tabernacle or temple courtyards (see Judg. 6:19-23; 13:19-20).

Altar of Incense

There are two types of altars associated with the tabernacle or temple. One type of altar is the altar of incense.

Exodus 37:25
They made the altar of incense out of acacia wood. It was square, a cubit long and a cubit wide, and two cubits high - its horns of one piece with it.

This altar is also called the golden altar. One was built for the tabernacle in Exodus 30:1-10 and 37:25-28 and one for Solomon's Temple in 1 Kings 7:48. The altar of incense was placed in the inner part of the tabernacle just outside the Holy of Holies.

Altar of Burnt Offering

The second type of altar is known as the altar of burnt offering. It is placed in the courtyard of the tabernacle (Ex. 27:1-8; 38:1-7). First Kings 8:64 also suggests that a courtyard existed and that an altar was made for the burnt offerings (see also 1 Ki. 8:22, 54; 9:25).

Exodus 38:1
They built the altar of burnt offering of acacia wood, three cubits high; it was square, five cubits long and five cubits wide.

1 Kings 8:64
On that same day the king consecrated the middle part of the courtyard in front of the temple of the LORD, and there he offered burnt offerings, grain offerings and the fat of the fellowship offerings, because the bronze

altar before the LORD was too small to hold the burnt offerings, the grain offerings and the fat of the fellowship offerings.

Altars for burnt offerings are made from different types of materials; stone (Ex. 20:25; Judg. 6:19-23; 13:19-20; 1 Sam. 14:31-35), earth (Ex. 20:24), and metal (altar of burnt offering for the tabernacle was overlaid with bronze).

SACRIFICE

The word sacrifice is defined because most offerings described in the Old Testament are sacrificial in nature (for the Lord) during both the tabernacle era and the temple era. Two of the offerings are not sacrificial in that they were monetary offerings used to restore tabernacles. Since Christians call their giving an offering, which according to the Bible is a sacrifice, the meaning of sacrifice needs to be established. This definition provides an understanding of the different offerings defined later, as well as what is actually *sacrificed*.

Sacrifice Defined

A generic definition of sacrifice is the slaughtering of an animal offered to God, with a specific ritual being performed depending on the type of offering. These are the offerings that require blood, but there are offerings that did include *non-blood* items. In many cases, the sacrifice is male, without blemish, and actually *eaten*. In no ritual is money *ever* the *sacrificial* item.

The Old Testament does not have a general word translated to mean 'sacrifice,' but the words used have the following general translations (in type of sacrifice and purpose):

1. That which is brought near. This includes the non-blood offerings such as the cereal offering, the firstfruits, the dough of the Feast of Weeks, and also includes the tithes.

2. That which is slain, as in the offerings where the sacrifice is eaten by both priests and worshippers.
3. That which goes up, as in the peace offering where the sacrifice is wholly burnt.
4. For guilt, as in the guilt offering where the sacrifice is eaten by the priests alone.
5. For sin, as in the sin offering where the sacrifice is eaten by the priests alone.

<u>Substances Used</u>

When required to give sacrificial offerings based on old covenant law, male animals are preferred most of the time. It is also emphasized that the sacrificial animals offered should have no blemish.

Leviticus 1:3
If the offering is a burnt offering from the herd, he is to offer a male without defect ...

Leviticus 3:1
If someone's offering is a fellowship offering, and he offers an animal from the herd, whether male or female, he is to present before the LORD an animal without defect.

If an individual cannot afford to provide the proper animal sacrifice, it can be substituted with a less expensive animal sacrifice such as doves or pigeons. In some cases, if the individual cannot afford even the doves, he can replace the animal substitute with a cereal offering.

Leviticus 5:7, 11
If he cannot afford a lamb, he is to bring two doves or two young pigeons to the LORD as a penalty for his sin - one for a sin offering and the other for a burnt offering.
... If, however, he cannot afford two doves or two young pigeons, he is to bring as an offering for his sin a tenth of an ephah of fine flour for a sin offering.

Notice in both cases how a poor individual can bring an offering unto the Lord because it is based on what the person can afford (see also Lev. 14:22). The idea of providing something 'according to a person's means' is addressed in Chapter 9, "Grace Giving."

Portions of the sacrifices are often eaten, as illustrated in the different offerings defined later in this chapter. There are other items used in conjunction with these rituals and are listed with each type of offering. The most important point to notice here is that money is never used as the sacrifice and later burnt or eaten - even though money is prevalent throughout the Old Testament. The primary substances for sacrifices under the law include fruit, animals, and grain.

Rituals Involved in Sacrifices

The typical ritual involving animal sacrifices requires the worshipper to bring the offering forward and lay his hands on it; and in some cases confess his sins. The animal is slaughtered, and the blood is handled by the priest. Quite often, portions of the animal are eaten. There are several offerings including this as part of the overall sacrificial ritual.

When and what parts of the animal are consumed depends on the occasion. However, the fat and the blood of the animal are never eaten (Lev. 7:22-27). Portions of the sacrifice are eaten either by the worshipper and the priest, or by the priests and their families, or by the priest alone. The priestly food must be eaten in certain places. If the food is for the priest's family, it must be eaten in a clean place. As for the food that could only be eaten by the priest, it is eaten within the designated areas.

Daily Ritual

The following describes the daily ritual of burnt offerings performed by the priest, which is accompanied with cereal and drink offerings (Ex. 29:38-42; Lev. 6:19-23; Num. 28:3-8). As an indication of how far Christians have modified and simplified biblical offerings, notice here the detail of the ritual, which indicates a part of the complexity of the sacrificial process.   The point here is that Christians claim to give offerings, as in 'tithes and offerings,' but are they really?

Leviticus 6:10-12
The priest shall then put on his linen clothes, with linen undergarments next to his body, and shall remove the ashes of the burnt offering that the fire has consumed on the altar and place them beside the altar.

Then he is to take off these clothes and put on others, and carry the ashes outside the camp to a place that is ceremonially clean.

The fire on the altar must be kept burning; it must not go out. Every morning the priest is to add firewood and arrange the burnt offering on the fire and burn the fat of the fellowship offerings on it.

BIBLICAL OFFERINGS

In the previous section, attention was given to the definition of sacrifice as it relates to the item literally being offered unto the Lord.   The term sacrifice was defined since most of the offerings listed below are actually animal sacrifices unto the Lord.   In addition, many people use sacrifice and offering interchangeably because 'sacrifice' is also an act of forfeiting something of value (Lev. 1:3). An offering, in general, is defined as a sacrificial present, something brought near the altar, a gift, a donation, and a few other definitions depending on the type of offering performed.

In this section, several types of offerings described in the Old Testament are listed.   In each of the following offerings, please note what is actually 'used as the sacrifice.' The goal of this section is to show that Christian giving should not be considered in the same sacrificial category as the sacrifices and offerings of the law.

Burnt Offering

The purpose of this offering is to make an atonement for sin (to pardon, reconcile, or purge). The fragrance of the burnt offering, an offering made by fire, is a pleasing aroma unto the Lord. Leviticus chapter 1 describes how the burnt offering is to be performed depending upon the type of sacrifice - whether it is a bull, a sheep or goat, a dove or pigeon. If the sacrifice is a bull, sheep, or goat, it must be male.

The fire upon the altar burns continually, as mentioned above in Leviticus 6:10-12 (see also Ex. 29:38-42). The animal sacrificed is wholly burnt except for the feathers of birds since they are plucked away (Lev. 1:16) and the skin since it is given to the priest (Lev. 7:8). See also Leviticus chapters 1, 6:8-13 and 8:18-21. Burnt offerings are also a part of the ceremonial purification or cleansing rites of individuals (Lev. 12:6, 8; 14:19, 22; 15:15, 30). Other offerings also include burning parts of the sacrificial item.

Cereal/Grain/Meal/Meat Offering

There are five kinds of meat or cereal offerings listed in Leviticus chapter 2. The word meat here is not equivalent to animal flesh, but is defined as a food offering of vegetables or grain and include the following:

1. Fine flour, oil, and frankincense (Lev. 2:1-3);
2. Unleavened cakes (Lev. 2:4);
3. Unleavened pan cakes (Lev. 2:5-6);
4. Unleavened fried pan cakes (Lev. 2:7-9); and
5. Firstfruits of crops (Lev. 2:12, 14-16). Further discussion of this type of offering is described in Chapter 5, "Firstfruit Defined."

Like the burnt offering, a portion of this type of offering is burned upon the altar. Typical ingredients for cereal offerings include wheat, corn, and barley. Every offering is seasoned with salt, but no leaven or honey can be used. This offering also produces a pleasing aroma unto the Lord. Remnants of the offering are eaten by the priest since only a portion of the cereal offering is burned upon the altar. This offering accompanies other offerings such as burnt and peace offerings. The poor can also participate in trespass offerings by providing a cereal offering instead. (Lev. 2; 5:11-12; 6:14-23; 10:12-13; 14:21; Num. 15:4, 8).

Peace/Fellowship Offering

The sacrificial item for this offering is of the herd (bull or cow) or of the flock (sheep or goat). It can be either male or female, but it must be without blemish. The Lord commands as a perpetual statute that no person shall eat the fat and blood of the animal. Therefore, the fat and blood are removed from the animal as part of the ritual prior to preparation. Part of the sacrifice is eaten by the priest and the rest by the person bringing the sacrifice. It must be eaten within one or two days. This offering is also made by fire and produces a pleasing aroma unto the Lord (Lev. 3; 7:11-21). The peace offering is also the premise for the thank offering, the free will offering, and the votive offering, depending on the purpose of the person bringing forth the offering.

Sin Offering

This offering takes place when someone unknowingly, or out of ignorance, breaks any commandment of the Lord and purification. There are four types of sin offerings depending on who commits the sin. The sin offering is performed in a manner similar to the peace offering, including the removal of the fat from the animal and the subsequent burning of the fat. Here is a list of sacrificial items corresponding to the person who sins:

1. Priest or whole congregation of Israel - young bull
2. A ruler - male goat
3. Common person - female goat
4. Cleansing ritual - lamb, pigeon, dove (and cereal offering)

When sin and burnt offerings are given on the same day, the sin offering is performed first. The sin offering, as well as the trespass offering, is eaten by the priest. (Ex. 29:10-14; Lev. 4; 6:24-30; 10:17; 12:6-7; 14:21; 15:29-30; 16:1-28; Heb. 13:11-12).

Guilt/Trespass Offering

A guilt offering is brought to the priest when one perjures oneself or touches something unclean, and the act involves something or someone else. This type of sin offering uses a ram for the sacrifice, requires reparation of damages, and a 20 percent monetary penalty, whether it involved a holy item or someone's property. In the case of a holy item, the monetary penalty goes to the priest. In the case of property owned by someone else, the monetary penalty goes to the person to whom the property belonged. In either case, the *money was not the sacrifice, it was an additional penalty.* A ram is used as the actual sacrifice. This offering, as in the sin offering, is eaten by the priest. (Lev. 5; 6:1-7; 7:1-7).

Please do not confuse the monetary penalty of this offering with actually paying for this offering 'in full' with money. Some believe this sacrifice could be paid for with money which is not correct. Instead, it is only the additional penalty that is paid for with money.

Drink Offering

Drink offerings accompany many other offerings and consist of libations of wine, which typically amounts to a fourth part of a hin (a hin is about five quarts). (Gen. 35:14; Ex. 29:40; Lev. 23:13; Num. 6:17; 15:5, 8-10).

Free Will Offering

The only special occasion for the free will offering is the Feast of Weeks/Pentecost (Deut. 16:10). Once someone commits to a free will offering, it must be fulfilled, much like a vow (Deut. 23:23). The sacrifice must be perfect unless it is a bull or lamb (Lev. 22:17-25), and is eaten by the priest sometime before the third day (Lev. 7:11-18). A cereal and drink offering accompany this offering (Num. 15:1-16).

Wave Offering

As its name suggests, a portion of the sacrifice is actually *waved* before the Lord. The wave offering is performed during other offerings including the peace offering (Ex. 29:22-28; Lev. 7:29-34; 9:19-21), jealousy offering (Num. 5:25), and the votive offering (Num. 6:19-20). This offering is also part of feasts including the Feast of the Passover (Lev. 23:10-11) and the Feast of Pentecost (Lev. 23:17-20). In addition, the wave offering is part of the consecration of the priest (Lev. 8:25-29). This offering, like many other offerings, is eaten by the priest in a clean place (Lev. 10:14).

The New International Version of the Bible specifies gold, gold jewelry, and bronze as items also used in a wave offering (Ex. 35:21; 38:24, 28). The King James Version does not use the word 'wave' in these same passages to describe the offerings. A more complete study on the wave offering relating to these Scripture references and their use of the word 'wave,' or the lack thereof, is needed to understand why the two translations differ. However, the intent here is to only point out the general definition of the wave offering.

Heave Offering

The heave offering is a gift or contribution to the priest, and as its name suggests, a portion of the sacrifice is actually *heaved* (lifted up or presented) into the air (Ex. 29:27; Num. 15:20). This offering is performed and eaten as part of several other offerings including the peace offering (Lev. 7:12-14), votive offering (Num. 6:20), the free will offering (Num. 18:29-30), and when tithing (Num. 18:24-28). Like the wave offering, it is eaten by the priest in a clean place (Lev. 10:14). This offering consists of the right thigh or hind quarter (Lev. 7:32; 10:14), or dough (Num. 15:21), or spoils of war (Num. 31:29, 41).

The King James Version of the Bible describes the Lord's portion in Numbers 31:28-41 as a 'heave' offering, while the New International Version calls this portion a tribute. Some of the items listed in Numbers did include people and may be confusing because people are not eaten as part of the ritual. A heave offering is also defined as just an offering or contribution to God as indicated in Numbers 31:28-41. As with the wave offering, additional study on this offering is needed to understand why these two translations differ.

Votive Offering

This offering is the fulfillment or repayment of a vow. Like the voluntary free will offering, the sacrificial item must be perfect, eaten by the priest prior to the third day, and the vow must be completed (Lev. 7:11-18; 22:17-22; Deut. 23:23). The votive offering also consists of a cereal and drink offering.

Here are some specific dedicated items used in vows: a person (Lev. 27:1-8); animals (Lev. 27:9-13); a house (Lev. 27:14-15); and a field (Lev. 27:16-25). The vows containing dedicated items can be redeemed, or bought back by the person who dedicated them unto God. The redeemer must pay the full price of the dedicated item with an additional 20 percent value added to it. The concept of 'redeeming' is studied in Chapter 4, "Tithing Defined."

Numbers chapter 6 describes the Nazarite vow, which is a vow of separation unto the Lord. During the vow, this person cannot eat or drink certain foods nor shave his head. Upon fulfillment of the vow, a votive offering is given to the priest, which consists of a burnt, sin, and peace offering. The sacrifice for each includes: a lamb of the first year for the burnt offering; a female lamb of the first year for the sin offering; and a ram for the peace offering. All items offered are without blemish. Upon completion of the vow, the Nazarite shaves his head, performs a wave offering, and subsequently drinks wine.

Thank Offering

This type of offering is a peace offering for a thanksgiving. It is given by a person's own free will. The flesh of the sacrifice is eaten in one day. This offering includes leavened bread with unleavened cakes (Lev. 7:11-13, 15; 22:29).

Ordination Offering

The ordination offering is a ritual involving several of the previously listed offerings. This ritual is performed for the anointing of a priest (Ex. 29; Lev. 6:19-23; 8).

Jealousy Offering

A jealousy offering takes place when a man becomes jealous of his wife, accusing her of fornication. The man provides barley without oil or frankincense for this offering. The priest puts holy water and dust from the floor into a vessel. Then the priest puts the offering into the woman's hand and has her take an oath. The oath states that if she has indeed been with a man other than her husband, then a curse would be upon her that would cause her thigh to rot and her belly to swell. The priest then writes the curses into a book, blots them out, and the ink used to write the curse is added to the water mixture in the vessel. The woman drinks the water, followed by the priest taking the offering from the woman and waving it before the Lord. If the woman is not defiled, she would then be clean (see law of jealousy - Num. 5:11-31).

Incense Offering

Incense offerings are burned on the altar of incense (Ex. 30:1-6; 37:25-28). Sweet incense is burned on this altar every morning (Ex. 30:7-9). The content of the holy incense (perfume) is described in Exodus 30:34-38. Nobody can duplicate this incense and smell it or they will be cut off from the people (Ex. 30:38). If someone offers strange incense, it would prove deadly, as it did in Leviticus 10:1-2 when a fire came out from the Lord and consumed Nadab and Abihu.

Some animal's blood is put on the horns of the altar of incense during the sin offering (Lev. 4:7). See also Malachi 1:11 and Luke 1:9-11.

Gift Offering

This offering is strictly a free will offering made by all people. Whoever wants to give for the purpose of building the tabernacle could offer several different types of items (Ex. 35:20-29; Num. 7:2-88).

Personal Offering

This offering consists of half a shekel given by everyone for the service of the tabernacle (Ex. 30:11-16). A shekel is about 64 cents. No matter how rich or poor people are, they are to give the same amount. See also 2 Kings 12:1-8 for a passage on the restoration of the temple.

CONTRAST WITH TODAY'S OFFERINGS

When a sacrifice is required for an offering, it is a food substance consisting of crops or livestock. In contrast, the only acceptable type of 'sacrificial' item for many churches today is money. The sacrificial item of the written law is, for the most part, *eaten,* and many times *burned* upon the altar. However, money was never treated in this manner, and neither is it treated this way in today's offerings. On the other hand, money is used to redeem dedicated items unto the Lord, and to build and restore the tabernacle.

For the most part, all of the tithes (as described in Chapter 4) are required of the Jewish community 'as a whole' before offerings are given by anyone in 'particular.' However, for each individual, offerings are not given or performed *above and beyond a tithe.* The person making the offering may not even be a tither if he does not have the required items.

Nevertheless, he could purchase what is needed for the offering. As it stands, offerings are not required to follow tithes.

Today, many Christians are taught that they are not true givers until they enter into the realm of *monetary* offerings which comes after giving the *monetary* tithe unto the Lord. The different types of offerings listed above, presented with scriptural passages and within context, show this not to be true. The tithe is another type of offering given unto the Lord when it is appropriate, and only required from those who own the legitimate items for the tithe.

Let us now look at the final two offerings mentioned - gift and personal offerings. These two offerings are used by some Christians to define the type of giving performed today, since they were used to build or restore the tabernacle. Some could argue that this is the same as restoring or building a local church facility today. After all, it appears that the contributions made to the church today take care of the four-walled church - not the people who make up the living church - so this is a fair comparison.

The question that comes to mind is the following, "Is today's offering freely given or is it required?" If it is freely given, then maybe Christians are performing a modified version of the gift offering. If it is required, then maybe Christians are performing a modified, but expensive version, of the personal offering. Nevertheless, these two offerings are for the benefit of the tabernacle or temple, which Christians have nothing to do with today. In addition, as with the other offerings, neither one of these two offerings was ever preceded with a tithe in biblical times. These two offerings were mostly monetary, but tithes were never monetary.

———————

Christians claim to bring tithes and 'offerings' to the local church, therefore, this chapter focused on the true meanings of the word 'offerings.' The different types of offerings defined in this chapter should not be confused with the monetary offering of today. A simple comparison was attempted and has shown them to be totally different. The old covenant law contains many different offerings for many occasions. However, some Christians have replaced all of them with just one monetary offering.

The Bible has given no indication in the New Testament that the offerings brought to the priests have been redefined from their old covenant meanings. Neither Jesus, nor the apostles, nor the Holy Spirit, presented a new way to do this. Monetary offerings used to support local churches are of human origin and tradition. Why? Because of rules like, "Offerings are above and beyond the tithe," which are not supported by the Bible. Nevertheless, giving money to support the local church is a good work that should continue - provided that the priority of the local church is to take care of the spiritual and physical needs of its members and the needy in their communities.

No old covenant tabernacle, temple, altar, or sacrifice, is meant to be part of the Christian experience. The monetary offering is not a replacement for all of the old covenant offerings. The church facility is not the equivalent of the old covenant tabernacle or temple. The pastor is not the equivalent of a priest. The offering plate is not symbolic of the old covenant altar. And money is not a substitute for the different sacrificial items.

When Jesus died on the cross, He did away with all of the rules and regulations concerning the rituals listed in this chapter - all of them. See Chapter 6, "Freedom Through Death," for complete details. The concluding point of this chapter is this: Christians should realize that their giving is actually an act of grace, not monetary offerings.

Leviticus 6:10-12

The priest shall then put on his linen clothes, with linen undergarments next to his body, and shall remove the ashes of the burnt offering that the fire has consumed on the altar and place them beside the altar.

Then he is to take off these clothes and put on others, and carry the ashes outside the camp to a place that is ceremonially clean.

The fire on the altar must be kept burning; it must not go out. Every morning the priest is to add firewood and arrange the burnt offering on the fire and burn the fat of the fellowship offerings on it.

4

Tithing Defined

The authors of this book have put some study into the subject of tithes and offerings, and in the area of giving. It was found through conversations on this subject that many people do not have a clear understanding of the practice of tithing or giving. The most problematic area is when Christians use the rules of tithing interchangeably with the concept of giving. The authors also learned that people who teach that Christians must "give of their firstfruits (which some say is the tithe) and offerings unto the Lord," do not actually perform other old covenant rituals. Moreover, they do not perform all of the rules and regulations associated with the tithe and offering rituals, but instead, are selective in which ones they perform.

The purpose of this chapter is to present a more complete definition of tithing than most people usually receive. It shows that the biblical tithe had a purpose and is clearly defined in Scripture. With this definition available, it will be apparent that tithing money has nothing to do with how Christians are to support the local church today.

As noted in Chapter 3, "Offerings Defined," the term 'offering' in today's church is different from all of the offerings described in Scripture. The Old Testament term 'tithe' has also been completely redefined by many of today's believers. This term, in addition to offerings, are among the most misunderstood terms in the Bible, in that they are not performed according to their biblical definitions.

This chapter also shows that money is not accepted nor required by the Lord as a tithe from Christians. Many

Christians create a form of tithes and offerings to fit into some form of a modern day giving theology. This chapter takes the unbiblical element out of tithing and defines it based on the Bible. Defining the term 'tithing' will help Christians understand what they are doing today, whether literally or in principle. They can then decide if the monetary tithing ritual performed in today's church is in accordance with the Bible, or if it is simply hand-me-down tradition. The goal of this chapter is to have Christians start calling their acts of giving what they actually are - not tithes and offerings, but Spirit-led giving or acts of grace.

SUBSTANCE OF THE TITHE

When asked why people should give 10 percent of their money as a tithe, some say it is because the financial situation has changed (recall Chapter 2, "Money and Occupations"). This is usually all that is stated with no elaboration. This almost always leads to confusion, requiring a follow-up question, "What financial situation?" Tithes and offerings were never based on finances. The currency of the world changes, but animals will be animals, and crops will be crops. People become poorer or richer, but a ram is still a ram, and a dove is still a dove.

The so-called financial situation cannot change the genetic make-up of the herd and flock, the grain from the soil, or the fruit of a tree. The sacrificial items used for offerings, and the materials given for tithes, remain the same throughout the Bible, whereas the standard for money and its value has changed. Since the tithe has not changed due to a financial situation, it is important to understand what items are acceptable as tithes.

A tithe literally means a tenth, or 10 percent, of 'something.' If this 'something' could be anything, then a person giving a tithe of his possessions simply gives 10 percent of what he owns to someone or something else. So a tithe of a person's garbage is 10 percent of the garbage. And, of course, the one everyone can relate to, a tithe of ten dollars is one dollar.

To describe the substance of the biblical tithe as only giving 10 percent of something, is actually incorrect. A tenth of garbage is actually not acceptable as a tithe according to how the Bible defines the tithe, simply because garbage is not what the Lord requires from those under the law. Neither is giving 10 percent of income to a church a valid tithe. The biblical definition of tithing specifies what is given as the tithe. Therefore, unless it is in accordance with Scripture, people cannot simply give what they want and appropriately call it a tithe.

Tithe is not Money

The definitions of sacrifice, the materials used for sacrifices, the rituals performed, and the types of offerings performed are listed in Chapter 3. From these definitions, clearly *no offering of money was accepted or required by the Lord* as part of the sacrificial ritual or 'blood offering.' The offering for the Lord, on the other hand, always consists of an edible substance, and is either eaten by the priests and worshippers or is burned. The required items for the tithe consist of the same items as offerings: seed of the land (crops), fruit of the trees, animals of the herd (i.e., cow or bull), or animals of the flock (i.e., sheep or goat).

Leviticus 27:30-32
A tithe of everything from the land, whether grain from the soil or fruit from the trees, belongs to the LORD; it is holy to the LORD.

If a man redeems any of his tithe, he must add a fifth of the value to it.

The entire tithe of the herd and flock - every tenth animal that passes under the shepherd's rod - will be holy to the LORD.

In addition to the items listed above in Leviticus chapter 27, Deuteronomy 14:22-23 includes new wine and oil in the list of items that are used as the tithe.

It is intriguing to hear someone, including a pastor, refer to these three verses in Leviticus chapter 27 and interpret *grain from the soil* and *fruit from the trees* as being equivalent to the money used in today's society. By doing this, they alter the tithe to mean something other than its true definition. The *grain* and *fruit* are the same grain and fruit people grow and consume today. The New Testament does not suggest, imply, or condone, such a change for the tithe. In addition, Chapter 2, "Money and Occupations," illustrates that money existed during the law, and Leviticus chapter 27 does not require money as a tithe.

As far as the monetary tithe is concerned, here is something to consider. When was the last time money was ever referred to as being *holy to the Lord* (as in Lev. 27:30, 32)? In many of today's churches it appears as if money is indeed that - holy unto the Lord. Chapter 2 points out money's role in society during Old Testament times. Money also has a role in the tithing ritual when it comes to redeeming the tithe, and when it is too far to carry. Each is discussed later in this chapter. However, money has nothing to do with what is considered holy unto the Lord.   Therefore, Christian contributions to the church should not be confused with the passages above in Leviticus and Deuteronomy.

TITHE TO BE EATEN

One of the main problems with today's form of tithing is how it is used. It is simply given to the local church. It is not used the way it was in Old Testament times, in that it does not go directly back to the giver. This section demonstrates that the tithe is partially for the one who gives it, although it is required by the Lord. Note in this section how the tithe is similar to the sacrificial nature of offerings - it is eaten.

Deuteronomy 12:17-19

You must not eat in your own towns the tithe of your grain and new wine and oil, or the firstborn of your herds and flocks, or whatever you have vowed to give, or your freewill offerings or special gifts.

Instead, you are to eat them in the presence of the LORD your God at the place the LORD your God will choose - you, your sons and daughters, your menservants and maidservants, and the Levites from your towns - and you are to rejoice before the LORD your God in everything you put your hand to.

Be careful not to neglect the Levites as long as you live in your land.

The tithe cannot be eaten in a person's own town, but rather *in the presence of the Lord* at a place where the Lord chooses. The tithe is *eaten* by those who bring it forward for the sacrificial ritual - similar in manner to the sacrificial offerings previously described. This tithe is 'offered and eaten' by all participants during years one, two, four and five of a seven year cycle. See also Deuteronomy 12:5-7 and 14:22-23.

As mentioned earlier, the tithe is an edible substance, such as grain, wine, oil, and animals. On the contrary, money is never eaten, salted, baked, etc. How many tithers today get to 'eat' their tithe, or share in the tithe, as was originally intended? How many people get to 'taste' their monetary tithe, or get a full stomach from their monetary tithe? The point is simply this: Christians today are not really tithing, so they should stop referring to their giving as tithing! When they stop calling their monetary gifts a tithe, other rules and regulations governing their giving will disappear.

Why Eating is Misunderstood

Ironically, Christians are told that 'eating the tithe is forbidden.' Unfortunately, many Christians are taught that eating the tithe is symbolic of keeping it for themselves. This way of thinking may come from the misinterpretation of

Leviticus 27:31 in relation to redeeming the tithe, which is discussed later in this chapter. This subsection, however, covers another verse that may lead to this misunderstanding.

Deuteronomy 26:12-14

When you have finished setting aside a tenth of all your produce in the third year, the year of the tithe, you shall give it to the Levite, the alien, the fatherless and the widow, so that they may eat in your towns and be satisfied.

Then say to the LORD your God: "I have removed from my house the sacred portion and have given it to the Levite, the alien, the fatherless and the widow, according to all you commanded. I have not turned aside from your commands nor have I forgotten any of them.

I have not eaten any of the sacred portion while I was in mourning, nor have I removed any of it while I was unclean, nor have I offered any of it to the dead. I have obeyed the LORD my God; I have done everything you commanded me.

Verse 14 is correct in suggesting there is no reason for someone to eat the tithe at the end of the 'year of tithing,' which is every third and sixth year of a seven year cycle. But the preceding verses, 12 and 13, explain how this particular tithe is for the Levites, the fatherless, the stranger, and the widow, to eat until they are full. The person providing the tithe does not eat it since it is designated for someone else to eat (see also Deut. 14:28-29). As stated in the passage above, even someone in mourning cannot use that as an excuse to eat this tithe. Furthermore, the tither is not allowed to use the tithe to feed participants of a funeral.

The real misinterpretation of Deuteronomy 26:14 is in its application to the monetary tithe. Many misinterpret the phrase, *I have not eaten any of the sacred portion*, when referring to this verse. Often Christians are told not to eat the tithe in an attempt to have them give monetary tithes to the church, and to show obedience to the Lord. As noted earlier, eating the tithe is permissible and, in fact, it is a natural part of the tithing ritual. Individuals who do not read verse 14 in context, and skip the previous two verses, will not be aware that the tithe is also eaten during this time. It is only the one 'giving the tithe' who does not eat it.

Being told not to eat the tithe is the complete opposite of God's intention. Today's believers are taught that eating the tithe is wrong due to the inappropriate use of the words 'eat' and 'tithe.' If people were living under the law, they would be in perfect agreement with old covenant law by eating the tithe with the appropriate participants. No matter how one studies the Bible, money can never be interpreted as being the substance of the tithe, nor has it ever been considered a consumable item.

PURPOSE OF THE TITHE

As noted above, the tithe is supposed to be consumed, so this concept is not covered again. On the other hand, who is supposed to eat the tithe is addressed, along with any other purpose of the tithe. Given the nature of the *legitimate* tithe, it is intuitively obvious that it does not provide for the upkeep of any physical facility - unlike the use of the *monetary* tithe today. As a reminder, the tithe in this book is not the same as 'giving' to the local church. This section describes the purpose of the true tithe as defined in the Bible. Giving to the local church is discussed in Chapter 9, "Grace Giving."

Support the Levites

Besides God giving commands to tithe in Leviticus 27, what is the purpose of the tithe? The first tithe the Israelites give unto the Lord is literally given to the Levites. This is in return for the work the Levites perform as an inheritance since they will not receive an inheritance among the Israelites.

Numbers 18:21, 23-24
"I give to the Levites all the tithes in Israel as their inheritance in return for the work they do while serving at the Tent of Meeting.

... It is the Levites who are to do the work at the Tent of Meeting and bear the responsibility for offenses against it. This is a lasting ordinance for the generations to come. They will receive no inheritance among the Israelites.

Instead, I give to the Levites as their inheritance the tithes that the Israelites present as an offering to the LORD. That is why I said concerning them: 'They will have no inheritance among the Israelites.'"

Here the tithe is given to the Levites for the work they perform at the Tent of Meeting. The tithe is actually given to people, not church building funds, light bills, etc. The Levite, which is not the same as a pastor, represents the Israelites at the tabernacle since the Israelites are not allowed to perform Levitical or priestly duties. There is no symbolic tabernacle or church today, however, that Christians cannot approach where a pastor is required to do something on their behalf - as the Levite does for the Israelites. Therefore, the pastor cannot require of Christians, nor should the church require of Christians, a tithe for the support of a pastor. How to correctly support a pastor, and those in the ministry, is covered in Chapter 9, "Grace Giving."

This tithe should not be confused with the tithe mentioned previously in Deuteronomy 12:17-19. The tithe mentioned there is the second tithe and follows the tithe mentioned above in Numbers chapter 18. *Be careful not to neglect the Levites as long as you live in your land* (Deut. 12:19). The inheritance for the Levites actually comes before the tithe for the people.

Tenth of the Tithe for Lord's Offering

As shown above, the tithe is collected by Levites as an inheritance. But a tenth of that tithe is given to Aaron the priest as the Lord's offering. This is the best and holiest part of the tithe.

Numbers 18:26, 28-29, 32

"Speak to the Levites and say to them: 'When you receive from the Israelites the tithe I give you as your inheritance, you must present a tenth of that tithe as the LORD's offering.

... In this way you also will present an offering to the LORD from all the tithes you receive from the Israelites. From these tithes you must give the LORD's portion to Aaron the priest.

You must present as the LORD's portion the best and holiest part of everything given to you.'

... By presenting the best part of it you will not be guilty in this matter; then you will not defile the holy offerings of the Israelites, and you will not die.'"

The tenth of the tithe is *the best part of it*, or the best part of the tithe. If the tithe did consist of money, then what is the 'best part' of money? Spending it? With true tithing, one can identify the best of the produce, but the best part cannot be identified when using money.

Every Three Years for the Needy

Not only did the Levites receive the first tithe as an inheritance, but every third and sixth year of a seven year cycle, the fatherless, the widows, and foreigners, who live in their towns eat from the tithe until satisfied (see Deut. 26:12-13).

Deuteronomy 14:27-29

And do not neglect the Levites living in your towns, for they have no allotment or inheritance of their own.

At the end of every three years, bring all the tithes of that year's produce and store it in your towns,

so that the Levites (who have no allotment or inheritance of their own) and the aliens, the fatherless and the widows who live in your towns may come and eat and be satisfied, and so that the LORD your God may bless you in all the work of your hands.

Every third year, those who need food receive it from the tithe, which is called the 'tithe of the poor.' With the church expenses that exist today, it is more convenient for many churches *not* to use their so-called tithe to feed the needy. Instead, many require a 'monetary benevolence offering' above and beyond the 'monetary tithe' to fulfill this need. This is actually backward from the true and accurate biblical purpose of tithing. In general, the tithe is shared in part with the worshipper who brings it forth, and, as in the case above, it is shared with those in need.

To further show that today's version of church contributions should not be called tithing, let us examine the case where people pick and choose certain verses of the old covenant law they want to perform. For example, revisiting Deuteronomy 26:14, it states, "I have not eaten any of the sacred portion while I was in mourning..." This verse is referring to the tithe for the needy every third year. If the church applies this verse to the monetary tithe of today and does *not eat it*, then why is the monetary tithe not given to strangers, the fatherless, and widows, every three years? This is the command given in Deuteronomy 26:12-13 and Deuteronomy 14:28-29. After all, if Christians are supposed to obey all of the commandments of the Lord, why not obey all the commands and regulations that apply to the tithe?

Imagine how many people would not need food stamps or welfare checks if Christians give a tenth of a year's income to those who need it every third and sixth year. However, since Christians should not give tithes and offerings, this book presents a better and more perfect way to share in the needs of the poor. There is only one purpose for mentioning the tithe of the poor. To simply show people that they really are not tithing when they do not take care of the needy.

Ungathered Harvest for the Needy

The previous subsection shows that the tithe provides food every three years for those who need it. In addition, harvest time also provides food for the needy throughout the season, since some of the remains are left over for the needy to gather.

Deuteronomy 24:19-21

When you are harvesting in your field and you overlook a sheaf, do not go back to get it. Leave it for the alien, the fatherless and the widow, so that the LORD your God may bless you in all the work of your hands.

When you beat the olives from your trees, do not go over the branches a second time. Leave what remains for the alien, the fatherless and the widow.

When you harvest the grapes in your vineyard, do not go over the vines again. Leave what remains for the alien, the fatherless and the widow.

If the tithe is indeed monetary and comes from the increase of an occupation, it would be nice to see during the harvest of that work some money 'left over and not picked up.' If all believers would cash their paycheck and 'leave some money on the ground,' then the fatherless and widows could come behind them and gather it up for themselves.

Unfortunately, some people even change the part of the law concerning the harvest of the produce by not participating in it. They have no problem interpreting the 'fruit of the tree' and 'seed of the land' as money. However, how much of the money (fruit and seed) is left ungathered for the poor at harvest time? This is one more example where certain parts of the old covenant law are practiced while the most important parts are overlooked. It is the overlooked parts that benefit others. See also Deuteronomy 26:12-13.

Seventh Year for You

To further emphasize how today's church is really not tithing, let us look at the Sabbath year. As noted above, every three years the entire tithe for that year went to the needy. This alone should be enough to cause most 'tithe requiring pastors' to re-evaluate what they are teaching. Now they know that an entire year's worth of tithes went to the poor, and not to the local church fund, or more accurately speaking, a tabernacle or temple fund. Well, it does not end here. It may also be troubling to know that every seventh year the agricultural tithe (grain and fruit) stays in the possession of the people since it is not required by the Lord!

Leviticus 25:2-7

"Speak to the Israelites and say to them: 'When you enter the land I am going to give you, the land itself must observe a sabbath to the LORD.

For six years sow your fields, and for six years prune your vineyards and gather their crops.

But in the seventh year the land is to have a sabbath of rest, a sabbath to the LORD. Do not sow your fields or prune your vineyards.

Do not reap what grows of itself or harvest the grapes of your untended vines. The land is to have a year of rest.

Whatever the land yields during the sabbath year will be food for you - for yourself, your manservant and maidservant, and the hired worker and temporary resident who live among you,

as well as for your livestock and the wild animals in your land. Whatever the land produces may be eaten.'"

The Lord said for six years, out of a seven year cycle, the land should be worked. In the seventh year, however, *the land itself must observe a sabbath to the LORD.* Nobody can claim any rights to, or use of, anything that grew by itself during this year - *Do not reap what grows of itself.* Therefore, tithing is not performed in the usual sense because no one is allowed to work the land and claim any rights to the harvest. But what grew on its own still provides food for the owner - *Whatever the land yields during the sabbath year will be food for you.*

If in fact it is appropriate for Christians to partake in the tithing ritual, the local church fails to teach its tithing members that every seventh year they are free from their obligation to tithe. Moreover, whatever residual income they earn that year is money for them. Tithers do not owe the Lord, or anybody, anything in the form of a tithe during this particular year.

Furthermore, the seventh year frees the Israelite from any debt he owes his brother. Deuteronomy chapter 15, starting at verse 1, states, "At the end of every seven years you must cancel debts." The creditor shall not require payment because, "the LORD's time for canceling debts has been proclaimed." As the Bible shows, the seventh year is a pretty good year for those who try to walk according to old covenant rules and regulations! The church that teaches about tithing should not tell their congregation they owe anything during this 'year of release,' or the sabbath year.

Since the church does not adhere to the entire ritual of tithing, it should not use any part of it to define how Christians ought to give today. It does not look good to only use selective parts of the tithing ritual to get Christians to support the church. Instead, simply ask the congregation, if they are willing, to support the ministries of the church. This is how it was done in the early church, and there were no needy persons among them (as in the Book of Acts).

BRING THE TITHE INTO THE STOREHOUSE

With a more complete understanding of tithes and offerings, the misinterpretation of Malachi 3:10 regarding the monetary tithe taught today can be understood. This passage says to *bring* the *tithes* into the *storehouse* that there may be *meat* in *mine house*. This passage is correct if not taken out of context. Since this passage is taken out of context, this section analyzes parts of the verse for clarification.

Malachi 3:10 NIV
Bring the whole tithe into the storehouse, that there may be food in my house.

Malachi 3:10 KJV
Bring ye all the tithes into the storehouse, that there may be meat in mine house

Behind the Word Bring

The study of this verse begins with the word *bring*. The worshipper is to literally *bring* the tithe into the storehouse, which is absolutely correct. Recall earlier that the people must travel to a place where the Lord put His name, since they cannot eat it in their home towns (Deut. 14:22-23). In a subsequent section, it is shown that if the tithe is too much for the individual to carry to the destination, it can be exchanged for silver, and then exchanged for food once the person reached the designated place (Deut. 14:24-26). Once there, it is collected by the Levites, but it is the priest that actually offers the tithe, taking it *into the storehouse* on behalf of the worshipper.

One Sunday a pastor thought it was correct to literally stand up and bring the tithe (money) to the front of the church because Malachi 3:10 uses the word *bring*. This pastor continued by saying that they will 'symbolically' bring their tithes as the plates were passed around! If this particular pastor believes his congregation should stand up and bring forward the tithes and does not do it, then to him it is sin (Jas. 4:17). How many people can get away with symbolically performing other such acts rather than actually doing them? Again, some believers pick and choose certain parts of particular verses to perform while ignoring other parts. The problem here is that 'bringing the tithe' is in reference to the real tithe, and not in reference to how Christians ought to support the church with their voluntary gifts.

Lame Tithes in the Storehouse

The next word in Malachi 3:10 that needs clarification is *storehouse*. The definition of this word depends on the particular verse of the Bible, and the word used depends on the particular translation of the Bible. The biblical definitions of storehouse are as follows:

1. Treasure - gold or silver (2 Ki. 20:13; Isa. 39:2);
2. Store - supplies of food or drink (Gen. 41:56; Jer. 50:26);

3. Barn - (Deut. 28:8);
4. Weapons storage - (2 Ki. 20:13; Isa. 39:2); and
5. God's storehouse - for the different elements of the earth relating to weather (Josh. 3:13, 16; Job 38:22; Psa. 33:6-7; Psa. 135:7; Jer. 10:13; 51:16).

To bring 'storehouse' into perspective, let us first visit Malachi chapter 1.

Malachi 1:6-8

"A son honors his father, and a servant his master. If I am a father, where is the honor due me? If I am a master, where is the respect due me?" says the LORD Almighty. "It is you, O priests, who show contempt for my name. "But you ask, 'How have we shown contempt for your name?'

"You place defiled food on my altar. "But you ask, 'How have we defiled you?' "By saying that the LORD's table is contemptible.

When you bring blind animals for sacrifice, is that not wrong? When you sacrifice crippled or diseased animals, is that not wrong? Try offering them to your governor! Would he be pleased with you? Would he accept you?" says the LORD Almighty.

As noted here, the Lord is speaking through Malachi against the priests - *It is you, O priests, who show contempt for my name.* The priests were allowing crippled animals to be offered, and therefore, the Lord was not accepting the offerings (Mal. 1:10,13, 2:13). "If an animal has a defect, is lame or blind, or has any serious flaw, you must not sacrifice it to the LORD your God" (Deut. 15:21).

In this context, the tithe of Malachi 3:10 is of livestock. Since this verse says to bring the *whole tithe* into the *storehouse*, God could not be instructing his people to load the storehouse with weapons or gold. The correct definition of storehouse here is 'store' or 'barn.' In addition, the 'whole tithe' means 'without blemish' (as noted above in Malachi chapters 1 and 2).

Genesis 41:56 and 2 Chronicles 32:28 are a couple of verses illustrating that food items are actually stored in storehouses. Therefore, they support the notion that the storehouse in Malachi 3:10 is equivalent to a barn. Yet, from the definitions of storehouse above, it is also the case that money is stored in storehouses, but money is not the topic of discussion in the book of Malachi.

Grain, corn, wine, oil, and animals are all stored in storehouses, and they are the same kinds of items God commands the people to tithe. Many people say that today's church is equivalent to the Old Testament storehouse. They believe this because of teachings stating that the *storehouse* in Malachi 3:10 is equivalent to *God's household* in 1 Timothy 3:15.

1 Timothy 3:15

if I am delayed, you will know how people ought to conduct themselves in God's household, which is the church of the living God, the pillar and foundation of the truth.

There is an obvious difference between the 'storehouse' in the book of Malachi and the 'church' (ekklesia) in First Timothy. A church is the gathering of a group of people in a public place - more specifically, a group of God's people.

Most Christians are not considered livestock, but Christians are considered people in *God's household, which is the church of the living God.* Hopefully it is becoming clear how outrageous some of these misinterpretations are, and how Christians should not use Old Testament passages like Malachi 3:10 to support how they should financially give to the church.

Spiritual Food or Literal Meat

The phrase, *that their may be meat in mine house*, is correct as stated. The word *meat*, like many other words and phrases, has also been redefined to mean something other than its original definition. Many believe the word meat is spiritual meat because people are told that the 'spiritual meat' mentioned here is 'the word of God.' As noted above, the New International Version uses the word *food* because it is literally something eaten and is stored in storehouses.

The word *meat* translates from several Hebrew words and is never used in reference to anything 'spiritual' or 'the word of God' anywhere throughout the Old Testament. The words *meat* and *tithes* always refer to something edible. On the other hand, the New Testament uses meat in the spiritual sense, and it does indeed relate symbolically to the word of God as seen in First Corinthians.

1 Corinthians 3:1-2 KJV
And I, brethren, could not speak unto you as unto spiritual, but as unto carnal, even as unto babes in Christ.

I have fed you with milk, and not with meat: for hitherto ye were not able to bear it, neither yet now are ye able.

1 Corinthians 3:1-2 NIV
Brothers, I could not address you as spiritual but as worldly - mere infants in Christ.

I gave you milk, not solid food, for you were not yet ready for it. Indeed, you are still not ready.

Reading before and after First Corinthians chapter 2, it is evident that this particular meat, or food, is indeed the word of God. See also 1 Corinthians 10:1-4. One can plainly see in this passage that the symbolic use of meat refers to the word of God. Malachi 3:10, on the other hand, plainly refers to natural food - the items required for tithing.

Malachi 3:10 NMV

Now let us put this into perspective. If the word 'tithe' is money, the word 'storehouse' is church, and the word 'meat' is the word of God, then no one should have a problem with the following interpretation in the New Money Version of the Bible.

Malachi 3:10 NMV
Bring 10 percent of your money into the church, that
there may be the word of God in my house.

It sounds a little ridiculous to pay for the word of God so
that it may come to church. Does this mean the more that is
paid, the more the 'word of God' will appear in the local
church? Or, does the 'word of God' require charging by the
hour? If a congregation has no money, do they receive no
'word of God?' The bottom line surrounding the word meat in
Malachi 3:10 is that meat (food) is not money and money is not
meat. Therefore, Christians should not equate their monetary
gifts to the church as meat, as something spiritual, or as
something that is edible. Nor should they equate their
monetary gift as an exchangeable commodity for the word of
God!

Rebuke the Devourer

It is time to take a look at who or what the devourer is as
mentioned in Malachi 3:11. Many Christians are taught that
this particular devourer is the same devourer mentioned in
First Peter.

Malachi 3:11 KJV
*And I will rebuke the devourer for your sakes, and he
shall not destroy the fruits of your ground; neither shall
your vine cast her fruit before the time in the field, saith
the LORD of hosts.*

1 Peter 5:8
*Be self-controlled and alert. Your enemy the devil
prowls around like a roaring lion looking for someone to
devour.*

A vast majority of Christians probably never question
whether or not the devourer mentioned in Malachi 3:11 is
actually the devil. Most Christians are taught not to think
otherwise, and with verses like 1 Peter 5:8 above, it is easy to
see why. Most say it must be the devil. Who else could 'he' be

referring to in Malachi 3:11 where it states *he shall not destroy the fruits of your ground?* The confusion starts with the word 'he,' and both verses above conclude by using the same root word, 'devour.'

The agent that actually does the devouring in Malachi 3:11 is not the devil, but is in fact locusts or similar pests that feed on crops. A few clear examples of locusts and other pests devouring crops are in these passages: Ex. 10:4-6; 10:12-15; Deut. 28:38, 42; 2 Chr. 7:13; and Amos 4:9; 7:1. Also, notice the *great army* mentioned in Joel 2:25 (KJV) is not that little devil, but consists of locusts and other pests.

The tithe is not money, but in fact crops and livestock. Money, our children, our health, etc., are not the items devoured in Malachi as Christians are taught today. In contrast, it is the substance of the real tithe that is actually being devoured. For further clarification, look at the NIV translation of Malachi 3:11.

Malachi 3:11 NIV
"I will prevent pests from devouring your crops, and the vines in your fields will not cast their fruit," says the LORD Almighty.

The Lord says to bring the whole tithe, a tenth of the crops of the field and livestock, into the storehouse and He *will prevent pests from devouring your crops.* Further review of Malachi 3:11, using other biblical resources, shows the devourer to be locusts. The devil is not the only thing that can cause problems in people's lives, but many Christians tend to blame the devil for everything that goes wrong.

Another thing Christians are taught about the devourer of Malachi 3:11 is that this devourer wreaks havoc in people's lives if they do not tithe money to the local church. Some of these misuses of what is devoured include children, financial situations, jobs, sleep, health, relationships, or just about anything that comes to mind.

It is erroneous to draw the conclusion that the devil wreaks havoc in any of these areas of our lives based on a correct interpretation of Malachi 3:10-11. The Lord does not say He is going to prevent the devil from doing anything in this verse, much less prevent the devil from devouring or eating crops. This is not to say that the devil cannot cause havoc in the lives of people, but misusing this passage is not the correct biblical way to illustrate this point.

If Christians do not read into this passage things that do not exist, then they can easily understand its literal meaning. If a Jewish person does not bring the required tithe into the storehouse, then it is prophesied that pests will devour the crops from which the required substance is supposed to come. Please do not misunderstand the intent of what is being explained here. The devil is indeed a pest! But that is another topic.

Robbing God of the Tithe

Before proceeding with Malachi 3:8-9, let us put this passage in context. Malachi 1:6-8 was presented earlier and shows that the prophet directed his message to the priests, not to the Jewish community at large. This is not to say that Jews cannot be affected by what was said.

The first mention of the curse is in chapter 1 at verse 14. Then the prophet speaks out against the priests further in chapter 2.

Malachi 2:1-2
"And now this admonition is for you, O priests.
If you do not listen, and if you do not set your heart to honor my name," says the LORD Almighty, "I will send a curse upon you, and I will curse your blessings. Yes, I have already cursed them, because you have not set your heart to honor me."

The priests were responsible for the actual offerings, and therefore, received the admonition. The context in which Malachi 3 is spoken is actually directed at the priests as well. Proceeding to Malachi 3:8-9, with the correct understanding of what tithes and offerings really are, one can see the true crime committed when the priest take tithes and offerings with defects into the storehouse, which are not accepted by the Lord.

Malachi 3:8-9
"Will a man rob God? Yet you rob me. But you ask,
'How do we rob you?' In tithes and offerings.
You are under a curse - the whole nation of you -
because you are robbing me."

Offering lame animals results in not giving the Lord His required tithes. In this case, the first part of the crime mentioned here does take place, that of not giving whole tithes - resulting in the Lord not accepting them. Since God does not want money, not giving a tenth of it to God does not subject anyone to the curse (even if that person is under the law).

Yet another crime is committed when tithes and offerings are not given. The tithe is not only given because it is required by the Lord, but it is also eaten by the one giving it, his family, and the Levites who received it as their inheritance. The tithe also takes care of the temple workers (Neh. 13:10-12). As for the priests, they receive a tenth of the tithe. In addition, every third year the tithe goes to the stranger, the widow, the fatherless, as well as the Levite.

Since the tithe is a food substance 'consumed' by many, robbing God, as it relates to the tithe, is, in effect, actually robbing those with whom God commanded his people to share. Compare this to how Jesus describes righteous people in Matthew 25:35-40.

MONEY AND ITS RELATION TO TITHING

This section focuses on situations where money is mentioned in relation to the tithe. Chapter 3, "Offerings Defined," shows that money has a role in the trespass offering (Lev. 5; 6:1-7), personal offering for the tabernacle (Ex. 30:11-16), and in the dedicated items used in vows (Lev. 27:1-29). This chapter shows that money has a similar use with the tithe.

Tithe Too Much to Carry

Deuteronomy chapter 14 shows a clear example of the tithe and money being two distinct entities. In this illustration, one is given permission to actually exchange his tithe for money.

Deuteronomy 14:24-26
But if that place is too distant and you have been blessed by the LORD your God and cannot carry your tithe (because the place where the LORD will choose to put his Name is so far away),

then exchange your tithe for silver, and take the silver with you and go to the place the LORD your God will choose.

Use the silver to buy whatever you like: cattle, sheep, wine or other fermented drink, or anything you wish. Then you and your household shall eat there in the presence of the LORD your God and rejoice.

The individual in this passage was blessed so much by the Lord (v24) that he could not carry his tithe to the designated place. If this place is too great of a distance to travel that it is impractical to carry the tithe, it can be sold for silver (money). The money is then carried to the designated place and used to purchase replacement food (v26).

If Christians are required to tithe today, then nothing about the passage above makes sense if the substance for the tithe is already money. In this passage, the tithe could *not* be carried, but the money *could* be carried. This means the tithe could not be money in the first place since the tithe in this passage was exchanged for money. In addition, it simply does not make sense for a monetary tithe to be *exchanged* for money. Finally, the tithe mentioned here is eaten *in the presence of the LORD your God*, so once again, the tithe is not money since people do not eat money.

Some authors feel that the tithe sold here required a 20 percent redemption fee. This is not correct in that the 20 percent fee is applied only if the person possessing the tithe wants to buy it back from the Lord. In the passage above, however, the person sold it to 'someone else' so that replacement food could be purchased once he reached the designated place. Leviticus 27:27 says in a similar situation, "If he does not redeem it, it is to be sold at its set value." Therefore, the tithe in this case is not purchased by the owner himself, and thus, no redemption fee is necessary.

Redeeming the Tithe

Taking a closer look at Leviticus 27, pay particular attention to verse 31. This verse, like many others, is almost always taken out of context. Many interpret Leviticus 27:31 as a penalty for one who keeps something that belongs to the Lord. Therefore, this person needs to repay (monetarily) the original monetary tithe, and then add a 20 percent penalty.

Leviticus 27:30-31
A tithe of everything from the land, whether grain from the soil or fruit from the trees, belongs to the LORD; it is holy to the LORD.
If a man redeems any of his tithe, he must add a fifth of the value to it.

To a certain extent, the previous argument is correct. The tithe does indeed belong to the Lord, and an additional 20 percent value is required if the person *chooses* to redeem the tithe from the Lord. The point that needs clarification is the following: the person giving the tithe has the 'option' to purchase or *redeem* the tithe with a monetary amount equivalent to the tithe, where the value is determined by a priest. If one exercises this option, then this person simply adds an additional 20 percent to the value of the tithe.

Redeeming the tithe is not a penalty as if one were in some sort of trouble. Verse 31 should be viewed as a choice provided under, and in accordance with, the old covenant law. This verse should not be interpreted to mean that if a person does not pay a monetary tithe on time, the person has to repay the money at a later time with a 20 percent penalty.

The reason people do not realize that this verse is dealing with two different concepts, i.e., the tithe and the redemption of a tithe, is because they do not take literally what the preceding verse states. Verse 30 states, *A tithe of everything from the land, whether grain from the soil or fruit from the trees, belongs to the LORD.* This verse clearly indicates items suitable for a tithe and what is *holy to the Lord.*   Money is not mentioned here as being holy to the Lord.

The main point to remember when reading through these subsections on 'redeeming the tithe' is the following: the person who redeems or purchases the tithe actually receives something in return, and that is the 'tithe' itself. If someone goes to market to buy something, the person expects to actually have something in his possession after the sale. This is also the case with purchasing the tithe. So if someone redeems a tithe of grain, this person gave the monetary equivalent of the tithe, plus a fifth of its value (20 percent), to the priest. In return for the money, the tither actually receives the grain, as opposed to offering it to the Lord.

Redeeming Dedicated Items

To further emphasize the need to read Bible passages in their entirety for a better understanding, let us continue to analyze Leviticus 27:31. Many of today's believers do not read all of Leviticus chapter 27 to really understand what is being said in this one verse. If they did, they would understand that other items are dedicated unto the Lord that could also be *redeemed* (purchased), not just the tithe from the land.

Leviticus 27 is *not* referring to redeeming money for money, or eating and not eating dedicated items.   Instead, it is referring to redeeming dedicated persons, dedicated animals, dedicated houses, dedicated fields, and the tithe from the land. When viewed in its entirety, chapter 27 shows that other redeemable items such as a person, animal, house, and field, are not translated into money, nor are these items symbolic of money. This is also the case for the seed of the land and the fruit of the tree, which are not symbolic of money either.

The money used to buy back these items in Leviticus chapter 27 is the same money that is used in everyday living as discussed in Chapter 2, "Money and Occupations." See Numbers 3:45-51 and 18:15-17 for other examples of redeeming.

What Are Tithers Redeeming Today?

Jewish people have the opportunity to redeem the tithe with the monetary value of it, plus an additional 20 percent of that value. As stated earlier, money is not required from the Lord as a tithe, but rather, the required items are produce and livestock.

What does the Lord require today that is in a person's possession and can be redeemed with money? Are tithers receiving wheat or corn in return for money, or a dedicated person, field, or house? The problem is that Christians hand over money and call it a tithe. But as recorded in Leviticus 27:30-31, when an individual gives the priest money, that person receives something tangible in return. When Christians give money during a tithing transaction, are they receiving something tangible in return? No. This is clearly not what the Lord has in mind. There is no choice today to keep anything in exchange for the money given, but instead, Christians are simply told that to be obedient they must give monetary tithes.

Some tithers claim to receive a 'spiritual blessing' in return for their tithe. If this is the case, this spiritual blessing must be something required from the Lord. It must also be in the person's possession to begin with since a person can only tithe something that the Lord has already blessed him with. In addition, the person must be given the ability to redeem the spiritual blessing with money, all of which must be defined somewhere in Scripture. This is obviously not the case.

Regarding the 20 percent interest, how does the church calculate how much this should be? If one is truly tithing today as defined in Scripture, the monetary amount given should be equivalent to the tithe, as determined by the priest, plus 20 percent. Since Christians have no legitimate tithe to offer - produce of the land for example - they cannot properly calculate what a true exchange should be for the tithe. Hence, Christians distort the whole tithing process and settle for 10 percent of how much money a person makes as an acceptable tithe. This is definitely not based on the Bible.

Today's tithers are told they cannot redeem or eat the tithe, but someone under the law can both redeem and eat the tithe when appropriate. And, when they give money to redeem the tithe, they actually receive something tangible in return, which is the tithe itself. In contrast, when Christian tithers give money, sad to say, they get short changed.

TITHE AS A TAX

Most people, including tithers, do not really enjoy paying taxes, and there is at least one author who sees the tithe as a tax. This author says the tithe is God's tax collected from Christians for living on Earth. This is an interesting way of viewing the monetary tithe and another good reason for not paying it today.

Is today's monetary tithe similar to a tax, or more specifically, similar to the temple tax? After all, a tax is collected to support a government run agency or to meet one's organizational expenses (recall Chapter 2, "Money and Occupations"). According to some, the temple tax is the atonement money collected in Exodus 30:11-16, which is used for the service of the tabernacle. Today, the tithe is used for the service of the church. The temple tax or atonement offering was instituted by the Lord, and the tithe of today is mandated by church leaders. Jews are required to give a specific amount of money for the service of the tabernacle. Similarly, Christians have a minimum amount of money they are required to give for the service of the church.

The authors are in agreement that today's version of the tithe is like a tax. It is indeed used by many churches to partly or fully fund the service of the church - the actual facility and support of the church workers. When church leaders require their members to give a minimum of 10 percent of their money to the church, then a tax exists.

The question is, "Do Christians have to pay this tax?" This section shows that Christians do *not* have to pay this tax, or the monetary tithe, for the service of the church. However, financial support for the church is a necessary work that should continue, but *without* the 'mandatory requirements' or 'minimum strings' attached (this is discussed further in

Chapter 9, "Grace Giving"). Since this other author did not provide Bible verses to support his idea of the tithe being a tax, there is not any discussion concerning his reasons for drawing this conclusion. Nevertheless, Bible passages are provided to refute this theology.

The King's Tenth

There is an example in First Samuel chapter 8 about a tenth of the fields and a tenth of the sheep collected by a king. This took place when Israel chose to have a king rather than continuing to have judges. This passage seems appropriate to discuss here because many believers associate giving a tenth with giving a tithe.

1 Samuel 8:14-17
He will take the best of your fields and vineyards and olive groves and give them to his attendants.
He will take a tenth of your grain and of your vintage and give it to his officials and attendants.
Your menservants and maidservants and the best of your cattle and donkeys he will take for his own use.
He will take a tenth of your flocks, and you yourselves will become his slaves.

At this point in history, the elders of Israel were not satisfied with how Samuel's sons were conducting themselves, and therefore, wanted a king like other nations. Samuel did not want the children of Israel to consider having a king, and prayed to the Lord. In response, the Lord told Samuel to give them what they wanted because they had rejected Him. Samuel then informed the people what a king would require from them, and a portion of the requirements are listed above in 1 Samuel 8:14-17.

Giving a tenth of anything to the king's *officials and attendants* is not the same as giving the tithe unto the Lord. The king's tenth was not holy, whereas the tithe given unto the Lord is holy (Lev. 27:30, 32). Likewise, the government collects more than a tenth of a person's income from many people today, but this does not constitute tithing to the government.

When Israel started giving a tenth of their fields and sheep to the king, they were not tithing either. Instead of wanting to follow the law of Moses, they wanted to be like other nations - to have a king judge them and fight their battles (1 Sam. 8:20). Therefore, they knowingly went away from the rule of the written law to have a king govern them instead (1 Sam. 8:7-8).

The tenth given to the king does not replace the tithe given to the Lord. Just because the children of Israel rejected the Lord does not mean the law was abolished and a new tithe instituted. They simply chose to follow a king, an earthly leader, and subsequently, they had to pay taxes to support their king.

Sons Are Exempt From Taxes

Romans 13:1-2 states that Christians are to obey those in authority because they are put there by God. See also 1 Peter 2:13-14. No governing power is in place that God does not want there, as they play roles in shaping world events, including biblical events. Paul continues with this letter to the Romans by pointing out the need to submit to these authorities because they are God's servants. People may not like the government they live under, but they need to pay all taxes actually owed (Rom. 13:5-7).

As mentioned earlier, the author of a certain book claims that the tithe is God's tax required of Christians for living on Earth. This is nothing more than another example of an honest mistake many people make when taught non-scriptural theology. The Bible does not point out everything that Christians *want* to know, but it contains enough to guide everyone along the narrow path. If there is an example in the Bible, apply it when appropriate. There is such a passage concerning the tax issue.

Many view the following passage from the book of Matthew as a 'Jesus paying the temple tax' story, but it is more than that. Please read it carefully (this passage is also quoted in Chapter 2 when discussing taxes in the New Testament).

Matthew 17:24-27

After Jesus and his disciples arrived in Capernaum, the collectors of the two-drachma tax came to Peter and asked, "Doesn't your teacher pay the temple tax?"

"Yes, he does," he replied. When Peter came into the house, Jesus was the first to speak. "What do you think, Simon?" he asked. "From whom do the kings of the earth collect duty and taxes - from their own sons or from others?"

"From others," Peter answered. "Then the sons are exempt," Jesus said to him.

"But so that we may not offend them, go to the lake and throw out your line. Take the first fish you catch; open its mouth and you will find a four-drachma coin. Take it and give it to them for my tax and yours."

Most probably do not realize that this passage holds the answer showing that God does not require a minimum or a mandatory amount of money from Christians for the support of the church. In this passage, Peter was asked if Jesus paid the temple tax. Peter replied, *"Yes, he does."* It is the dialogue that takes place inside the house that provides a very profound revelation. Before Peter could ask Jesus anything, Jesus asked the first question, *"From whom do the kings of the earth collect duty and taxes - from their own sons or from others?"* Peter responded by saying, *"From others."* Then Jesus followed with, *"Then the sons are exempt."*

Notice that Jesus asked a question concerning *earthly kings*, although the tax collectors came for the temple tax. Jesus is the Son of God; therefore, He was explaining to Peter that He is exempt from paying this tax because of His sonship (see Jn. 1:14, 18; 3:16-18). The children of Israel were not referred to as sons and daughters like Christians are today. Jesus is the first son, and after His death and resurrection, believers in Christ are also sons and daughters (see Rom. 8:15-17; Gal. 4:4-7).

In Matthew 17:24-27 above, Jesus used earthly kings and sons to illustrate a spiritual parallel relationship between Him and His Father, the God of the temple. Jesus was saying that He did not have to pay the required amount of taxes, or money, to His Father because sons are exempt from such taxes! Since the atoning sacrifice of Jesus, followers of Christ are also sons and daughters of the living God. Consequently, Christians do not have to pay any required amount of money to God in the form of a tax, much less a tithe as a tax - *Then the sons are exempt.* However, in order not to offend the tax collectors, Jesus instructs Peter to go to the lake and get the required tax from the mouth of a fish.

The New Temple

Another reason Christians are not required to pay any form of a tax for the service of the tabernacle, temple, or church, is because there exists a new temple. This new temple is not made of hands, but is of flesh, and is in fact the human body. The first body that was referred to as a temple made of flesh was the body of Jesus (Jn. 2:21).

Jesus was accused of plotting to destroy the temple of God - the physical building - and then rebuild it in three days (Matt. 26:60-64; 27:40). Those He spoke to did not realize Jesus was speaking of His own body, and the disciples did not realize this either until after Jesus was raised from the dead (Jn. 2:22).

Jesus foretold of a new kind of temple in John 2:21. Would people pay for service on a building if they knew it would be replaced soon? This could be another reason why Jesus was not eager to pay this temple tax of Matthew 17:24-27. Jesus knew things were about to change dramatically, but since Jesus did not want to offend them, He paid the tax (Matt. 17:27).

All Christians are recipients of this change in temple. For the bodies of all Christians are temples of God - temples of the Holy Spirit.

1 Corinthians 3:16-17
Don't you know that you yourselves are God's temple and that God's Spirit lives in you?

If anyone destroys God's temple, God will destroy him; for God's temple is sacred, and you are that temple.

1 Corinthians 6:19-20
*Do you not know that your body is a temple of the
Holy Spirit, who is in you, whom you have received from
God? You are not your own;*
*you were bought at a price. Therefore honor God with
your body.*

This new temple is sacred, so Christians should take care
of their temple like people used to take care of the temple of
God made with hands. ⸱ God mandates that Christians *Honor
God with your body.* In other words, if you want to pay a
temple tax, then take that tax money and use it for the service
of this new temple. For example, Christians can buy a comb
for their hair, clothes to hide their nakedness, toothpaste to
clean their teeth, soap for a bath, and perfume or cologne to
hide what the soap missed! If there is a temple tax for today's
Christians, it should be spent for the upkeep of each person's
temple! Although this book mentions how Christians can
spend their temple tax dollars, there are other ways Christians
can honor God with their bodies, such as keeping in good
health, not using drugs, watching what is said to one another,
etc.

No New Taxes

Are today's Christians tithing money as if it were a tax so
they will not offend someone? Perhaps this person is their
spouse, their friend, or maybe their pastor. "No new taxes"
may sound like a political slogan, but church leaders should
stop taxing followers of Christ.

Today, the tabernacle, or the temple of God, is not used by
Christians to perform old covenant rituals. Therefore, the
upkeep of an earthly man-made temple is not a requirement.
The new temple is made of flesh and Christians are required to
keep it holy. Earlier parts of this chapter demonstrate that the
church is not equivalent to a storehouse. Likewise, neither is
the church equivalent to the temple or tabernacle.

Are Christians paying tithes to the church the way they pay
taxes to a government? People pay taxes to the government
and expect the government to solve their problems. This

mentality has carried over into Christianity by giving the so-called required tenth of a person's income to the church as if it were a tax. As a result of giving this tenth, Christians act as if God will solve all of their problems, as well as the problems of their communities. However, if people do not allow God to use them to solve the needs of their communities, then it is very possible that many needs will never be met.

For those individuals who want to pay a tithe unto the Lord as if it were a mandated tax, they should check their new family tree and see whether their Father is in heaven or on Earth. If in heaven, then these individuals are tax exempt (Matt. 17:24-27). Otherwise, like the children of Israel, one may pay a monetary tithe, or tax, as if it were paid to a king and fall into the same situation that Israel did. "When that day comes, you will cry out for relief from the king you have chosen, and the LORD will not answer you in that day" (1 Sam. 8:18).

Christians need to get out of the 'tax mentality,' and start giving from the desires of their hearts. If Christians want to really do something positive, they ought to become new covenant givers as discussed in Chapter 9, "Grace Giving." In fact, some Christians are probably already giving to the church according to the way of the gospel. Any required form of tax unto the Lord, or unto the Father, is totally unbiblical and should not be mandated by church leaders.

OTHER MISUSES OF THE WORD TITHE

Christians give a tenth of their money to the local church and call it a tithe. Many also give additional money to the church, evangelists, TV ministries, etc., and call that an offering above and beyond the monetary tithe. Let us look at additional misuses of the word tithe to see how far from the true definition of tithing Christians have strayed.

Tithing Time and Talent

There is the misconception that Christians can actually tithe their time and talent, which is just as misleading as the monetary tithe itself. This section starts off by asking, "How does one actually tithe time and talents to the Lord?" If people tithe their time, do they literally give 2.4 hours of every day to the Lord? Or do they make up the time for a whole week by giving the entire 16.8 hours to the Lord on Sunday?

When Christians tithe talents, what talents do they actually perform? Does the 16.8 hours a week include singing, ushering, helping with the church finances, etc.? Do not forget that a tithe is literally 10 percent of something. What happens if someone gives 20 hours of time and talent to the church for an entire week? Is the additional 3.2 hours considered an offering above and beyond this tithe? Should the first 16.8 hours be declared a tithe and the rest declared an offering before the Lord will accept the 3.2 hours as an offering? The more one searches God's word, the more confusing today's tithing theology becomes.

People cannot give only 10 percent of their talent to the Lord. For example, if someone has the talent to sing, this person should not spend 10 percent of his 'singing time' singing for the Lord, and the other 90 percent of his 'singing time' singing for Satan. A second example would be the one who wants to lead a Sunday school class. Nobody can measure the amount of time needed for preparation, and the actual time giving the lesson, and possibly come out to 10 percent of their time per day per week.

The individuals who say they tithe their time and talents to the Lord are actually *giving,* and *not tithing,* their time and talents to the Lord or to the church. It is very difficult to regulate 10 percent of someone's time and talents for the Lord's use, so Christians are urged to stop trying to regulate their spiritual walk. Chapter 8, "New Covenant Commands," will provide additional information concerning a Christian's daily walk in the Spirit.

Tithes Representing Time and Talent

Stated above are ways some Christians claim they can tithe their time and talent. Equally as unbiblical is the notion that the monetary tithe can actually represent time, talent and energy. According to the biblical definition, this is simply not possible. The Lord does not give those under the law the option of exchanging time with the required tithing items. Nor did He allow the use of talent and energy as replacements for the original tithe. The only way these things can replace the required tithed items is if there is truly a new way to tithe. Since there is no biblical passage to validate a change in the tithing requirements, this can only be of human origin and tradition, and should therefore be terminated.

Some of God's people do have the gift of giving, so let them give accordingly. But in general, using the monetary tithe to represent time, talent, and energy is the lazy person's way of not participating in the work of the church. The kind of tithing mentioned here furthers the mentality that if a person goes to church and pays a tithe, then this person has done his job until the next paycheck - he has given his time, talent and energy to the church through his monetary tithe. It also furthers the 'Sunday only' Christian mentality. What about the rest of the week? The local body, as well as the church in general, needs everyone's time, talent, and energy throughout the week - not just on Sunday. Giving money to the local church is not going to clean the sanctuary or take care of the community's needs. It takes everyone's time and talent to accomplish these tasks.

Tithing More Than 10 Percent

There are occasions when stories are told of people being blessed, and because of this blessing, they tithe more than 10 percent of their income. But if people wait long enough during the same conversation, these individuals will also say a tithe is only 10 percent of one's income, thus contradicting themselves.

A pastor once told a story of a person who had a business. The businessman tithed from the revenue of the business.

Every two years he increased his tithe by 10 percent. Thus, he started off by tithing 10 percent, then 20 percent the third year, 30 percent the fifth year, until he reached a point where he tithed 100 percent of the revenue from the business. The pastor also added that during this time the person made investments into other money-making ventures, so he did not totally rely on his earnings from this particular business. This same pastor also mentioned earlier in his sermon that "you cannot tithe 9 percent or 11 percent," but contradicting himself, he said this particular individual tithed 100 percent of his revenue!

Tithing, by definition, means 10 percent or one-tenth of something. According to the old covenant law, a tithe is one-tenth of livestock, produce, oil, etc. Today the tithe is considered 10 percent of one's income. Moreover, stories are told of how blessings come as a result of tithing and as blessings continue, the tithe increases to more than 10 percent.

This kind of giving leads many to believe that all giving should be done at the local church - tithing up to 100 percent of one's income. This is especially harmful if the church does not help the needy in its community. Are people supposed to tell their neighbor they have no extra food to give because they saved money on the food bill in order to tithe more at the church?

If Christians only give money to support traditional church activities, then they have not yet experienced the true joy of giving. The true joy of giving is when a person gives to someone else on the 'individual' level, or on a personal, one-on-one basis. In addition, until all Christians participate in giving at the individual level, it is very likely that the needy will continue to be overlooked in favor of traditional church expenses.

Another problem with the concept of tithing more than 10 percent is the idea that the amount of the tithe can change. Further problems arise when the tithe is not only interchanged with firstfruit, but also with the offering. The latter interchange exists despite the fact that the monetary offering is taught to be above and beyond the monetary tithe. This is very confusing to new and old believers alike, especially when the terms *tithing, offering* and *giving* are used interchangeably. To summarize this accurately, a tithe is a tenth of the required items offered; an offering is regulated by the particular ritual performed (Chapter 3); and Christian giving is not regulated at all (Chapters 8 and 9).

The Pharisees Gave Tithes

In the book of Matthew, many say Jesus had the opportunity to tell the scribes and Pharisees not to tithe. Instead, He told them tithing is what they ought to have done. If tithing should not be practiced today, why did Jesus *not* tell them to discontinue tithing? The answer is simple. The Pharisees were under the law, therefore, *they had to tithe.* The complete explanation is provided in Chapter 9 as to why Jesus did not tell the Pharisees to *stop* tithing.

The real question here is whether or not the Pharisees were actually offering real tithes, or doing what Christians do today - giving a monetary tithe. Since many pastors read only the King James translation, two versions of Matthew 23:23 are presented here. Although the New International Version is a little more self-explanatory, many people still miss what Jesus is saying due to traditional teaching on the monetary tithe.

Matthew 23:23 KJV
Woe unto you, scribes and Pharisees, hypocrites! for ye pay tithe of mint and anise and cummin, and have omitted the weightier matters of the law, judgment, mercy, and faith: these ought ye to have done, and not to leave the other undone.

The King James Version uses the word 'pay' which misleads some into thinking the tithe of the Pharisees was money. Since today money is used to pay for goods, and since the word tithe is misinterpreted to mean the phrase '10 percent of one's income,' Christians automatically think Jesus told the Pharisees to continue paying 10 percent from whatever means they had of making a living. Now look at the New International Version.

Matthew 23:23 NIV
Woe to you, teachers of the law and Pharisees, you hypocrites! You give a tenth of your spices - mint, dill and cummin. But you have neglected the more important matters of the law - justice, mercy and faithfulness. You should have practiced the latter, without neglecting the former.

Let us take a closer look at what was actually being tithed. They were not tithing money of any kind, but in this passage, they gave a tenth of their spices - *mint, dill and cummin.* Yet, many believers do not see that the Pharisees gave a true tithe which came from the seed of the land, not the money earned from an occupation. Old covenant law commands them to do this, and everyone knows they followed the letter of the law.

Today's monetary tithing practice does not have anything in common with the true act of tithing as performed by the Pharisees and others in the Bible. Therefore, to quote Matthew 23:23 in order to support today's form of monetary tithing would actually be quoting this verse out of context.

NO NEW TITHE

Many churches today require Christians to give 10 percent of their money to the local church and call it a tithe. But as shown by definition in this chapter, the tithe is not, was not, and should never be, interpreted as 10 percent of a person's income. The passages cited in this chapter clearly show that the tithe comes from what is produced in the fields each year, as well as from livestock. It is an edible substance such as wheat or bulls. It does not take an agricultural expert to realize that the field produces such things as corn and wheat - not money. After all, money does not grow on trees! Moreover, nobody should add to or take away from the commands given by God (Deut. 4:2; 12:32). "Do not add to his words, or he will rebuke you and prove you a liar" (Prov. 30:6).

This chapter covers quite a few items concerning the old covenant practice of tithing, starting with the word tithe.

Tithing, according to old covenant law, is a tenth of the grain of the soil, of the fruit of trees, of the herd and flock, and of new wine and oil. In years one, two, four, and five of a seven year cycle, the tithe is *not* to be *eaten* in the hometown of the person supplying the tithe. Instead, it is *eaten* at a place God chooses. The worshipper, his family and servants, and the Levites participate in the eating of the tithe, as it is always something that can be consumed.

The purpose of the tithe is to support the Levites, and every three years to support the needy and the Levites. In addition, when gathering the harvest, crops are left over for those who are in need. Also, a tenth of the tithe collected by the Levites is presented to the priest as the Lord's offering, and every seventh year the agricultural tithe is not required by the Lord at all. In comparison with today's version of tithing, tithing in biblical times provided more support for people than does the monetary tithe of today!

This chapter also covers a few common misinterpretations such as 'eating the tithe,' 'bringing the tithe into the storehouse,' 'tithe as a tax,' and 'redeeming the tithe.' The following clarifications were made: eating the tithe is, in fact, supposed to be done; the phrase to 'bring the tithe into the storehouse' (Mal. 3:10) is often used out of scriptural context, where storehouse here is actually a place used to store crops and livestock; Christians tithe as if it is a tax and was declared not necessary because of their sonship; and the 20 percent redemption fee is *not a penalty* for not tithing, but it is part of an option under the law to purchase the tithe wherein 20 percent is added to the value of the tithe.

It should also be noted how offerings were not given or performed 'above and beyond a tithe.' For example, the giving of the tithe was not required before the ritual of the burnt offering, the peace offering, or the sin offering. In addition, the one responsible for providing an offering can purchase it. This clearly implies that this particular person must not have been able to tithe of this item. Today, Christians are told they are not true givers until they enter the realm of monetary offerings, which comes after a monetary tithe unto the Lord. Chapters 3 and 4 show, by the definitions of offerings and tithing, that this is not biblically based.

Christians should be liberal givers, but the method Christians have adopted, in the form of monetary tithes and offerings, does more harm than good. It is very confusing when Christians replace the tithe with money. Proceeding into the later chapters of this book, the harm caused by giving in the name of monetary tithes and offerings is further demonstrated. This includes the strict nature of tithes preventing Christians from being led by the Spirit in the area of giving. It is simply an unacceptable Christian practice if one is to walk in the Spirit.

It is time to stop the tradition of monetary tithing and the monetary offering because tradition is what makes the commandments of God of no effect (Matt. 15:3-9). Hopefully this book has shown, and will continue to show, that today's version of the tithe is man-made and passed along by tradition.

To date, Christian giving has been disguised as tithes and offerings, and as a result, people have added unnecessary regulations to it. These unnecessary rules prevent Christians from experiencing true Spirit-led giving. Tithing is simply one of the many rituals performed under old covenant law, and like the other rituals, is not required of Christians (Chapter 6, "Freedom Through Death"). Giving, on the other hand, is required of Christians and is covered in Chapter 9, "Grace Giving," where the Spirit-led way to give is discussed.

Deuteronomy 14:28-29

At the end of every three years, bring all the tithes of that year's produce and store it in your towns,

so that the Levites (who have no allotment or inheritance of their own) and the aliens, the fatherless and the widows who live in your towns may come and eat and be satisfied, and so that the LORD your God may bless you in all the work of your hands.

5

Firstfruit Defined

Let us start this chapter by getting straight to the point - tithes and firstfruit have two different meanings. Many tithers use these terms interchangeably when, in fact, they should not. Tithing has already been defined in the previous chapter. It is now time to define firstfruit according to what is written in the Bible.

The misinterpretation of several Bible verses dealing with the firstfruit is why Christians tend to have an inaccurate definition of it. This chapter clears up many misunderstandings concerning the use of firstfruit. Many people mistakenly use this word in defining the tithe, and in defining how Christians give. By defining the word firstfruit, the reader can see the problem with using this term to describe the tithe and how Christians ought to support the church, especially when it comes to tithing money. This kind of mistake happens when Christian giving is called something other than what it is, and in this particular case, calling it 'firstfruit.'

At the conclusion of this chapter, the reader will see that referring to the biblical firstfruit when talking about monetary income is inappropriate and has nothing to do with traditional monetary giving. This clarification will help guide the followers of Christ back to biblical forms of Christian stewardship in relation to economics.

One passage covered in this chapter is Genesis 4:3-4. It deals with the offerings of Cain and Abel and how God looked with favor on Abel. The main passage, however, from which firstfruit is taught to be 10 percent of a person's income is

Proverbs 3:9-10. It states, "Honor the LORD with your wealth, with the firstfruits of all your crops; then your barns will be filled to overflowing, and your vats will brim over with new wine."

SUBSTANCE OF THE FIRSTFRUIT

Firstfruit is the first of the crops or fruit that ripen and is subsequently gathered. It is an edible substance such as wheat, oil, wine, corn, etc. (Lev. 2:14, 23:17; Num. 18:12; Deut. 18:4; 2 Chr. 31:5), and is grown in the land or soil (Ex. 23:16, 19; 34:26; Deut. 26:10). The giving of the firstfruit is seasonal and it is gathered year by year (Neh. 10:35).

Firstfruit is the kind of fruit that is literally *eaten* and also permissible to eat, not the forbidden kind like that in the garden of Eden, nor the monetary kind some people teach today. The following verses in this section show the firstfruit as being crops from the field or fruit from the tree.

Exodus 23:16
Celebrate the Feast of Harvest with the firstfruits of the crops you sow in your field. Celebrate the Feast of Ingathering at the end of the year, when you gather in your crops from the field.

Crops are gathered at the beginning of the season, and for the Feast of Ingathering, the last of the *crops* are also gathered. However, the Bible gives no indication when giving the firstfruit as to how much should be gathered (i.e., one bushel or ten).

Most conclusions concerning the amount of the firstfruit have included assumptions. The problem with making an assumption is that one may assume something as true and fail to study the validity behind the assumption. For example, one may assume that tithing money is something Christians are required to do today when, in fact, this is not the case.

Best of the Firstfruit

In Malachi it states that all of the tithes should be delivered to the storehouse. If tithe and firstfruit are indeed the same, then can they be interchanged in the following passage and still make sense?

Exodus 23:19
Bring the best of the firstfruits of your soil to the house of the LORD your God. ...

According to this verse, one is to *bring the best of the firstfruit*. Recall in the book of Malachi that God commands the people to "bring the whole tithe into the storehouse" (Mal. 3:10). If tithe and firstfruit are the same, then Exodus 23:19 would read, *"Bring the best of the* tithe *of your soil to the house of the LORD your God."* The question then becomes, "How much is the best of the tithe?" Is it 8 percent, or maybe just 3 percent? Are God's people commanded to bring the tithe into the storehouse in Malachi while commanded to bring the best of the tithe to the house of the Lord in Exodus?

There is already enough confusion in thinking that tithes and firstfruit have something to do with the amount of money earned - they are both actually edible substances. The concept of the tithe and firstfruit being interchangeable only adds to the confusion. This is expected when Christians refer to their giving as tithes and/or firstfruit.

Storeroom for the Firstfruit

The following verse indicates that men were in charge of the storerooms that housed different types of contributions. Notice how the storerooms were for the *firstfruits and tithes.*

Nehemiah 12:44
At that time men were appointed to be in charge of the storerooms for the contributions, firstfruits and tithes. From the fields around the towns they were to bring into

*the storerooms the portions required by the Law for the
priests and the Levites, for Judah was pleased with the
ministering priests and Levites.*

As noted here, the contributions are gathered *from the
fields.* The items gathered are food substances, which are put
into storerooms, not money put into bank accounts. *They
were to bring into the storerooms the portions required by the
Law,* which are actual *firstfruits and tithes.*

What is required by the law for the tithe (Lev. 27:30, 32;
Deut. 14:22-23), and for the firstfruit (Lev. 2:14, 23:17; Num.
18:12; Deut. 18:4; 2 Chr. 31:5), has already been established.
Nehemiah indicates that firstfruits and tithes are different.
However, many of today's believers have combined the two
words, firstfruit and tithe, into one meaning - 10 percent of a
person's income.

PURPOSE OF THE FIRSTFRUIT

Nehemiah 10:35-37

*We also assume responsibility for bringing to the
house of the LORD each year the firstfruits of our crops
and of every fruit tree.*

*As it is also written in the Law, we will bring the
firstborn of our sons and of our cattle, of our herds and of
our flocks to the house of our God, to the priests
ministering there.*

*Moreover, we will bring to the storerooms of the house
of our God, to the priests, the first of our ground meal, of
our grain offerings, of the fruit of all our trees and of our
new wine and oil. And we will bring a tithe of our crops
to the Levites, for it is the Levites who collect the tithes in
all the towns where we work.*

The purpose of the firstfruit is to support the priest. The
firstfruit is given to the priests as an offering from the Jewish
community *(to the priests ministering there),* not from the Levite.
The Levite receives a tithe from the people, a tenth of which

goes to the priests. The tenth given to the priest from the Levite (a tithe of the tithe) should not be confused with firstfruit, which is offered by the people.

Best of the Firstfruit for Priest

Recall Numbers 18:26-29 and compare it with this verse from Ezekiel.

Ezekiel 44:30
The best of all the firstfruits and of all your special gifts will belong to the priests. You are to give them the first portion of your ground meal so that a blessing may rest on your household.

Here Ezekiel says the *best of all the firstfruits will belong to the priests* (offered by Jewish worshippers). It should not be translated 'the best of the tithe' because the passage in Numbers states that the *tithe of the tithe* is given to the priest (offered by the Levites). In addition, Numbers 18:26-29 should not be translated 'the tithe of the firstfruit,' nor 'the firstfruit of the tithe.'

According to Ezekiel 44:30, the best of the firstfruit belongs to the priest. Numbers 18:26-28 also states the priest was to receive a tenth of the tithe. Furthermore, Numbers 18:21 states that the Levites receive the tithe as an inheritance. Nehemiah confirms what is already required, while showing there is a difference between what the priests receive and what the Levites receive from the people. One received produce from the firstfruit and a tenth of the tithe (the priest) while the other received produce from the tithe (the Levite).

To support today's version of tithing, people use the word firstfruit to mean tithe. If 'tithe' is used instead of 'firstfruit' in Exodus 23, then it would read, "Celebrate the Feast of Harvest with the tithe of the crops you sow in your field." The problem here is that the word 'tithe' is not used when referring to what the people should offer the priests. Therefore, Exodus 23 would have a whole different meaning if firstfruit and tithe were, in fact, interchangeable.

Some of the Firstfruit for Priest

The following passage is similar to that of Exodus 23:19 and Ezekiel 44:30, except it says 'some' instead of 'best' of the firstfruits.

Deuteronomy 26:1-4

When you have entered the land the LORD your God is giving you as an inheritance and have taken possession of it and settled in it,

take some of the firstfruits of all that you produce from the soil of the land the LORD your God is giving you and put them in a basket. Then go to the place the LORD your God will choose as a dwelling for his Name

and say to the priest in office at the time, "I declare today to the LORD your God that I have come to the land the LORD swore to our forefathers to give us."

The priest shall take the basket from your hands and set it down in front of the altar of the LORD your God.

If firstfruit and tithe are equivalent, then a similar question can be asked, "How much is *some* of the tithe?" In addition, the firstfruit mentioned here is given to a priest, whereas the tithe is collected by the Levites. *And we will bring a tithe of our crops to the Levites, for it is the Levites who collect the tithes in all the towns where we work* (Neh. 10:37).

If people stop redefining the words tithe and firstfruit to be equivalent, and stop converting them from edible items to currency, then the previous passages would make sense. In either case, the best and some of the firstfruit came from the soil of the land because they consisted of crops - *take some of the firstfruits of all that you produce from the soil of the land.* Please do not translate 'soil of the land' into 'checkbook', 'bank account', or 'occupation.'

NEW COVENANT FIRSTFRUIT

The term firstfruit is used differently in the Bible depending on where it is located. In the Old Testament, firstfruit is as defined above, but in this section, the symbolic use of firstfruit is addressed. Please note, firstfruit is never 'defined' as being the first part of someone's income. This does not imply that Christians cannot use the word firstfruit symbolically in reference to the first part of their income. However, Christians should not take what is said about the firstfruit and use it as a requirement to give 10 percent of their money. Everyone should stop at the symbolic use of the word firstfruit when describing monetary gifts.

With this said, here is the chance for those who want to take the word firstfruit to another level.

Romans 16:5 KJV
Likewise greet the church that is in their house. Salute my wellbeloved Epaenetus, who is the firstfruits of Achaia unto Christ.

Here is an example of the use of firstfruit to describe someone as first to convert to Christ in Asia. However, in order to understand the symbolic use of the term firstfruit in this passage, one must first understand the true definition as described earlier. See also 1 Corinthians 16:15. In the next example, firstfruit is used to describe Christ as the first person raised from the dead.

1 Corinthians 15:20-23
But Christ has indeed been raised from the dead, the firstfruits of those who have fallen asleep.

For since death came through a man, the resurrection of the dead comes also through a man.

For as in Adam all die, so in Christ all will be made alive.

But each in his own turn: Christ, the firstfruits; then, when he comes, those who belong to him.

The following verses also use the word firstfruit: Romans 8:22-23, James 1:18, and Revelation 14:4. Notice that in none of these passages can the firstfruit be interpreted as being money.

PROVERBS 3:9-10 EXPLAINED

Proverbs 3:9-10 NIV
Honor the LORD with your wealth, with the firstfruits of all your crops;
then your barns will be filled to overflowing, and your vats will brim over with new wine.

Proverbs 3:9-10 KJV
Honour the LORD with thy substance, and with the firstfruits of all thine increase:
So shall thy barns be filled with plenty, and thy presses shall burst out with new wine.

Honor the Lord With Your Wealth

Many Christians think that the only type of wealth or substance is money. This incorrect thinking, along with other inaccurate teachings on this subject, is the reason this passage is so highly misinterpreted by many believers today. The definition of wealth or substance is literally any tangible good belonging to a person. The fact-of-the-matter is, neither this nor any other verse in the Bible supports present day tithes and offerings.

In Proverbs 3:9 are the words: *honor the Lord with your wealth.* The question then becomes, "How does one honor the Lord with his wealth or substance?" To honor the Lord with wealth, or to show gratitude towards God, one can provide a free will offering. There is no set amount to give in this type of offering. "From what you have, take an offering for the LORD. Everyone who is willing is to bring to the LORD an offering of gold, silver and bronze" (Ex. 35:5). In addition, a person can give a thank offering unto the Lord, or even a gift offering. Those under the law have plenty of ways to honor the Lord with their substance or wealth.

Honor the Lord With Your Firstfruit

This chapter defined and presented examples of the firstfruit. In light of these definitions and examples, it is erroneous to consider firstfruit and tithe synonymous terms. Accordingly, Proverbs 3:9 does not suggest that a person give 10 percent of his income to the Lord. The firstfruit is a food substance, and according to the Bible, it is not a specific amount (see Ex. 23:16, 19; Deut. 26:2; Neh. 10:37; 12:44).

Barns, Vats, Bank Accounts

Quite often, verses and words in the Bible are redefined. The same is true of Proverbs 3:9-10. In the world today, too much emphasis is placed on making money, and consequently, Scripture is redefined to relate to making money. In Proverbs 3:10, the words 'barn' and 'vat' have been redefined to mean 'bank account,' and thus used to support today's version of tithes.

Proverbs 3:10
then your barns will be filled to overflowing, and your vats will brim over with new wine.

A barn is a barn, and a vat is a vat (winepress). People do not put money into either of these. Livestock and produce are stored in these places, and money is put into a wallet or purse.

Proverbs 3:9-10 NMV

If one applies all that Christians are taught concerning Proverbs 3:9-10, with all its misinterpretations, then the New Money Version of the Bible would interpret this passage as follows:

Proverbs 3:9-10 NMV
Honour the LORD with your money, with the first 10 percent of all the money you make;
then your bank accounts will be filled with plenty, and your wallets shall burst out with new money.

The Bible says to honor the Lord with one's wealth and with the firstfruits of one's *crops*. In return, his/her *barns* will be *filled*. Instead, Christians give Him 10 percent of their money, which is *not* what the Lord asked for as a tithe or the firstfruit. Then they expect to find their bank accounts filled with plenty.

If a person does not have the necessary crops, then Proverbs 3:9 cannot be performed. Hence, Proverbs 3:10 cannot work either. In any case, Christians should concern themselves with walking in the Spirit and getting necessary instructions from new covenant commands (Chapter 8). Most importantly, Christians need to stop giving under the guise of 'firstfruit,' since this is not the manner in which Jesus or the disciples instructed Christians to give under the new covenant.

FIRSTBORN AND FIRSTLING

Those who teach on giving monetary tithes and offerings usually select any passage in the Bible where someone is required to give unto the Lord and then use it to support their view. This includes passages containing the terms 'firstborn' and 'firstling.' Examination of the Bible shows that firstborn or firstling are quantities, ranging from one to many, of the same item. Firstborn or firstling can be either man or animal.

Deuteronomy 15:19-22 is translated from Hebrew to both firstborn and firstling depending on the Bible translation. These old covenant terms in this passage have an attribute similar to sacrifices used in offerings - they can be *eaten*. The following is an example of the firstborn consisting of the male of the herd (i.e., bull and cow) and flock (i.e., sheep and goat). Notice what is done to the firstling and who participates in this ritual.

Deuteronomy 15:19-22

Set apart for the LORD your God every firstborn male of your herds and flocks. Do not put the firstborn of your oxen to work, and do not shear the firstborn of your sheep.

Each year you and your family are to eat them in the presence of the LORD your God at the place he will choose.

If an animal has a defect, is lame or blind, or has any serious flaw, you must not sacrifice it to the LORD your God.

You are to eat it in your own towns. Both the ceremonially unclean and the clean may eat it, as if it were gazelle or deer.

The person providing the offering, along with the person's family, *eats* the *firstborn* at a place God chooses. On the other hand, a family can eat the firstborn of the herd and flock in their home town if it had a defect, and must not be sacrificed. The participants are not told to bring a tenth of the herd or flock, nor were they told to bring money. Once again, people do not eat money, and when has money ever been described as having *a defect*, being *lame or blind* (v21)?

The main difference between Leviticus 27:32-33 and Deuteronomy 15:19 is that Leviticus 27:32 specifies a 'tenth' of the herd and flock, or a tithe, while Deuteronomy 15:19 only requires the 'first' of the herd and flock. Recall that Leviticus 27:32 mentions counting the herd and flock as it passed under the rod and took every tenth animal as the tithe. It is entirely possible that if the owner of the herd possesses only nine animals, then a tithe of the herd is not offered since a tenth animal could not pass under the rod. In contrast, the firstborn of the herd always results in at least one animal if there are any 'firstborn' animals.

Terms Used Interchangeably

Firstborn and firstling are used interchangeably in several verses of the Bible, and the word used typically depends on the version of the Bible. In most cases, firstborn refers to man while firstling typically refers to animals. Some translations also use the words or phrases 'oldest,' 'older,' and 'first offspring' when talking about the firstborn of man. However, firstborn and firstling never refer to money.

Firstborn is used to translate several different words from Hebrew. The following verses are examples of the use of firstborn in the King James Version where it refers to man: Gen. 10:15; 22:21; 25:13; 27:19, 32; 35:23. The following verses use firstborn in reference to man and beast: Ex. 11:5; 12:12, 29; 13:15. There are also passages in reference to women: Gen. 19:31-38; 29:26; 1 Sam. 14:49. In Deut. 21:16-17, the word firstborn is translated as the child who has the right of the firstborn, or birthright. Finally, firstborn is used to refer to Jesus as being the firstborn of man or creation: Matt. 1:25; Lk. 2:7; Rom. 8:29; Col. 1:15, 18; Heb. 11:28; 12:23.

The term firstling is typically used in the King James Version when referring to animals. The following verses use the word firstling: Ex. 13:12-13; 34:19-20; Lev. 27:26; Num. 18:15, 17; Deut. 15:19; 33:17. With the exception of the aforementioned Exodus passages, these verses in the New International Version use the word firstborn instead.

The firstborn is the first of something, not a tenth of something. The main point is that there is no quantity associated with the firstborn except for the quantity of 'one.' In addition, passages containing the word firstborn should not be used to validate the monetary tithe, or used in regard to a person's income.

The Offerings of Cain and Abel

A common misuse of the word firstborn, or firstling, is in Genesis 4:3-4 regarding what Abel offered unto the Lord.

Genesis 4:3-4
In the course of time Cain brought some of the fruits of the soil as an offering to the LORD.

But Abel brought fat portions from some of the firstborn of his flock. The LORD looked with favor on Abel and his offering,

Many Christians claim that Abel brought a tithe unto the Lord. Others say Abel brought a portion unto the Lord as if he were tithing. Both cases are clearly wrong because it states that Abel *brought fat portions from some of the firstborn*, not a tithe, nor a portion considered a tithe.

From the definitions of firstling and firstborn covered in this chapter, it is obvious that Abel did not tithe anything in any sense of the word. The Bible does not say how many of his flock were used in the offering, it simply says he brought fat portions from *some* of the firstling, or the *firstborn*, of his flock. Furthermore, it does not make biblical sense when this passage is misconstrued to support monetary tithing. Changing the meaning from 'offering fat portions from the firstborn' to 'tithing money' is simply not biblically sound.

Exodus 23:16, 19 and Deuteronomy 26:2 specify that the firstfruit comes from the soil. When people plant seed for an upcoming harvest, it is done so in the ground. People of Old Testament times planted and grew the same types of crops and fruit as farmers do today, and in the same way - in the ground.

Recall in Chapter 2, "Money and Occupations," that money was used before, during, and after the writing of the law, and yet is not a requirement for the tithing ritual. Neither is money a requirement for the firstfruit, otherwise it may be called 'firstshekel' or something similar.

Hopefully Christians stop using the term firstfruit to validate today's monetary tithe, or use it to promote Christian giving. It has nothing to do with either one of them. Making reference to the biblical firstfruit when talking about a person's income is inappropriate and has nothing to do with how a Christian ought to give.

Proverbs 3:9-10 KJV

Honour the LORD with thy substance, and with the firstfruits of all thine increase:

So shall thy barns be filled with plenty, and thy presses shall burst out with new wine.

6

Freedom Through Death

In seeking to do God's will, some Christians mistakenly believe that righteousness comes from obeying certain regulations under the old covenant. They find justification in adhering to Old Testament rules and regulations. Two such groups of people in the Bible were the Pharisees and Sadducees. For the most part, they only observed the letter of the law and Jesus referred to them as vipers. They are the epitome of those who say unto the Lord, "Lord, Lord," yet will not enter into the kingdom of heaven. Also, there are people who cast out demons and perform miracles in the name of Jesus who will not make it into heaven (Matt. 7:21-23). Why is it, then, that Christians think performing works to find favor with God - such as giving monetary tithes and offerings - will have any effect today?

The misuse of Bible passages causes Christians to perform acts contrary to what God requires. Continuing the process of steering Christians away from tithes and offerings, this chapter first points to the new covenant and the freedom it gives Christians from old covenant laws and practices. Further, this chapter addresses the freedom from the curse that Christians enjoy as well as the righteousness they have apart from the law.

THE NEW COVENANT

Old covenant rules and regulations do not lead to true acts of righteousness for those who believe in the risen Savior. Christians are not to abide by old covenant law as a means for justification, righteousness, or judgment, since they are under a new covenant.

Old Covenant Attraction

According to Hebrews 13:8, "Jesus Christ is the same yesterday and today and forever." And in Luke 6:46 Jesus asks, "Why do you call me, 'Lord, Lord,' and do not do what I say?" Because of these verses, many Christians believe that they are obligated to follow old covenant rules and regulations. They fail to realize that although Jesus is the same, God's people have changed due to the sacrifice of Jesus.

Many Christians adhere to some old covenant commands because they seem to relate to today. For example, Christians refer to Deuteronomy 8:11:

Deuteronomy 8:11
Be careful that you do not forget the LORD your God, failing to observe his commands, his laws and his decrees that I am giving you this day.

According to this verse, God's people are to *observe his commands* that He is giving *this day.* This coupled with Jesus being the *same yesterday and today and forever* lead Christians to follow some commands throughout the Old Testament. The problem is that the commandments under the old covenant for the Jewish community are not the same as those under the new covenant for Christians. Chapter 8, "New Covenant Commands," shows that Christians also have a set of instructions to observe, as a result of the new covenant.

Christians are often faced with undue pressure to follow old covenant laws. Fellow saints accuse them of not believing in the whole Bible and of not following all of God's commands. Believers succumb to this pressure out of guilt and fear, and consequently abide in old covenant laws and practices.

Tithes and offerings, or a modified version of them, is one area of old covenant law where Christians are being pressured to follow. Today, Christian giving is commonly taught from Proverbs 3:9 - "Honor the LORD with your wealth, with the firstfruits of all your crops." According to some, this specifically requires Christians to pay God first and then pay personal debts afterwards since, "God always wants the first and the best of a person's increase or money."

Tithers also refer to Leviticus 27:30 when they want to emphasize how important the tithe is to the Lord - "A tithe of everything ... is holy to the LORD." Combining the ideas from Proverbs and Leviticus, one is led to believe that God commands Christians to give tithes and that it is important. Verses such as these, and their application to Christianity, make it important to understand the freedom Christians have through the death of Jesus Christ.

Change in the Priesthood

Notice in Hebrews chapter 7 that the priesthood of Jesus is 'like' that of Melchizedek, but not the 'same' as Melchizedek - Melchizedek's priesthood was not in conjunction with blood for the remission of sins.

Hebrews 7:11
If perfection could have been attained through the Levitical priesthood (for on the basis of it the law was given to the people), why was there still need for another priest to come - one in the order of Melchizedek, not in the order of Aaron?

This verse states that *perfection* was not attained *through the Levitical priesthood.* So another priest was to come, but *not in the order of Aaron.* The burnt and sin offerings performed under the Levitical priesthood could not take away sins. "For if there had been nothing wrong with that first covenant, no place would have been sought for another" (Heb. 8:7).

"And what we have said is even more clear if another priest like Melchizedek appears, one who has become a priest not on the basis of a regulation as to his ancestry but on the basis of the power of an indestructible life" (Heb. 7:15-16). Therefore, this new priest (Jesus) became a priest with an oath.

Hebrews 7:21-22
but he became a priest with an oath when God said to him: "The Lord has sworn and will not change his mind: 'You are a priest forever.'"
Because of this oath, Jesus has become the guarantee of a better covenant.

Change of the Law

Hebrews 7:12, 18-19
For when there is a change of the priesthood, there must also be a change of the law.
...
The former regulation is set aside because it was weak and useless
(for the law made nothing perfect), and a better hope is introduced, by which we draw near to God.

Beginning with Hebrews 7:1, the only regulations mentioned up to this point are tithing and the regulation in regard to the ancestry of the priesthood. The priesthood and its regulation in regard to ancestry *is set aside because it was weak and useless.*

Notice Hebrews 7:19. It states that *the law made nothing perfect,* which stems from the fact that perfection was not attained through the Levitical priesthood. This affirms what Paul told the Romans. "For sin shall not be your master, because you are not under law, but under grace" (Rom. 6:14). Therefore, tithing is also useless because it is part of the law. However, this change in the law does not allow Christians to convert the real tithe into a monetary tithe or the real offerings (all of them) into one combined monetary offering.

The New Covenant With Israel

A better covenant is now available to Christians. "By calling this covenant 'new,' he has made the first one obsolete" (Heb. 8:13). This new covenant is described in Hebrews (see also Jer. 31:31-34).

Hebrews 8:6-11

But the ministry Jesus has received is as superior to theirs as the covenant of which he is mediator is superior to the old one, and it is founded on better promises.

For if there had been nothing wrong with that first covenant, no place would have been sought for another.

But God found fault with the people and said: "The time is coming, declares the Lord, when I will make a new covenant with the house of Israel and with the house of Judah.

It will not be like the covenant I made with their forefathers when I took them by the hand to lead them out of Egypt, because they did not remain faithful to my covenant, and I turned away from them, declares the Lord.

This is the covenant I will make with the house of Israel after that time, declares the Lord. I will put my laws in their minds and write them on their hearts. I will be their God, and they will be my people.

No longer will a man teach his neighbor, or a man his brother, saying, 'Know the Lord,' because they will all know me, from the least of them to the greatest."

Chapter 8, "New Covenant Commands," covers the conscience and its role in knowing good from evil. Notice here, however, that the Lord has written His laws in the believer's mind and heart (v10). Therefore, *no longer will a man teach his neighbor.* Since they know the Lord, Christians rely on the law written on their hearts instead of relying on old covenant laws.

The problem with the first covenant is that the people did not remain faithful to it, hence, *God found fault with the people.* The Lord made a new covenant where He wrote His laws on hearts and minds, therefore, keeping His people faithful to it - Christians cannot turn away from a law that is within them. Christians have a new covenant and possess the law of Christ.

2 Corinthians 3:6
He has made us competent as ministers of a new covenant - not of the letter but of the Spirit; for the letter kills, but the Spirit gives life.

Jesus, the Final Sacrifice

God presented Jesus as a sacrifice of atonement through faith in His blood (Rom. 3:22-25). Jesus died as the ultimate sacrifice, once and for all - unlike the sacrifices and offerings of the old covenant, which had to be offered repeatedly.

Hebrews 10:9-12
Then he said, "Here I am, I have come to do your will." He sets aside the first to establish the second.
And by that will, we have been made holy through the sacrifice of the body of Jesus Christ once for all.
Day after day every priest stands and performs his religious duties; again and again he offers the same sacrifices, which can never take away sins.
But when this priest had offered for all time one sacrifice for sins, he sat down at the right hand of God.

Many people interchange the phrases 'New Testament' with 'new covenant' and 'Old Testament' with 'old covenant.' This may confuse some people because the first four books of the New Testament portion of the Bible include Jesus' ministry in the flesh. For clarification, the new covenant did not come into being until the sacrifice of Jesus - *He sets aside the first to establish the second.*

For everyone who believes in Jesus, the sacrifice of Jesus set them free from sins committed under the old covenant, and it made His followers *holy through the sacrifice of the body.* The religious duties of the priest offering the same sacrifices again and again can never take away sins. On the other hand, Jesus *had offered for all time one sacrifice for sins* (see Heb. 9:1 - 10:23 for complete details).

Hebrews 7:23-25
Now there have been many of those priests, since death prevented them from continuing in office;

but because Jesus lives forever, he has a permanent priesthood.

Therefore he is able to save completely those who come to God through him, because he always lives to intercede for them.

Priests under the old covenant actually die and are replaced by other priests who also die. However, Jesus has a permanent priesthood. He saves completely, and He forever intercedes on the behalf of believers.

Significance of the Lord's Supper

In Matthew 26:26-28, Jesus made a reference to this new covenant while talking to His disciples in the upper room.

Matthew 26:26-28
While they were eating, Jesus took bread, gave thanks and broke it, and gave it to his disciples, saying, "Take and eat; this is my body."

Then he took the cup, gave thanks and offered it to them, saying, "Drink from it, all of you.

This is my blood of the covenant, which is poured out for many for the forgiveness of sins."

In 1 Corinthians 11:23-29, Paul shared with the Corinthians information about the Lord's Supper, explaining that it is in recognition of the Lord's death. He reminded them of what Jesus told the disciples, stating in verse 26, "For whenever you eat this bread and drink this cup, you proclaim the Lord's death until he comes." He continued by saying that Christians are to examine themselves before taking part in the supper to prevent them from sinning against the body and blood of the Lord. Paul concluded in verse 29, "For anyone who eats and drinks without recognizing the body of the Lord eats and drinks judgment on himself."

The idea behind today's communion is to *proclaim the Lord's death until he comes.* Can Christians truly recognize the body of the Lord through communion of a new covenant when they observe the rules and regulations under the old covenant? Are Christians eating and drinking judgment on themselves by symbolically performing or emulating the sacrificial rituals of tithes and offerings?

For those who want to truly sacrifice something, consider sacrificing praise from your lips (Heb. 13:15), or offering your bodies as living sacrifices (Rom. 12:1). Christians should operate under the permanent priesthood, a priesthood that saves completely, and not under the old priesthood requiring tithes and offerings.

FREEDOM FROM THE LAW

The previous section shows a change in the priesthood, a change in the law, and a change from the old covenant to a new covenant. This new covenant is the reason that Christians do not need old covenant rules or regulations to govern their spiritual walk. This includes the rules associated with tithes and offerings.

Purpose of the Law

The old covenant law cannot replace the Holy Spirit as the governing agent for Christians. This leads to the question, "Where does the law come in and why?"

Galatians 3:19
What, then, was the purpose of the law? It was added because of transgressions until the Seed to whom the promise referred had come...

In response, the law was added because of transgressions (sin) until Jesus had come (Rom. 5:18-21; 6:19). Although people know good and evil apart from the law through their conscience, the law also makes people aware of sin as stated by Paul in Romans 6:20 and Romans 7:7-12.

On the other hand, the Bible teaches that the law still exists, so it must have a purpose despite Christianity. Therefore, the next question to answer is, "Who is the law made for?" The book of Timothy provides the answer.

1 Timothy 1:9-10

We also know that law is made not for the righteous but for lawbreakers and rebels, the ungodly and sinful, the unholy and irreligious; for those who kill their fathers or mothers, for murderers,

for adulterers and perverts, for slave traders and liars and perjurers - and for whatever else is contrary to the sound doctrine

Do tithers really want to identify themselves with those who are *ungodly, liars* and *perverts?* These are the types of people required to use the law. Christians definitely do not fall into this category. In contrast, Christians are told in Romans 6:13, "Do not offer the parts of your body to sin, as instruments of wickedness, but rather offer yourselves to God, as those who have been brought from death to life; and offer the parts of your body to him as instruments of righteousness." Therefore, the law is for those who have *not believed* in Jesus, and *not* Christians who are using their bodies as instruments of righteousness - the *law is made not for the righteous.*

Fulfillment of the Law

Matthew 5:17-18

Do not think that I have come to abolish the Law or the Prophets; I have not come to abolish them but to fulfill them.

I tell you the truth, until heaven and earth disappear, not the smallest letter, not the least stroke of a pen, will by any means disappear from the Law until everything is accomplished.

Jesus did not come to destroy or overthrow *(abolish)* the Law, but He came to complete or satisfy *(fulfill)* the Law. For those in Christ Jesus, nothing else remains to be accomplished on their own. "For he who loves his fellowman has fulfilled the law" (Rom. 13:8). Therefore, the law no longer requires observance for judgment, righteousness and justification - the blood of Christ was shed for sins. On the other hand, those under the law should use it for discipline. Once they turn to Christ and believe, they are no longer under the custody of the law.

Galatians 3:25
Now that faith has come, we are no longer under the supervision of the law.

Jesus, Our Husband

In an illustration about marriage, Paul explains how believers are released from the law by the ultimate sacrifice of Jesus. Thus, Christians died to the law through their Savior. However, please do not confuse a Christian's freedom from the old covenant law with having no law at all. Chapters 8 and 9 discuss the new guidelines and how they relate to this new husband Christians have in Jesus Christ.

Romans 7:1-4
Do you not know, brothers - for I am speaking to men who know the law - that the law has authority over a man only as long as he lives?
For example, by law a married woman is bound to her husband as long as he is alive, but if her husband dies, she is released from the law of marriage.

So then, if she marries another man while her husband is still alive, she is called an adulteress. But if her husband dies, she is released from that law and is not an adulteress, even though she marries another man.

So, my brothers, you also died to the law through the body of Christ, that you might belong to another, to him who was raised from the dead, in order that we might bear fruit to God.

Like a woman who becomes a widow, followers of Christ become widows. The widow is no longer bound to the law concerning marriage because her husband died. Similarly, Christians are no longer bound to the law because Christ died. Christians *died to the law through the body of Christ*. Those who are widowed can marry again. Therefore, Christians, too, can marry again and have another husband. For them, the one who rose from the dead is that new husband! They are released from the requirements of the previous law in order to serve in the new way.

Romans 7:5-6

For when we were controlled by the sinful nature, the sinful passions aroused by the law were at work in our bodies, so that we bore fruit for death.

But now, by dying to what once bound us, we have been released from the law so that we serve in the new way of the Spirit, and not in the old way of the written code.

People who trust in the Lord *died to the law* and now belong to the risen Christ. They now *bear fruit to God* whereas before they *bore fruit for death*. Christians cannot simultaneously be *released from the law* and be under the law, nor can they simultaneously serve *in the new way of the Spirit* and *in the old way of the written code*. Therefore, the concept of Christians giving tithes and offerings conflicts with the way of the Spirit since these practices are a part of the written code.

Nailing It to the Cross

Jesus paid the price for everyone's release from the law and gave Christians the rights of sons and daughters. Recall from Chapter 4 that the reason for not paying the tithe as a tax is due to a Christian's sonship status. With the redemption from the law, followers of Christ are no longer slaves to the basic principles of the world. Instead, God made everyone alive with Christ (Gal. 4:3-5). Therefore, take heed of the following words from Paul to the Colossians.

Colossians 2:13-17

When you were dead in your sins and in the uncircumcision of your sinful nature, God made you alive with Christ. He forgave us all our sins,

having canceled the written code, with its regulations, that was against us and that stood opposed to us; he took it away, nailing it to the cross.

And having disarmed the powers and authorities, he made a public spectacle of them, triumphing over them by the cross.

Therefore do not let anyone judge you by what you eat or drink, or with regard to a religious festival, a New Moon celebration or a Sabbath day.

These are a shadow of the things that were to come; the reality, however, is found in Christ.

Jesus *canceled the written code* (old covenant law), *that was against us and that stood opposed to us, nailing it to the cross.* Therefore, do not please men, but please God, and do not let anyone pass judgment based on the written regulations in regard to tithes and offerings. *These are a shadow of the things that were to come; the reality, however, is found in Christ.*

FREEDOM FROM THE CURSE

Many tithers believe the curse of the law can apply to Christians - to those who believe in the risen Christ. Quotes are taken from Malachi 3:8-9 and Deuteronomy 11:26-28, implying that Christians will be cursed for not obeying the commandments of the Lord. The fact is, only those who are under the written law, or those who obey just parts of it, are under that curse.

Jesus Became a Curse

Christians have accepted Jesus as Lord and Savior, and in doing so, they have accepted the fact that He became sin for them, thereby washing their sins away (2 Cor. 5:21). Those who say Christians can actually be cursed fail to realize that Jesus was made a curse for them. In fact, Jesus redeemed followers of Christ from the curse of the law. Galatians 3:10-14 clears this up immediately.

Galatians 3:10-14
All who rely on observing the law are under a curse, for it is written: "Cursed is everyone who does not continue to do everything written in the Book of the Law."

Clearly no one is justified before God by the law, because, "The righteous will live by faith."

The law is not based on faith; on the contrary, "The man who does these things will live by them."

Christ redeemed us from the curse of the law by becoming a curse for us, for it is written: "Cursed is everyone who is hung on a tree."

He redeemed us in order that the blessing given to Abraham might come to the Gentiles through Christ Jesus, so that by faith we might receive the promise of the Spirit.

Christ redeemed us from the curse of the law. Therefore, He became a curse for His followers since, *"Cursed is everyone who is hung on a tree."* As a result, Christians cannot be cursed and the power of sin has been disabled. "The sting of death is sin, and the power of sin is the law" (1 Cor. 15:56). So with the removal of the curse, the power of the law has been disabled. Therefore, sin has no power over those in Christ since there is no curse for those who believe.

The curse is a direct result of not doing *everything written in the Book of the Law* (see also Deut. 27:26, Jas. 2:10). Since it is difficult to obey the entire law, those trying to observe it are going to trespass against God on at least one occasion - and with this trespass comes the curse. Also note that a person cannot live by the law and live by faith because *the law is not based on faith.* Relying on the works of the law will not result in justification from God since *the righteous will live by faith.* So those who rely on tithes and offerings are placing a curse upon themselves since the work they are doing is not by faith, but instead, it is of the law.

No Condemnation for Christians

There is no concept of a cursed Christian. Either a person relies on the law, or the person is led by the Spirit - promised to those who believe in Christ. Jesus redeemed His followers *so that by faith we might receive the promise of the Spirit.* All Christians make mistakes during their lifetime, but rest assured a curse will *not* come to those who believe in Jesus. On the contrary, God sent his Son into the world so that the followers of Christ might have eternal life, not a curse (Jn. 3:16-17).

Condemnation is a thing of the past for those who believe in the Son of God. Whoever believes in Him is not condemned. Those who do not believe in the name of God's one and only Son are condemned already (Jn. 3:18). Romans 8:1 adds to this, "Therefore, there is now no condemnation for those who are in Christ Jesus." There is no reason to fear the curse of the law for not giving tithes and offerings. On the contrary, as pointed out in Galatians 3:10-14 above, it is the act of giving tithes that actually brings a curse upon the believer! This results from modern day tithers not continuing to do everything written in the book of the law, since they rely on observing only selective (and misinterpreted) parts of the law.

This is yet another reason for Christians not to perform their giving in the name of tithing. Tithing obviously contains rules associated with it that do not apply to followers of Christ.

Christians should stop putting themselves in a position to be cursed, and start calling their giving what it is - an act of grace.

RIGHTEOUSNESS APART FROM THE LAW

Every command within the law is good, requires holiness, and provides a form of order for the world (Rom. 7:12). The problem is that those under the law use it inappropriately by trying to establish their own form of righteousness. Nevertheless, no one is justified before God by the law because, "The righteous will live by faith" (Gal. 3:11). There is a new righteousness apart from the law. But first, let us look at a righteousness that was of the old covenant.

Old Covenant Righteousness

Romans 10:3-5
Since they did not know the righteousness that comes from God and sought to establish their own, they did not submit to God's righteousness.

Christ is the end of the law so that there may be righteousness for everyone who believes.

Moses describes in this way the righteousness that is by the law: "The man who does these things will live by them."

Although the law was meant to help, it turned out to be a stumbling block for God's people. It took Christ to fulfill - end, complete, or satisfy the requirements of - the law that righteousness might be available to all who believe. In the above passage, the Israelites sought to establish their own righteousness as opposed to submitting to God's. They did not obtain the true knowledge of the law, which was to use it as a vehicle for the restraint of sins and to convict them of guilt. Instead, they created a legalistic approach concerning the law and expected justification by the works of it.

Moses describes the righteousness that is by the law (v5). In Leviticus 18:5 God says to, "Keep my decrees and laws, for the man who obeys them will live by them. I am the LORD." Similar words are found in Deuteronomy chapter 6.

Deuteronomy 6:24-25

"The LORD commanded us to obey all these decrees and to fear the LORD our God, so that we might always prosper and be kept alive, as is the case today.

And if we are careful to obey all this law before the LORD our God, as he has commanded us, that will be our righteousness."

Under the old covenant, God's people have to obey the rules and regulations in order to live. *For the man who obeys them will live by them, that we might always prosper and be kept alive.* This is also their righteousness (v25) if they obey *all the law.* In contrast, today's Christian does not *live by them,* but lives by faith as a result of the new found freedom in Christ Jesus.

New Covenant Righteousness

Christian righteousness must surpass that of the Pharisees. "For I tell you that unless your righteousness surpasses that of the Pharisees and the teachers of the law, you will certainly not enter the kingdom of heaven" (Matt. 5:20). Some Christians fail to realize that it is with their heart they believe and are justified, and fail to understand that the law cannot impart life (Gal. 3:21). Romans chapter 3 adds to this by revealing a new righteousness from God, apart from the law, which is through faith in Jesus.

Romans 3:19-24

Now we know that whatever the law says, it says to those who are under the law, so that every mouth may be silenced and the whole world held accountable to God.

Therefore no one will be declared righteous in his sight by observing the law; rather, through the law we become conscious of sin.

> *But now a righteousness from God, apart from law,*
> *has been made known, to which the Law and the*
> *Prophets testify.*
>   *This righteousness from God comes through faith in*
> *Jesus Christ to all who believe. There is no difference,*
>   *for all have sinned and fall short of the glory of God,*
>   *and are justified freely by his grace through the*
> *redemption that came by Christ Jesus.*

Life for the person under the law is gained by living according to the law, but no Christian is declared righteous by observing it. *But now a righteousness from God, apart from law, has been made known.* This righteousness comes to all who believe. The righteousness that eluded everyone who relied on observing the law, is now available to everyone. There is nothing a person can do, nor a work to perform, to help a person obtain righteousness. This includes giving tithes and offerings and modified versions of them.

Christians should stop trying to find righteousness, justification, or any form of satisfaction, from the rituals of the old covenant law. Instead, Christians should give freely - for God loves a cheerful giver. Also remember, all *are justified freely by his grace through the redemption that came by Christ Jesus.* See Philippians 3:5-9 concerning Paul's 'righteous' conversion from legalistic righteousness to that which is by faith.

Must Be Born Again

This new covenant righteousness is only available to Christians. One might ask, who are true Christians? They are those who are born again. In John 3:3-8, Jesus tells Nicodemus, "No one can see the kingdom of God unless he is born again." Jesus also says, "No one can enter the kingdom of God unless he is born of water and the Spirit."

In order to be born again, one must believe in the name of God's one and only Son (Jn. 3:18; Mk. 16:16). "Whoever believes in the Son has eternal life, but whoever rejects the Son will not see life, for God's wrath remains on him" (Jn. 3:36).

Romans 10:9-10

That if you confess with your mouth, "Jesus is Lord," and believe in your heart that God raised him from the dead, you will be saved.

For it is with your heart that you believe and are justified, and it is with your mouth that you confess and are saved.

Christians receive salvation through the sanctifying work of the Spirit and through belief in the truth (2 Thes. 2:13). The belief and confession of Jesus is necessary for people to become born again, and thus, they are children of God. "Yet to all who received him, to those who believed in his name, he gave the right to become children of God - children born not of natural descent, nor of human decision or a husband's will, but born of God" (Jn. 1:12-13). In addition, Christians are children of Abraham (Gal. 3:7).

Titus 3:4-7

But when the kindness and love of God our Savior appeared,

he saved us, not because of righteous things we had done, but because of his mercy. He saved us through the washing of rebirth and renewal by the Holy Spirit,

whom he poured out on us generously through Jesus Christ our Savior,

so that, having been justified by his grace, we might become heirs having the hope of eternal life.

"For it is by grace you have been saved, through faith - and this not from yourselves, it is the gift of God - not by works, so that no one can boast" (Eph. 2:8-9). Also, 1 Peter 1:23 states, "For you have been born again, not of perishable seed, but of imperishable, through the living and enduring word of God."

The result of being born again is that the Spirit of God lives in each Christian. "If anyone does not have the Spirit of Christ, he does not belong to Christ" (Rom. 8:9-11). Since Christ is in them, their bodies are dead to sin, but their spirits are alive because of righteousness.

Once people believe and become Christians, they are compelled from within to do the will of the Father (see Chapters 8 and 9) and they are to listen to the teachings of Jesus. The main way Christians carry out the will of the Father is to love one another. "Let us love one another, for love comes from God. Everyone who loves has been born of God and knows God," and, "Whoever does not love does not know God, because God is love" (1 Jn. 4:7-8).

LISTEN TO JESUS

With all the biblical support to keep Christians from turning to the law for righteousness or justification, Christians still turn to it for one reason or another. They revert to the law that was opposed to them, in spite of Paul stating in Romans 7:6, "But now, by dying to what once bound us, we have been released from the law so that we serve in the new way of the Spirit, and not in the old way of the written code."

Acts 15:1-21 shows that Christians in the early church addressed the same issues discussed in this chapter of the book. "Then some of the believers who belonged to the party of the Pharisees stood up and said, 'The Gentiles must be circumcised and required to obey the law of Moses' " (v5). Peter addressed the crowd, saying, "No! We believe it is through the grace of our Lord Jesus that we are saved, just as they are" (v11). James also spoke up and said, "It is my judgment, therefore, that we should not make it difficult for the Gentiles who are turning to God" (v19).

When giving presents a dilemma for Christians, the New Testament should be the primary source of guidance. Unfortunately, some turn to the old covenant law and do what is required of those under the law. Even more unfortunate is that some ministers actually tell followers of Christ to obey the laws of old, and Christians tend to believe their ministers.

Some Christians forget that those in leadership positions are human, too, and that they can also make mistakes. Sadly, members of the flock do not usually double check what is being taught. Therefore, they usually make the same mistakes by taking for granted that what people teach is correct. Let us go to the book of Hebrews.

Hebrews 1:1-2

In the past God spoke to our forefathers through the prophets at many times and in various ways,

but in these last days he has spoken to us by his Son, whom he appointed heir of all things, and through whom he made the universe.

Under the old covenant, God spoke through *the prophets at many times and in various ways* to communicate his will to men. God chose certain people, qualified by him, for the purpose of revealing his will. This is how people received the word of God in Old Testament times. In addition, Jesus made reference to those living under the old covenant as having Moses and the prophets to listen to when He was telling the parable of the rich man and Lazarus (Lk. 16:19-31).

Under the new covenant, however, believers receive the word directly from God through the Spirit. No longer are the mysteries of God kept from them since they received a complete teaching in Christ Jesus.

Things of God or Things of Men

Peter was one of the twelve apostles, and was therefore, in the inner circle. Since Peter had access to the Teacher when others did not, he was privy to information prior to the rest of the population. During Jesus' walk in the flesh, God's chosen people, including Peter, were still under the law since Jesus had not been sacrificed yet. Nevertheless, Peter knew the truth of what was to come because of his relationship with Jesus.

In Mark chapter 8, Jesus and his disciples were on their way to the villages around Caesarea Philippi. They were having a discussion about who Jesus was, when Jesus asked Peter, "Who do you say I am?" (Mk. 8:29). Peter answered, "You are the Christ." Jesus then proceeded to teach them about His death.

Mark 8:31-33

He then began to teach them that the Son of Man must suffer many things and be rejected by the elders, chief priests and teachers of the law, and that he must be killed and after three days rise again.

He spoke plainly about this, and Peter took him aside and began to rebuke him.

But when Jesus turned and looked at his disciples, he rebuked Peter. "Get behind me, Satan!" he said. "You do not have in mind the things of God, but the things of men."

Here is an apostle who was instructed first hand by Jesus, that Jesus rebukes. Jesus just finished *plainly* explaining that He must be *killed and after three days rise again.* Peter actually started to rebuke Jesus concerning this, which is surprising since Peter had just confessed that Jesus is the Christ. So Peter knew what it meant for Jesus to be the Christ.

Peter could not have had in mind the gospel of Jesus. Instead, he was thinking about himself, which is more typical of the teachers of the law. As a result, Jesus said to Peter that he did *not have in mind the things of God, but the things of men.* When teachers today talk about Christian economics, do they have in mind the *things of God* or the *things of men?* Moreover, when they teach monetary tithes and offerings, are they teaching the gospel of Christ or rules taught by men?

Listen to Him!

In Mark chapter 9 (see also Matt. 17), Jesus takes Peter, James and John up a high mountain. The transfiguration of Jesus took place there and His clothes became dazzling white.

Mark 9:4-7

And there appeared before them Elijah and Moses, who were talking with Jesus.

Peter said to Jesus, "Rabbi, it is good for us to be here. Let us put up three shelters - one for you, one for Moses and one for Elijah."

(He did not know what to say, they were so frightened.)

Then a cloud appeared and enveloped them, and a voice came from the cloud: "This is my Son, whom I love. Listen to him!"

The events on the mountain were so overwhelming that they did not know what to say. Peter, however, did manage to say that they should *put up three shelters - one for you, one for Moses and one for Elijah.*

When there is dialog in the Bible, the response to a situation, or question, helps determine the real meaning of a passage. In this case, notice there was no response directly concerning whether or not three shelters were required. The response from the *cloud* did not waste any time in getting straight to the point. The first part of the response was, *This is my Son, whom I love.* The second part of the response could indicate that Peter did not understand fully what Jesus taught regarding the gospel. Notice that Peter wanted to put up a shelter for Elijah and Moses. The second part of the response states emphatically, *Listen to him!*

Those under the law listened to the word of God as presented through people specifically chosen by God. Under the new covenant, however, believers are to listen to Jesus. Jesus said that when He leaves He will send the Comforter to guide and to remind His followers of what He taught. When Christians give monetary tithes and offerings, are they listening to people chosen by God under the old covenant, or are they understanding the teachings of Jesus and listening to the Comforter?

Peter Performing Lawful Acts

Some time had passed now and Jesus was sacrificed for the remission of sins. Peter was one of many who believed in his heart that God raised Jesus from the dead, and confessed with his mouth that Jesus is Lord. Nevertheless, Peter still fell to the pressures of his peers and tried to force Christians to follow Jewish customs and obey the law for justification.

Being an apostle, Peter had great influence over the people and could easily persuade them to do questionable things. Christians are also easily persuaded to perform Old Testament rituals by church leaders instead of operating under the influence of the Holy Spirit.

Galatians 2:16
Knowing that a man is not justified by the works of the law, but by the faith of Jesus Christ, even we have believed in Jesus Christ, that we might be justified by the faith of Christ, and not by the works of the law: for by the works of the law shall no flesh be justified.

Peter knew that no one was justified before God by the law. Due to his fear of the circumcision group, however, he began pushing Jewish customs and laws onto the Gentile Christians. Today, there is a fear of the tither group and their claims of non-tithers being disobedient and cursed. This prompts some to push the monetary tithe and offering onto today's believers. Nevertheless, when Peter was in Antioch, Paul opposed him to his face "because he was clearly in the wrong" (Gal. 2:11). Paul also said that Peter and the others "were not acting in line with the truth of the gospel" (Gal. 2:14).

Tithers, and ministers in a position like Peter, can be misled at times. This causes many people to stray from the truth because of their teaching. Those who force old covenant rules and regulations upon Christians, such as tithes and offerings, are clearly wrong, and are not acting in line with the truth of the gospel.

The rules and regulations of the law were never meant for the righteous, but for the lawless. If each Christian loves the Lord and thy neighbor as thyself, there is no need for laws instructing people on how and what to do in every situation. For example, if people love their neighbor as themselves, which includes their spouse, then they do not need laws on domestic violence. If they love the Lord, they would automatically do the things that please Him.

One of the works that pleases the Lord is grace giving and is discussed in detail in Chapter 9, "Grace Giving." Giving is one area where Christians started with the Spirit, but have corrupted themselves by adding selective parts of tithing to regulate what, how, how much, when, and to whom to give.

Nothing people do today - no works whatsoever - will help them obtain righteousness. At the same time, the absence of obeying Old Testament law will not result in a curse, since Christians are not under that law. Too many Christians concern themselves with performing the works of monetary tithes and offerings, thinking they will be cursed. Jesus removed the yoke of slavery and sin along with the curse. He also redeemed those under law that they might receive the full rights of sons. So Christians serve in the new way of the Spirit and bear good fruit to God.

Do not give power to sin by trying to obey the law, and thus fall subject to the curse. The one who tries to obtain justification by the law will be alienated from Christ and fall away from grace (Gal. 5:4). Remember the words spoken by Paul to the Galatians.

Galatians 2:21
I do not set aside the grace of God, for if righteousness could be gained through the law, Christ died for nothing!

Romans 7:1-4

Do you not know, brothers - for I am speaking to men who know the law - that the law has authority over a man only as long as he lives?

For example, by law a married woman is bound to her husband as long as he is alive, but if her husband dies, she is released from the law of marriage.

So then, if she marries another man while her husband is still alive, she is called an adulteress. But if her husband dies, she is released from that law and is not an adulteress, even though she marries another man.

So, my brothers, you also died to the law through the body of Christ, that you might belong to another, to him who was raised from the dead, in order that we might bear fruit to God.

7

430 Years Before The Law

Even though Christians claim freedom from the law through the death of Jesus, many still abide under old covenant commands - including a modified version of tithing. One reason for this is the notion that 'tithing existed before the law.' Some Christians say tithing started before the law and should continue today, since the law does not abolish the rituals that were already in effect.

Interestingly, when tithers claim that tithing occurred prior to the law, they fail to mention, or perform, any other commands given or acts done prior to the law - even those acts performed by Abraham himself. Most say the reason for not performing other pre-law acts are the defining passages found in the New Testament that refute the need to continue something practiced during the law or prior to the law.

This chapter focuses on several acts performed prior to the law that are not required of Christians today. It also points out the related New Testament passages that explain why Christians do not need to continue these practices - including clarifications of passages used to support the practice of tithing.

This chapter starts with Abraham and some of the acts he performed other than, and including, giving a tenth of the spoils of war to Melchizedek. The reason to focus on Abraham's life-style and acts is that Christians tend not to use Abraham as an example in all areas of their lives - just in the area of giving. Some quote John 8:39 when encouraging Christians to tithe:

John 8:39 KJV

They answered and said unto him, Abraham is our father. Jesus saith unto them, If ye were Abraham's children, ye would do the works of Abraham.

For clarification, Galatians 3:6-9 and Hebrews 11:1-3, 6, and 8, explain that the children of Abraham are those that have the 'faith' and 'obedience' of Abraham. Faith and obedience are the 'works of Abraham' mentioned in John chapter 8, and not the actual act of giving a tenth to Melchizedek.

Special attention is given to Hebrews 7:8 and Galatians 3:17. Hebrews 7:8 states, "In the one case, the tenth is collected by men who die; but in the other case, by him who is declared to be living." Whereas Galatians 3:17 reads as follows: "What I mean is this: The law, introduced 430 years later, does not set aside the covenant previously established by God and thus do away with the promise." These two verses cause quite a stir for believers when discussing traditional tithes and offerings and are covered completely in this chapter.

This chapter continues with Jacob, Adam and Eve, and any relationship they may have with tithing, followed by examples of pre-law altars and offerings. In contrast, Christians do not build altars for sacrificial offerings today because it was 'done before the law.'

ABRAHAM'S PRE-LAW ACTS

If Christians claim to tithe because Abraham 'gave a tenth' prior to the law, do they also believe they can have more than one wife or some concubines? What about circumcision that was a practice God started with Abraham as a sign in the flesh of an everlasting covenant? These specific issues are covered here.

Circumcision, an Everlasting Covenant

Circumcision was a sign of an 'everlasting covenant' between Abraham and his descendants in the flesh, and consisted of the removal of the foreskin of all males. Please read all of Genesis 17:10-29 for more detail.

Genesis 17:10-13
This is my covenant with you and your descendants after you, the covenant you are to keep: Every male among you shall be circumcised.

You are to undergo circumcision, and it will be the sign of the covenant between me and you.

For the generations to come every male among you who is eight days old must be circumcised, including those born in your household or bought with money from a foreigner - those who are not your offspring.

Whether born in your household or bought with your money, they must be circumcised. My covenant in your flesh is to be an everlasting covenant.

When God made this covenant with Abraham, all males who were eight days old or older required circumcision. This included Abraham who was 99 years old at the time. Today, many newborn males are circumcised on the eighth day, or even on the first day. Some are circumcised for biblical reasons and others for health reasons. Not many are circumcised because of the everlasting covenant with Abraham, or because he was circumcised prior to the law.

Circumcision was incorporated into the written law. Any stranger who wants to partake in the Lord's Passover must be circumcised (Ex. 12:43, 48-49). Also, on the eighth day of life, male children are circumcised (Lev. 12:3).

The only good circumcision does today is related to health reasons or if someone observes the law of Moses. If someone breaks the law, however, it is as if the person was not circumcised at all (Rom. 2:25). Since it is impossible not to break at least one commandment of the law, Christians should not consider circumcising male children for the sake of the law.

Romans 2:28-29

A man is not a Jew if he is only one outwardly, nor is circumcision merely outward and physical.

No, a man is a Jew if he is one inwardly; and circumcision is circumcision of the heart, by the Spirit, not by the written code. Such a man's praise is not from men, but from God.

Circumcision, the everlasting covenant made in the flesh, is no longer of the foreskin for those who believe, but *circumcision is of the heart*. God had already mentioned this, surprisingly enough, in Deuteronomy 10:16. This new way of circumcision is performed by the Spirit, not by a surgical tool commanded in *the written code*. Since Christians are in Jesus, neither circumcision nor uncircumcision has any value (Gal. 5:6; 6:15).

Multiple Wives

The situation concerning Abraham (Abram), his wife Sarai, and Hagar, is in Genesis chapter 16. In Genesis chapter 15, God informed Abraham of the 'Abrahamic Covenant' concerning his offspring. Since Sarai could not conceive, she advised Abraham to sleep with her handmaid to fulfill this covenant. Abraham accepted the idea and took Hagar to be his wife.

Genesis 16:1-4

Now Sarai, Abram's wife, had borne him no children. But she had an Egyptian maidservant named Hagar;

so she said to Abram, "The LORD has kept me from having children. Go, sleep with my maidservant; perhaps I can build a family through her." Abram agreed to what Sarai said.

So after Abram had been living in Canaan ten years, Sarai his wife took her Egyptian maidservant Hagar and gave her to her husband to be his wife.

He slept with Hagar, and she conceived. ...

The question now becomes, "Since Abraham and his wife, Sarai, agreed to this act, can Christian men take on new wives as well?" After all, this was practiced before the law by Abraham. Continuing in Genesis chapter 16, one will notice that this is not what God intended. Abraham's seed was to come through his wife, Sarai. Jacob, like Abraham, also had more than one wife (Gen. 29).

The book of Exodus makes it evident that multiple wives are permitted for men under the law. All one has to do is provide a woman with food, clothing, and marital rights (Ex. 21:10-11). Furthermore, husbands can divorce their wives for simply disliking them or finding them displeasing. A man can write one of his wives a certificate of divorce and literally send her on her way. The only way this man can marry her again is if she does not marry another man (Deut. 24:1-4).

For the new covenant believer, text concerning how many wives one can have is in First Corinthians chapter 7. It clearly states that each man can have but one wife, and each wife but one husband. Once a man and woman marry, the body of one now belongs to the other as well. For both the man and the woman, separation or divorce should not be considered (1 Cor. 7:1-11) except for marital unfaithfulness (Matt. 19:3-9).

Having multiple wives is another example of something permissible for Abraham but is not acceptable for the new covenant believer. Therefore, the statement, "Polygamy started before the law," is not a justifiable reason for Christians having multiple wives.

Concubines

Abraham had concubines before the law. Does this mean Christians can have them? After the death of Sarah - named Sarai previously - in Genesis chapter 23, Abraham married Keturah (Gen. 25:1). As stated in 1 Chronicles 1:32, she was first his concubine. This was apparently not Abraham's only concubine as shown in Genesis 25.

Genesis 25:5-6
Abraham left everything he owned to Isaac.
But while he was still living, he gave gifts to the sons
of his concubines and sent them away from his son Isaac
to the land of the east.

Compare this to Jacob's relationships with his wives' handmaids in Genesis 30. Notice above that Abraham gave gifts unto *the sons of his concubines*. Does this suggest that Christian men may have multiple woman on the side so-to-speak? No. Paul said to the unmarried and widows that it is good for them to stay unmarried. If they cannot control themselves, however, then they should marry (1 Cor. 7:8-9, 36-39), and only have one spouse.

Can Abraham have concubines today and be considered obedient and in agreement with New Testament teachings? No. Neither should men today if they are followers of Christ. This is another example of something permissible before the law that is not allowed for Christians.

Abraham's Tenth

Tithers make non-tithers fully aware of the fact that Abraham gave a tenth of the spoils of war to Melchizedek, a priest.

Genesis 14:20
"And blessed be God Most High, who delivered your
enemies into your hand." Then Abram gave him a tenth
of everything.

According to tithers, this verse supports their claim that Christians should give one tenth of their monetary income to the local church. They base this on two premises: 1) Abraham gave a tenth of the spoils to Melchizedek and so Christians should give likewise, and 2) Giving a tenth shows that Christians have the faith and obedience of Abraham. Further evaluation of this verse shows the error in these two premises.

As previously stated, Abraham (Abram) gave a tenth of the spoils of a war to Melchizedek, a priest (Heb. 7:1, 4). But what specifically was given to this priest no one knows. Did Abraham tithe by definition as defined in Chapter 4, or did he simply give a tenth of everything obtained from the war? If Abraham tithed by definition - where the only clear definition came during Moses' day - he could not have given Melchizedek any 'money' because the definition of tithe does not include money.

If Abraham did not tithe by definition, he could have given a tenth of anything from the spoils of the war, which could have even included people. Yet, the question still remains, "Why do Christians tithe money today?" Abraham's tenth came from the spoils of a war, but today's tenth comes from the income of honest labor. Although spoils can include money, it is not certain whether Abraham gave any money to Melchizedek. What is certain is that spoils of war contain other items as well (see Josh. 8:1, 27; 11:14; Num. 31).

Having the faith and obedience of Abraham is usually misunderstood. Having obedience like that of Abraham does not mean emulating the 'actual acts' he performed. The Bible provides guidelines for Christians to follow, which cover Christian economics. Christians should do what is required of them according to the will of God. These righteous acts are how Christians show that they have faith and obedience like Abraham - not by trying to do what he actually did.

Since the practices of Abraham are not examples for Christians in all areas of life, then it does not make biblical sense to use this one 'actual act of giving' as an example either. It makes even less sense that 'giving the tenth of the spoils' is an example of what Christians should do with their 'monetary income.' Abraham walked this planet during a different biblical period when certain acts were permissible for him. Some people may choose to emulate specific practices of Abraham. However, their desire to emulate one specific way of doing something does not constitute a biblical ritual that all others are to perform. Neither does it mean that they have the faith and obedience of Abraham.

GIVING A TENTH TO A LIVING PRIEST

Based on Hebrews 7:8, some people say Christians are required to give a tenth because Jesus himself received a tenth.

Hebrews 7:8
In the one case, the tenth is collected by men who die; but in the other case, by him who is declared to be living.

Melchizedek Received a Tenth

The verse above has caused confusion in the area of giving. The phrase, *by him who is declared to be living*, has some thinking this is referring to Jesus, and therefore, tithing must continue today. It is time to correct this misinterpretation.

First, each verse in Hebrews 7:1-10 focuses on the subject of Melchizedek, and is comparing his priesthood to that of the Levitical priesthood. When reading along in chapter seven, the subject does not remain the same for verses one through seven, and for verses nine and ten, but change specifically for verse eight. In addition, to show that the word *him* in verse eight is actually Melchizedek, return to the beginning of chapter seven.

Hebrews 7:1-3
This Melchizedek was king of Salem and priest of God Most High. He met Abraham returning from the defeat of the kings and blessed him,
and Abraham gave him a tenth of everything. First, his name means "king of righteousness"; then also, "king of Salem" means "king of peace."
Without father or mother, without genealogy, without beginning of days or end of life, like the Son of God he remains a priest forever.

Notice immediately how Melchizedek is the subject as Hebrews 7 starts with, *This Melchizedek.* Abraham *gave him a tenth of everything*, where the word *him* is still referring to Melchizedek.   Then verse two gives a description of Melchizedek and what *his* name means.

Hebrews 7:3 follows and clears up Hebrews 7:8. It says, *like the Son of God he remains a priest forever.* The Son of God is Jesus, so the word *he* cannot be Jesus also, or the comparison would not make sense. In fact, the word *he* is the subject of this section in Hebrews, which is Melchizedek, and *he* remains a priest forever. Furthermore, he, Melchizedek, *is without father or mother, without genealogy, without beginning of days or end of life* (Heb. 7:3). As a result, the one *declared to be living* in Hebrews 7:8 is, in fact, Melchizedek.

Now let us return to Abraham's giving a tenth to further clarify the phrase, 'declared to be living' from a different angle.

Genesis 14:18-20
Then Melchizedek king of Salem brought out bread and wine. He was priest of God Most High,

and he blessed Abram, saying, "Blessed be Abram by God Most High, Creator of heaven and earth.

And blessed be God Most High, who delivered your enemies into your hand." Then Abram gave him a tenth of everything.

Abraham gave a tenth of the spoils to Melchizedek. This is the same Melchizedek that is the subject of Hebrews 7:1-10 - the *priest of God Most High.* When reading Hebrews chapter 7, clearly the subject of verse eight is Melchizedek and not Jesus. It should now be evident that Abraham gave a tenth to a living priest, prior to the Levitical priesthood, namely, Melchizedek. Therefore, this one verse should not be used out of context by switching the subject to Jesus in order to justify offering monetary tithes. It simply is not biblically sound.

Jesus Never Received a Tenth

Although the tithe is holy unto the Lord, it is always literally given to someone in the natural. Before the law, Abraham gave a tenth to Melchizedek - whether or not this was a legitimate tithe is still debatable. Under the law, the tithe is given to the Levites, shared with the priesthood, shared with the tither including his family and servants, and provides for the needy every third and sixth year. Somewhere along the way the tithe has evolved from supporting people with food to financing church building funds and padded pews.

Today, Christians supposedly give the tithe to Jesus by giving to the local church based on the so-called storehouse/church connection. Some also believe Jesus should receive tithes because He is supposedly the one 'declared to be living' in Hebrews 7:8. When Jesus walked the earth and was under the law of Moses, the tithes were gathered by the Levites, and a tenth of the tithe along with the firstfruits were given to the priests. Jesus, on the other hand, was from the tribe of Judah, not the tribe of Levi. Since Jesus was not from the tribe of Levi, He could not have been an earthly priest. Therefore, Jesus could not have received tithes while simultaneously conforming to the law - only the Levites collected tithes.

Since Jesus did not receive tithes while He was in the flesh, how did He receive support? He received the same type of support He expected His disciples to receive. "Go! I am sending you out like lambs among wolves. Do not take a purse or bag or sandals" (Lk. 10:3-4). The disciples needs were met from gifts of various people as they traveled.

Luke 8:1-3
After this, Jesus traveled about from one town and village to another, proclaiming the good news of the kingdom of God. The Twelve were with him,

and also some women who had been cured of evil spirits and diseases: Mary (called Magdalene) from whom seven demons had come out;

Joanna the wife of Cuza, the manager of Herod's household; Susanna; and many others. These women were helping to support them out of their own means.

Notice these people supported Jesus and His disciples *out of their own means*, not by giving tithes or monetary tithes. This concept resurfaces in Chapter 9, "Grace Giving."

Jesus did not require tithes while He walked the earth, so why would He require them now that He is in heaven? After all, earthly priests that eventually die are responsible for the tithe while living, not those priests that have already passed away. There is another good reason Jesus does not need the legitimate tithe. Earthly priests have earthly bodies that need natural food! Do not forget all of the other humans fed by the tithes including the people who give the tithes, their families, and the needy. Jesus does not require natural food or money while in Heaven.

PROMISES SPOKEN TO ABRAHAM

Now the focus shifts to another New Testament passage many people use to justify the monetary tithe. Some pastors teach from the following passage in Galatians, using it to illustrate how tithing started 430 years before the law, specifically with Abraham, and should therefore continue today.

Galatians 3:15-18
Brothers, let me take an example from everyday life. Just as no one can set aside or add to a human covenant that has been duly established, so it is in this case.

The promises were spoken to Abraham and to his seed. The Scripture does not say "and to seeds," meaning many people, but "and to your seed," meaning one person, who is Christ.

What I mean is this: The law, introduced 430 years later, does not set aside the covenant previously established by God and thus do away with the promise.

For if the inheritance depends on the law, then it no longer depends on a promise; but God in his grace gave it to Abraham through a promise.

Some tithers say Abraham tithed 430 years before the law, and the law cannot do away with practice of tithing. A tenth went to a priest or king before the law, to the Levites under the law, and now supposedly to the church or to Jesus for Christians. Some claim that Christians should follow Abraham's gratitude in the area of tithing, and in doing so, they will be considered cheerful givers.

The tenth Abraham gave to Melchizedek has already been covered. The problem covered in this section is centered on the misunderstanding of what was actually 'promised' to Abraham. The law *does not set aside the covenant previously established by God and thus do away with the promise.*

Promises, Not Tithing

Some congregations think the promise in Galatians chapter 3 above is referring to the tithing practice. This mis-information leads many Christians to give 10 percent of their income to the church under false pretenses. This section shows that the promise referred to in Galatians 3:15-18 is definitely not any form of tithing. The call of Abraham and the correct promises are in Genesis chapters 12 and 13.

Genesis 12:1-3

The LORD had said to Abram, "Leave your country, your people and your father's household and go to the land I will show you.

"I will make you into a great nation and I will bless you; I will make your name great, and you will be a blessing.

I will bless those who bless you, and whoever curses you I will curse; and all peoples on earth will be blessed through you."

Abraham did what the Lord asked and traveled to Canaan, where the Lord said to him, "To your offspring I will give this land" (Gen. 12:7). Later in Genesis 13:15-17, the Lord told Abraham that all the land he saw will be given to him and his offspring forever, and that his offspring, like the dust of the earth, would be too numerous to count. Clearly the tithing ritual had nothing to do with the promises made to Abraham.

Let us return to Galatians chapter 3. Paul starts off this chapter by calling the Galatians foolish for being bewitched (tricked) into following the law after receiving the Spirit by the hearing of faith (Gal. 3:1-3). Verse 13 states that Christ redeemed His followers from the law, and verse 17 states that the law does not do away with the *promises* given to Abraham. Verse 19 states the purpose of the law - that it was added because of transgressions until the seed should come to whom the *promise* was made. Verse 22 continues by explaining that the whole world is a prisoner of sin, so that what was *promised* might be given to those who believe in Jesus Christ. In conclusion, verse 29 declares Christians heirs according to the *promise*, not according to tithing or any other pre-law practice.

It is clear that the promises spoken to Abraham and to his seed were indeed actual promises. Tithing has absolutely nothing to do with the promises, with anything in this passage, or with anything in this particular chapter of Galatians. On the other hand, tithing is a work of the law, the same law that Paul called the Galatians foolish for reverting back to obeying. So do not be mislead into tithing money by someone who says, "The law, introduced 430 years later, does not set aside the covenant previously established by God." If they stop here, then remind them of the following - "and thus do away with the promise. For if the inheritance depends on the law, then it no longer depends on a promise" (Gal. 3:17-18). This is actually what is being taught in that passage.

JACOB'S VOW - ADAM & EVE

Prior to the written law, there is at least one person in the Bible who gave a tenth to a priest or king - Abraham. Another person, Jacob, made a vow to give a tenth (Gen. 28:22). This section addresses whether or not Jacob or Adam and Eve were tithers. Although this section covers pre-law tithes, it does not discuss Abel's offering because Chapter 5, "Firstfruit Defined," already showed that Abel did not tithe - but instead he brought fat portions from some of the firstborn of his flock.

Jacob Vowed a Tenth

Jacob is the only person other than Abraham in the recorded history of the Bible, prior to the law, to have anything to do with giving a tenth.

Genesis 28:20-22
Then Jacob made a vow, saying, "If God will be with me and will watch over me on this journey I am taking and will give me food to eat and clothes to wear

so that I return safely to my father's house, then the LORD will be my God

and this stone that I have set up as a pillar will be God's house, and of all that you give me I will give you a tenth."

At the time of this passage, Jacob was fleeing for his life because his brother Esau wanted to kill him (Gen. 28:10-19). He ends up in a place called Luz. Jacob found himself in such poor living conditions that he used a stone for a pillow. One night he had a dream that God made promises to him similar to those made to Abraham and Isaac. When Jacob awoke from his dream, he realized that "this is none other than the house of God." He then took the stone he used as a pillow and used it as a pillar, and called the place Bethel. God assured Jacob in the dream that he would watch over him wherever he went. But Jacob, fleeing for his life, did what many people of Old Testament times did when in trouble, and that was to make a vow.

It should already be clear that Christians should *not* perform certain rituals simply because someone else in the Bible did them. This includes Jacob's vow to give a tenth. The Bible does not tell followers of Christ to do what Jacob did. Nevertheless, many Christians are taught to give a tenth of their income to the local church and call it a tithe based on Jacob's vow.

The question is whether or not Jacob 'was required to tithe.' If Jacob was *not* already required to tithe by this time, then why do some tithers refer to this passage in connection with a 'mandatory' monetary tithe today? Some say Abraham was supposedly tithing before the date of this passage. If so, why would he not teach the people, especially his own relatives, to tithe after him? If Jacob made a vow to give a tenth of his possessions, then it stands to reason that it was not already required of him. Why, then, are Christians 'required' to tithe money today based upon this passage?

On the other hand, if Jacob *was* required to tithe at the time of his vow, then Abraham may have passed down some form of a tithing tradition (although there is no Scripture to support this). If this is the case, why did Jacob make a vow to tithe when the tithe was already required? People cannot vow an item unto God if it already belongs to Him (see Lev. 27:26). This includes tithes. Some tithers may cite Jacob as someone who was supposed to tithe as an example for Christians today. If so, they need to explain why Jacob made a vow to tithe since the tithe already belonged to the Lord. In addition, there is no evidence in the Bible that the vow Jacob made was passed on to his offspring, somehow making its way through the law and subsequently into Christianity.

Were Adam & Eve Tithers?

A well-known author of biblical economics wrote a book in which he claims God expected Adam and Eve to tithe! Wow! Reading through, a revelation is anticipated because this is something people rarely hear. The author continued by mentioning how it was Adam and Eve's job to take care of the garden. They could not eat from one particular tree, yet they were to take care of it. The author concluded by saying this was their tithe to God. That is it! Taking care of the garden and not eating from a particular tree was their tithe unto the Lord!

Upon looking for something profound to be written by the author, nothing substantial or useful was revealed. He did not even cite a passage in support of what he was saying. It is possible that he was referring to the following passage.

Genesis 2:15-17
The LORD God took the man and put him in the Garden of Eden to work it and take care of it.

> *And the LORD God commanded the man, "You are free to eat from any tree in the garden;*
> *but you must not eat from the tree of the knowledge of good and evil, for when you eat of it you will surely die."*

If this author was not referring to this passage, then it is not known on what Scripture he was basing his claim. Nevertheless, it is evident there is nothing in this passage that has to do with tithing. The truth is, there are no passages that even imply that Adam and Eve tithed. Some people will distort anything to validate why Christians must give a tenth of their income to the church, instead of letting Christians give as they have decided in their hearts to give (as led by the Spirit). This is yet another reason why everyone should study the Bible for themselves.

Imagine cleaning and managing a home, being told not to eat a cookie from the cookie jar, and having that be considered a tithe. That is similar to what Adam did - not to make light of his work. According to any recorded definition in the Bible, this is definitely not tithing. If they were tithing, where was the Levite or priest associated with this tithe? The Israelites need the Levitical priesthood, and Abraham gave a tenth to Melchizedek, a priest (and a king). Where, or who, was the equivalent of the Levite to whom Adam and Eve were to give the tithe? This line of questioning may sound strange since Adam and Eve did not 'give' something as a tithe. Instead, they 'did not eat of a certain tree and took care of the garden.' This particular author, however, called these acts a tithe.

Based on the Bible, Adam and Eve did not give tithes to anyone. This is another obvious example of the mis-interpretation of Scripture to fit a personal theology. The Bible does not tell Christians everything they *want* to know, but it does tell them everything they *need* to know. In this case, the Bible does not tell Christians how much to give in any particular situation. Still, this does not give anyone the right to draw their own conclusions, and in turn tell Christians to do something based solely on these conclusions.

OFFERINGS BEFORE THE LAW

Offerings were made prior to the Mosaic Law and include some of the terms defined in Chapter 3, "Offerings Defined." These include altar, sacrifice, offering, burnt offering, drink offering, and firstborn. All of these terms were in use prior to the law and subsequently incorporated into it. If tithers claim to offer tithes because this practice supposedly occurred before the law, then what about these items in particular? These items or acts are totally ignored by tithing Christians.

Altars Used

As defined in Chapter 3, altars are used for sacrificing items unto God. Several prominent people of the Bible built altars prior to the law. Recall that the tabernacle and temple structures were constructed with altars in their courtyards. However, altars can be built without either of them, especially during the biblical times when tabernacles and temples did not exist.

Genesis 13:18
So Abram moved his tents and went to live near the great trees of Mamre at Hebron, where he built an altar to the LORD.

Abraham also built altars in Genesis 12:7-8 and Genesis 22:9 (see also Gen. 13:3-4). Isaac built an altar in Genesis 26:25, Jacob built altars in Genesis 33:18-20 and Genesis 35:1-7, and Moses built an altar in Exodus 17:14-15. In addition, Noah built an altar in Genesis 8:20.

Sacrifices Offered

Sacrifices were common before the law for individuals who worshipped God in those days, such as Jacob - who was later named Israel (see also Gen. 31:53-55).

Genesis 46:1

So Israel set out with all that was his, and when he reached Beersheba, he offered sacrifices to the God of his father Isaac.

The children of Israel continued this practice during their captivity by Pharaoh. They wanted to go on a three-day journey into the desert to offer sacrifices to God. It took many plagues before Pharaoh let the people go on this journey (Ex. 3:18-19; 5:7-8, 16-17; 8:8, 24-28).

Substances Used

The substances used during the law for sacrifices were also used prior to the law for sacrifices and offerings unto God. This is evident early in the Bible when Cain and Abel brought offerings unto the Lord (Gen. 4:3-4). Cain, who was a tiller of the ground, brought 'fruit of the ground' as an offering. Abel, who was a keeper of sheep, brought 'fat portions from some animals' as an offering.

In addition, Abraham used a ram as a sacrifice instead of his own son, Isaac (Gen. 22:13). Isaac even questioned Abraham concerning the whereabouts of the lamb they needed for the offering (Gen. 22:7-8). These offerings occurred well before the establishment of the law and were incorporated into it similar to other pre-law acts. Also, while the children of Israel were held captive by Pharaoh, they requested to sacrifice 'livestock' as an act of worship unto the Lord.

Exodus 10:24-26

Then Pharaoh summoned Moses and said, "Go, worship the LORD. Even your women and children may go with you; only leave your flocks and herds behind."

But Moses said, "You must allow us to have sacrifices and burnt offerings to present to the LORD our God.

Our livestock too must go with us; not a hoof is to be left behind. We have to use some of them in worshiping the LORD our God, and until we get there we will not know what we are to use to worship the LORD."

Burnt Offerings

One of the most common offerings of the Mosaic Law is the burnt offering. It, too, was performed prior to the law as indicated in Exodus 10:24-26 above. Abraham was tested by God to offer his own son Isaac as a burnt offering (Gen. 22:1-2), but a ram was provided for the offering instead (Gen. 22:13).

The final example that ties together the building of an altar, a sacrifice, substances used for a sacrifice, and the burnt offering, all occurring before the law by one individual, is in Genesis chapter 8.

Genesis 8:20-21
Then Noah built an altar to the LORD and, taking some of all the clean animals and clean birds, he sacrificed burnt offerings on it.

The LORD smelled the pleasing aroma and said in his heart: ...

Note that the sacrificial items used by Noah were clean animals and birds. Compare this to the written law concerning clean and unclean animals in Leviticus 11:1-23. Also note how the burnt offering provided a pleasing aroma unto the Lord similar to the burnt offering of the written law.

Firstborn and Firstling

Giving the firstborn or firstling unto the Lord did not start with the Mosaic Law. In fact, it began early in Genesis chapter 4. Recall that Abel brought an offering of the firstborn, or firstlings (KJV), of his flock unto the Lord.

A more prominent reason for giving the firstborn of both man and animal relates to the Passover. When Pharaoh did not let the children of Israel go, God delivered a deadly plague that resulted in the death of all the firstborn. Read Exodus 11 through Exodus 13:16 for additional details.

Exodus 11:4-5

So Moses said, "This is what the LORD says: 'About midnight I will go throughout Egypt.

Every firstborn son in Egypt will die, from the firstborn son of Pharaoh, who sits on the throne, to the firstborn son of the slave girl, who is at her hand mill, and all the firstborn of the cattle as well.

The children of Israel would suffer the same fate unless they complied with the rule the Lord gave to Moses and Aaron in Exodus chapter 12. Each household had to apply the blood of a lamb on the two side posts and upper doorpost of their homes. They also had to eat the flesh of the lamb on the tenth day of April. All the firstborn of Egypt, including the children of Israel, would die that night except for the households with the blood around the door. This day was to be celebrated throughout all generations as an everlasting ritual (Ex. 12:14, 24-27).

Exodus 13:14-15

"In days to come, when your son asks you, 'What does this mean?' say to him, 'With a mighty hand the LORD brought us out of Egypt, out of the land of slavery.

When Pharaoh stubbornly refused to let us go, the LORD killed every firstborn in Egypt, both man and animal. This is why I sacrifice to the LORD the first male offspring of every womb and redeem each of my firstborn sons.'

The sacrificing of the firstborn was incorporated into the law of Moses similar to many other rituals that were 'done prior to the law.' This is also true of the firstborn male of the herd and flock, and is in Deuteronomy 15:19-22. As far as the firstborn sons are concerned, they are redeemed as part of the law as well (Ex. 34:19-20; Num. 18:15-18).

Pre-Law Offerings Not Performed Today

Every aspect covered in this section was incorporated into the law of Moses and is discussed in Chapters 3 and 5. Not one of these rituals is performed by Christians today. Yet, many tithe - or more correctly, give a tenth of their income - because it was supposedly done before the law.

How many Christians still build altars? How many still perform animal sacrifices? How many call these animal sacrifices an offering unto the Lord? How many perform burnt offerings that provide a pleasing aroma unto the Lord? How many celebrate the day the Lord brought the Israelites out of Egypt? After all, all of these things were a part of life prior to the written law.

Once again, just because something was done before the law does not mean followers of Christ should perform them. Christians have the law of Christ in their hearts to instruct and guide them in their Spirit-led walk (see Chapter 8, "New Covenant Commands").

For some, Abraham is an example of *what* to do in the normal course of Christian living. This chapter explained why doing something today just because it was practiced before the law, or because it was performed by Abraham, is not a valid reason for today's believer. God's people have changed since the death, burial, and resurrection of Jesus.

One might argue that tithing is different. In fact, when talking to 'serious' tithe believers, tithing seems segregated from everything else before the law and during the law - as if tithing is the only carry over into the new covenant. These people are simply holding onto tradition, and a false sense of security or comfort based on a righteousness that is of the law. What most people misunderstand is that giving a tenth is not what made Abraham a righteous man, but it was his belief in God (Jas. 2:23).

This chapter covered several passages that may have something in common with tithing prior to the old covenant law. If the Lord had intended for tithing to exist prior to the law, then so-be-it. However, the Bible does not indicate whether or not there existed a tithing ritual prior to the law. Nevertheless, if tithing did exist, it still falls into the same category as all the other practices and rituals performed prior to the law. That is, it was subsequently incorporated into the law, and obeying it makes nobody perfect (Heb. 7:19).

If Christians want to continue giving, or start giving as the Spirit leads them, then they need to start doing it in accordance with the gospel of Christ. The next couple of chapters cover how one ought to give in relation to Christianity - showing how Christians should support the church and one another.

Galatians 3:17-18

What I mean is this: The law, introduced 430 years later, does not set aside the covenant previously established by God and thus do away with the promise.

For if the inheritance depends on the law, then it no longer depends on a promise; but God in his grace gave it to Abraham through a promise.

8

New Covenant Commands

This chapter introduces issues related to giving under the new covenant, or true Christian giving. Therefore, to bring closure to the previous chapters, a brief synopsis is provided here. Earlier chapters cover the existence of money in the Bible, the definition of biblical offerings, including firstfruits and tithes, freedom from the old covenant law, and righteousness apart from the law. Chapter 2 clears up any ideas about society changing from a bartering society to a monetary one. Because it is important to accurately define the terms discussed in this book, Chapters 3, 4 and 5 define offerings, tithes, and firstfruit. These chapters show that today's offerings, tithes, and firstfruits, do not correspond to their biblical definitions.

As Chapter 6 demonstrates, legitimate tithes, offerings, and firstfruits, are only mandated under old covenant law. Since Christians enjoy freedom from that law, they are no longer required to provide these three types of offerings. It also describes a new righteousness not of the law, but of God. This righteousness is freely given through faith (in Christ Jesus) to those who believe in Him, and therefore, Christians should stop trying to obtain righteousness via old covenant law. Furthermore, Chapter 7 shows why Christians should refrain from doing something simply because it was done prior to the law. The conclusion surrounding monetary offerings, tithes, and firstfruits, is that they are of human origin, and Christians should not give in the names of any of these terms.

Not all Christians know God's will and rules for Christian living. As a result, they mistakenly turn to the old covenant law for guidelines, even in the area of giving. This chapter shows that Christian stewardship, in respect to finances, does not resemble the legalistic rituals of the Old Testament. This chapter presents a new way to walk for those who convert to Christianity.

Christians need a relationship with God and with one another in order to walk under the influence of the Holy Spirit, not a relationship with old covenant laws. Christ set Christians free from the law and made them slaves to righteousness. Therefore, they are obligated to give, and give responsibly within their freedom in Christ. Although Christians possess this freedom from the law, they are still bound to God's requirements and the demands of love, some of which are listed in this chapter.

Throughout this chapter, emphasis is placed on how written laws are for the lawless and not for Christians. It shows a Christian's requirement to support one another, and provides some correct motivational reasons for giving. In addition, this chapter demonstrates that each Christian knows the difference between right and wrong, good and evil - all without written rules and regulations to govern every detail of one's walk in Christ.

IMPORTANCE OF GOD'S WILL

Monetary tithes and offerings are given for many reasons. They are given because some feel they are doing God's will (being obedient to the Lord). However, such 'acts' are actually replacing the true Christian calling to give. They also result in a form of self justification. For example, people may give monetary tithes and offerings and focus on the good they think they are doing. When in reality, they ought to deal with a problem area of their lives - such as over drinking once in a while. Instead of dealing with the occasional drinking problem, they credit themselves for tasks achieved, such as giving a tenth of their income to the local church.

Unfortunately, pleasing God is far from happening in this case - whether giving a certain amount of money to the church or avoiding the drinking problem. Monetary tithing is not commanded of God, and offering it is not a replacement for doing God's will.

Mark 3:31-35

Then Jesus' mother and brothers arrived. Standing outside, they sent someone in to call him.

A crowd was sitting around him, and they told him, "Your mother and brothers are outside looking for you."

"Who are my mother and my brothers?" he asked.

Then he looked at those seated in a circle around him and said, "Here are my mother and my brothers!

Whoever does God's will is my brother and sister and mother."

The will of God is the only thing Christians should concern themselves with, and every good work is derived from this concern. In the passage above, Jesus said whoever does God's will is His mother, brother and sister. Since Christians desire to be brothers and sisters of Christ, then God's will deserves more attention than it usually receives. There are several verses in the New Testament explaining what God's commands are for those who look to the Son and believe in Him.

Romans 4:23-25

The words "it was credited to him" were written not for him alone,

but also for us, to whom God will credit righteousness - for us who believe in him who raised Jesus our Lord from the dead.

He was delivered over to death for our sins and was raised to life for our justification.

Jesus was crucified and raised to life to justify those who believe in Him, and thus, *God will credit righteousness.* Since God freely gave righteousness to the followers of Christ, obeying old covenant laws cannot add anything useful to the Christian experience - the goal of righteousness has already been obtained. Under the old covenant law, everyone is a slave to sin and free from righteousness. As a result of salvation, however, Christians are slaves to righteousness. This releases believers from the rules and regulations under the old covenant - as clarified in Chapter 6 - and frees them to do the will of God under the new covenant.

1 John 2:17
The world and its desires pass away, but the man who does the will of God lives forever.

THE CONSCIENCE

Everyone probably knows people who knowingly do wrong. The claim is that they are not violating any laws of the country in which they live. This can lead to disorderly conditions and is a good reason there are so many laws in today's societies. Similarly, Christians are free from old covenant law, but that does not mean they can use their freedom to indulge in whatever acts enter into their minds. Even if certain acts are permissible by law for Christians, that does not mean it is beneficial (1 Cor. 10:23).

Christians cannot hide behind the laws of the land to justify their actions, especially in the sight of God. Even if no laws exist, there is no excuse for committing acts of evil. If no one is ever caught stealing, cheating on their spouse, etc., they are still guilty in the sight of God. Taking this a step further, if one lives by faith and walks by the Spirit, then no written laws are necessary to guide the person from day to day.

Everyone's conscience makes them aware of good and evil, which is the focus of this section. This section explains, in particular, that Christians do not require written rules, whether on paper or on stone, to regulate their actions or how to give. God's laws written in their hearts and on their minds (Heb. 8:10) will guide them into making decisions in line with the will of God, and the conscience will convict them when they are doing wrong or evil.

To Know Good and Evil

To explain the work of the conscience, or this 'governing agent,' let us return to when being aware of good and evil started - with Adam and Eve. Genesis 2:9 states that there were trees in the garden and some of them provided food. One tree in particular consisted of the 'knowledge of good and evil.' Adam and Eve knew specifically not to eat of this tree. If they did, they would surely die (Gen. 2:15-17). As found in Genesis 3:6, however, Adam and Eve ate from this tree, their eyes were opened, and they knew they were naked.

Genesis 3:7-11
Then the eyes of both of them were opened, and they realized they were naked; so they sewed fig leaves together and made coverings for themselves.

Then the man and his wife heard the sound of the LORD God as he was walking in the garden in the cool of the day, and they hid from the LORD God among the trees of the garden.

But the LORD God called to the man, "Where are you?"

He answered, "I heard you in the garden, and I was afraid because I was naked; so I hid."

And he said, "Who told you that you were naked? Have you eaten from the tree that I commanded you not to eat from?"

Prior to eating from this tree, Adam and Eve saw no need for clothing. Now they could see, or had knowledge of good and evil. Therefore, they hid themselves because of their nakedness.

The Lord asked Adam, *"Who told you that you were naked?"* There is no clear explanation for how Adam knew of his nakedness. The Lord did not tell him and the law of Moses had not been established. There were also no national laws in existence for the land or even local church rules in place. Furthermore, the Comforter (Holy Spirit) had not come yet. It can only be concluded that this awareness came from within.

Genesis 3:22

And the LORD God said, "The man has now become like one of us, knowing good and evil. He must not be allowed to reach out his hand and take also from the tree of life and eat, and live forever."

Adam and Eve became like God in one respect - they knew *good and evil.* Their own consciences told them of their nakedness. Because they were now aware of good and evil, they could literally make a conscious choice concerning their everyday activities - and be held accountable for them. From this time forward, everyone has known the fundamental difference between good and evil.

The obvious side effect of knowing good and evil is the penalty of death. *He must not be allowed to reach out his hand and take also from the tree of life and eat, and live forever.* The penalty of death is inevitable for all since everyone has knowledge of good and evil.

Conscience Convicts

Today, as with Adam and Eve, conscious decisions are made whether to do good or evil, regardless if it is lawful or not. The following passage shows how the conscience convicts non-Christians of doing wrong even though the 'act' itself was in accordance with the law. According to John 8:5, the people brought an adulteress to Jesus, asking, "In the Law Moses commanded us to stone such women. Now what do you say?"

John 8:6-9

...But Jesus bent down and started to write on the ground with his finger.

When they kept on questioning him, he straightened up and said to them, "If any one of you is without sin, let him be the first to throw a stone at her."

Again he stooped down and wrote on the ground.

At this, those who heard began to go away one at a time, the older ones first, until only Jesus was left, with the woman still standing there.

The law of Moses deems stoning appropriate, and therefore, the people were completely justified in stoning this woman. Jesus, however, asked those who were without sin to throw the first stone. Notice how the law convicted the adulteress of her sin, but everyone's own conscience convicted them of their sinful ways. Nobody knows what Jesus actually wrote on the ground, but some believe He wrote down the people's sins. Nevertheless, the point here is that the people who caught this woman in sin were not actually caught themselves. Therefore, their own consciences convicted them since no witnesses came forward.

Many believe the first time Jesus *bent down and started to write on the ground with his finger* is symbolic of the old covenant laws written on stone tablets (ref. Ex. 32:15-16). Then Jesus straightened up and said, *If any one of you is without sin, let him be the first to throw a stone at her. Again he stooped down and wrote on the ground.* The second time He wrote on the ground may be symbolic of Jesus foretelling of God writing his laws on the people's hearts and minds. Soon afterwards, they *began to go away one at a time.* Once again, what Jesus wrote is unknown. However, this interpretation of John 8:6-9 reiterates how even non-Christians do not need laws to govern their actions.

Conscience is a Witness

The conscience acts as a witness to what is true (Rom. 9:1). In order to witness something, one must either see or hear the act. In the same way, the conscience witnesses to what is good and evil, and right and wrong, and therefore, no one will have an excuse on judgment day for their actions.

Romans 2:14-16
(Indeed, when Gentiles, who do not have the law, do by nature things required by the law, they are a law for themselves, even though they do not have the law,

since they show that the requirements of the law are written on their hearts, their consciences also bearing witness, and their thoughts now accusing, now even defending them.)

This will take place on the day when God will judge men's secrets through Jesus Christ, as my gospel declares.

God is going to judge the secrets of men, using each person's conscience as a witness against them or to defend them. The conscience is actually how certain people are a law unto themselves who do not have the old covenant law. This is the case with the Gentiles - *they are a law for themselves.*

Guided by the Spirit

In Jeremiah 31, starting at verse 31, the Lord said that a time is coming when He will make a new covenant with the house of Israel. This covenant is not like the earlier covenant, because with the new one, He put His law on the people's minds and wrote it on their hearts (see also Heb. 8:6-11). The new covenant was ushered in by the outpouring of the Holy Spirit, which is available to all who believe.

Joel 2:28-29
'And afterward, I will pour out my Spirit on all people. Your sons and daughters will prophesy, your old men will dream dreams, your young men will see visions.
Even on my servants, both men and women, I will pour out my Spirit in those days.'

These events are foretold again by Jesus in the book of John when He said, "If anyone is thirsty, let him come to me and drink. Whoever believes in me, as the Scripture has said, streams of living water will flow from within him" (Jn. 7:37-38). The Scripture Jesus referred to came from Isaiah 44:3, where it states, "For I will pour water on the thirsty land, and streams on the dry ground; I will pour out my Spirit on your offspring, and my blessing on your descendants."

John chapter 7 continues by stating that believers are going to receive the Spirit later since it had not yet been given. Furthermore, in John chapter 16, Jesus refers to the Spirit as the Counselor saying that the Counselor will not come until after He leaves. "But I tell you the truth: It is for your good that I am going away. Unless I go away, the Counselor will not come to you; but if I go, I will send him to you" (Jn. 16:7).

What was foretold in the above passages came to pass at Pentecost, when, "a sound like the blowing of a violent wind came from heaven" (Acts 2:1-4). The people saw what appeared as tongues of fire come to rest on each person there. All of the believers were filled with the Holy Spirit as foretold, but others thought they were drunk. In response, Peter addressed the crowd, explaining that they were in fact witnessing what had been spoken of by the prophet Joel (Acts 2:14-18).

Returning to the book of John, Jesus says in John 14:26 that, "the Counselor, the Holy Spirit, whom the Father will send in my name, will teach you all things and will remind you of everything I have said to you." This follows from what is mentioned in Chapter 6, "Freedom Through Death," in the section "Listen to Jesus." That section states that Christians are to listen to Jesus, as opposed to listening to something else, such as old covenant laws. Note also John 10:27, wherein Jesus says, "My sheep listen to my voice; I know them, and they follow me."

Furthermore, John chapter 16 states that Christians can still listen to Jesus. Although Jesus is gone and with the Father, the Spirit is available to believers for counseling and teaching during their lifetime. Notice, however, that Jesus never mentioned 'leaving the written law' to counsel believers.

John 16:12-15

"I have much more to say to you, more than you can now bear.

But when he, the Spirit of truth, comes, he will guide you into all truth. He will not speak on his own; he will speak only what he hears, and he will tell you what is yet to come.

He will bring glory to me by taking from what is mine and making it known to you.

All that belongs to the Father is mine. That is why I said the Spirit will take from what is mine and make it known to you."

Keep Your Conscience Clear

The Pharisees and Sadducees followed all, or as many, of the rules and regulations of their time as Christians attempt to follow today. Since the new laws of the Spirit are written in hearts and on minds, Christians actually walk in the Spirit. It is the conscience and Spirit that govern a person's daily walk, and not old covenant regulations. In essence, Christians do good works that go beyond what is stated as part of old covenant law because Spirit-led works start within the heart. Since Christians walk under the influence of the Spirit, and subsequently produce fruit of the Spirit (Gal. 5:22-23), they cannot possibly have any use for the regulations of old.

A question may be asked, "Can a Christian know when they are sinning (where sin is the transgression of what is pleasing to God)?" Yes, there are many times Christians know they are sinning. James 4:17 states, "Anyone, then, who knows the good he ought to do and doesn't do it, sins." Again, no law is necessary since it is their own conscience, guided by the Spirit, convicting them to do what is right. However, their conscience must be pure and not corrupt with the desires of the world.

Through grace, Christians can do righteous acts, while refraining from those that lead to death. Hebrews 9:14 states that the blood of Christ offered "unblemished to God, can cleanse our consciences from acts that lead to death." Christians should follow Paul's example where he has a hope in God of a resurrection and, "So I strive always to keep my conscience clear before God and man" (Acts 24:16).

Nobody can keep their conscience clear before God and man by offering monetary tithes. Nevertheless, several radio shows, television shows, pastors, and evangelists, give the impression that all is good, or one's conscience is clear, if each person pays the monetary tithe before all else. However, the Bible clearly states that consciences are cleansed by the blood of Christ, not by actions.

COMMANDMENTS FOR BELIEVERS

The word of God in its fullness has been kept hidden until now (Col. 1:24-28). Therefore, Christians have a complete teaching in Christ Jesus not available to all in Old Testament times. Paul's letters in the Bible are one way to learn about this teaching since he was given the task from the Lord of "testifying to the gospel of God's grace" (Acts 20:24). "For I have not hesitated to proclaim to you the whole will of God" (Acts 20:27).

Romans 12:2
Do not conform any longer to the pattern of this world, but be transformed by the renewing of your mind. Then you will be able to test and approve what God's will is - his good, pleasing and perfect will.

Christians should be transformed by the renewing of their minds (see also Eph. 4:21-24). This implies growth for the believer leading them to *be able to test and approve what God's will is - his good, pleasing and perfect will.* Therefore, it should not be surprising that the New Testament contains several guidelines for believers.

Obeying new covenant commands prevents Christians from becoming a part of this world with its sinful and wicked ways. At the same time, these commands help to build up and support fellow believers. The law of Christ starts with the heart, and therefore, cannot be performed grudgingly, nor performed out of a habit without the love of God present.

Contrast With Old Covenant Commands

The new covenant commands (law of Christ in the heart) contain no strict regulations, nor is there a harsh penalty - for those who are saved - for not performing any particular one (at any particular time). In contrast, the old covenant law, for example, sentenced people to death for attacking or cursing their parents, and for kidnapping (Ex. 21:15-17).

The commands under the new covenant leave room for Christians to act according to their individual faith and according to their individual means. "Therefore, as we have opportunity, let us do good to all people, especially to those who belong to the family of believers" (Gal. 6:10). Compare this with the rules concerning conduct toward one another in Exodus chapters 21, 22, and 23.

Notice, while reading new covenant commands, the lack of corresponding requirements given to fulfill each instruction. Also try applying the following questions to each command.

1. When must it occur?
2. How does one specifically perform it?
3. What amount of effort is required?
4. When is it satisfied?
5. Who is the recipient?

Attempting to answer these questions will show the simplicity of new covenant commands and our flexibility in carrying them out. Also, determine the penalty or reward for each command. This is an indication of the freedom Christians have to operate under the influence of the Spirit and without fear of retribution. After weighing the consequences of living under the two covenants, why would anyone choose to obey the old covenant law?

List of Commands

A partial list of commands is presented here, of which there are well over 100 within the New Testament.

- Be imitators of God and live a life of love, clothing yourselves with compassion, kindness, gentleness, humility, and patience. (Col. 3:12; Eph. 5:1-2)
- Rid yourselves of anger, rage, slander, malice, filthy language, sexual immorality, lust, impurity, evil desires, and greed. Instead, honor God with your body. (Col. 3:5-8; Eph. 4:31, 5:3-4; 1 Cor. 6:12-20; Titus 3:1-2; Jas. 1:21)

- Let the peace of Christ rule in your hearts and let the word of Christ dwell in you. (Col. 3:15-16)
- Whatever is true, pure, noble, right, lovely, or admirable, think about such things. Whatever you have learned from, received from, or seen in, me, put it into practice. Be ready to do, and devote yourselves to doing, whatever is good. (Phil. 4:8-9; Titus 3:1, 8)
- As often as you can, do good to all people, especially to believers. Let us not become weary in doing this, but continue to do good even when suffering. (Gal. 6:9-10; 1 Pet. 4:16-19)
- Forgive one another as the Lord forgave you, and be kind to one another. (Col. 3:13; Eph. 4:32)
- You were called to be free, so use your freedom to serve, and submit to one another in love, and in so doing you will fulfill the law of Christ. The whole law is summed up in this command: "Love your neighbor as yourself." (Matt. 22:37-40; Mk. 12:29-34; Jn. 13:34-35; 15:12-13,17; Gal. 5:13-14; 6:2; Eph. 5:21)
- Love your enemies. (Matt. 5:44)
- Do not utter unwholesome words when talking to one another. Only use words helpful for the building up of others. (Eph. 4:29; 1 Thes. 5:11)
- Do not tell lies to each other. (Col. 3:9; Eph. 4:25)
- Do not become conceited, or provoke or envy each other. (Gal. 5:26)
- Do not repay someone wrong for wrong. (1 Thes. 5:15)
- Do not argue about the law. (Titus 3:9)
- Do not let anyone deceive you with empty words. (Eph. 5:6-7)
- Do not show favoritism. (Jas. 2:1)
- Do not swear by heaven or by earth or by anything. Simply let your yes be yes, and your no be no. (Jas. 5:12)
- Speak to one another with psalms, hymns and spiritual songs, and let your conversation be full of grace. (Eph. 5:19; Col. 4:6)
- If someone has been caught in a sin, restore him gently. (Gal. 6:1-2)

- Everyone should test his own actions, without comparing himself to anyone else. Each person should carry his own load. (Gal. 6:4-5)
- A person shall reap what he sows. Sowing to please the sinful nature shall reap destruction. Sowing to please the Spirit, shall from the Spirit reap eternal life. (Gal. 6:7-8)
- Live by the Spirit and not by the sinful nature. The fruit of the Spirit is love, joy, peace, patience, kindness, goodness, faithfulness, gentleness and self-control. Against such things there is no law. (Gal. 5:16-23)
- Since we live by the Spirit, keep in step with the Spirit and worship in spirit and in truth. (Gal. 5:25; Jn. 4:24-25)
- Do not grieve the Holy Spirit. (Eph. 4:30)
- Do what the word says, do not merely listen to it. (Jas. 1:22)
- Obey the gospel of God. (1 Pet. 4:17)

Give According to Your Heart

There is an additional command concerning Christian giving.

- "Every man according as he purposeth in his heart, *so let him give*; not grudgingly, or of necessity: for God loveth a cheerful giver" (2 Cor. 9:7 KJV).

This verse may appear on tithing envelopes at church labeled, 'Tithes and Offerings,' but without the first part of the verse - "... *so let him give*; not grudgingly, or of necessity: for God loveth a cheerful giver." Quoting only part of the verse is very misleading, and very deceptive, since the meaning when stated this way (on tithing envelopes) is that Christians should give monetary tithes and offerings cheerfully.

Concerning the collection of money, the problem is twofold. The first problem concerns the written text. This verse is quoted out of context by the absence of the first part of it; the first part is key to Christian giving. The second problem is that it is taken out of context concerning its meaning. The sacrificial acts of tithes and offerings were not performed in the early church, neither literally or symbolically. In this verse, the Corinthians freely gave some of their monetary blessings to fellow Christians as an act of charity, not as an act of tithes and offerings.

The New International Version prints this verse as follows:

2 Corinthians 9:7

Each man should give what he has decided in his heart to give, not reluctantly or under compulsion, for God loves a cheerful giver.

When viewed in its entirety, and taken within context, the meaning of this passage is clear. It has nothing to do with giving 10 or more percent of a person's income to the local church. Neither does it have anything to do with the sacrificial practice of tithes and offerings. If the Corinthians did indeed practice these old covenant rituals, Paul would not have coordinated the 'collection' and the 'giving' of them. Instead, each Corinthian would have taken the tithes and offerings to a place where the Lord put his name and eaten them there.

On the contrary, the Corinthians took up a collection to assist their brother and sisters financially. In addition, the amount given by each individual was determined independently of one another, and without the rules of the law. *Each man should give what he has decided in his heart to give.* Furthermore, the gifts were offered freely and cheerfully, as opposed to grudgingly given according to some rule. For further study on this offering, known as the 'Jerusalem offering,' see Acts 24:17; 2 Corinthians 8:23; and Romans 15:26-27.

LOVE THY NEIGHBOR

A Top Priority

The following passages illustrate the importance of shifting the priority of individual Christian and organized church responsibilities to that of the less fortunate. Until this change occurs, Christians may find themselves neglectful concerning the needs of others, as well as irresponsible with money collected at the corporate level. In addition, they may actually become overcommitted to any and everything else other than human concerns and needs. Some of these commitments may at times be highly questionable.

Matthew 22:36-40

"Teacher, which is the greatest commandment in the Law?"

Jesus replied: "'Love the Lord your God with all your heart and with all your soul and with all your mind.'

This is the first and greatest commandment.

And the second is like it: 'Love your neighbor as yourself.'

All the Law and the Prophets hang on these two commandments."

Notice that the second command, to *love your neighbor as yourself* is as important as the first command, to *love the Lord your God with all your heart and with all your soul and with all your mind.* Proverbs 19:17 states, "He who is kind to the poor lends to the LORD." Today's Christians must cease giving the Lord and their neighbor 'leftover' consideration after all else has been done. The Lord and the needy deserve to be a top priority, not an afterthought. Otherwise, Christians may miss out on their reward - "and he will reward him for what he has done" (Prov. 19:17 cont.).

Luke 10:25-28

On one occasion an expert in the law stood up to test Jesus. "Teacher," he asked, "what must I do to inherit eternal life?"

"What is written in the Law?" he replied. "How do you read it?"

He answered: "'Love the Lord your God with all your heart and with all your soul and with all your strength and with all your mind'; and, 'Love your neighbor as yourself.'"

"You have answered correctly," Jesus replied. "Do this and you will live."

Examination of the new covenant commands for Christians reveals devotion towards one another. Further examination shows that giving to the poor is a requirement, especially to those who are in Christ. The expert in the law asked, *"what must I do to inherit eternal life?"* The answer by the expert was to love the Lord 'and' thy neighbor. Jesus responded favorably and said, *"Do this and you will live."* Moreover, "The entire law is summed up in a single command: 'Love your neighbor as yourself' " (Gal. 5:14).

More Important Than Tithes & Offerings

In Mark chapter 12, one of the teachers of the law asked Jesus, "Of all the commandments, which is the most important?" Everyone knows that tithes are holy unto the Lord and that a curse awaits those who did not offer them. However, giving tithes and offerings was not the answer to the question. Instead, to love the Lord and to love thy neighbor were the answers Jesus provided.

Mark 12:29-34

"The most important one," answered Jesus, "is this: 'Hear, O Israel, the Lord our God, the Lord is one.

Love the Lord your God with all your heart and with all your soul and with all your mind and with all your strength.'

The second is this: 'Love your neighbor as yourself.' There is no commandment greater than these."

"Well said, teacher," the man replied. "You are right in saying that God is one and there is no other but him.

To love him with all your heart, with all your understanding and with all your strength, and to love your neighbor as yourself is more important than all burnt offerings and sacrifices."

When Jesus saw that he had answered wisely, he said to him, "You are not far from the kingdom of God." And from then on no one dared ask him any more questions.

Jesus says there is no commandment *greater than these* two, and the teacher of the law agreed. But notice what the teacher added. He says that these two commands are *more important than all burnt offerings and sacrifices.* Even the teacher of the law admitted that loving the Lord and loving thy neighbor is more important than offerings and sacrifices. In contrast, most Christians today would easily conclude that monetary tithes and offerings are clearly more important than anything else; thus demonstrating how highly Christians value these monetary rituals in many of today's churches.

Oddly enough, Christians should become like the teachers of the law in one respect - to conclude that loving their neighbor is more important than monetary tithes and offerings. Maybe Jesus would then think of His followers as being wise, and eventually tell them what He told the teachers of the law. *"You are not far from the kingdom of God."*

How the Righteous Will Answer

Since Christians bring nothing into this world and will take nothing out of it, it only makes sense to use their material possessions for the benefit of others. Christians should assist as many as possible with basic human needs to enrich human life, while pursuing the truth of Christ Jesus. Then they can look forward to hearing these words from the Master.

Matthew 25:21
"His master replied, 'Well done, good and faithful servant! You have been faithful with a few things; I will put you in charge of many things. Come and share your master's happiness!' "

Christians must acknowledge the demand of love and their responsibility to carry the burdens of others. If Christians desire true joy, they ought to take care of one another by any means available and not hoard all that God has blessed them with (Lk. 12:16-21).

Matthew 25:35-40
For I was hungry and you gave me something to eat, I was thirsty and you gave me something to drink, I was a stranger and you invited me in,

I needed clothes and you clothed me, I was sick and you looked after me, I was in prison and you came to visit me.'

"Then the righteous will answer him, 'Lord, when did we see you hungry and feed you, or thirsty and give you something to drink?

When did we see you a stranger and invite you in, or needing clothes and clothe you?

When did we see you sick or in prison and go to visit you?'

"The King will reply, 'I tell you the truth, whatever you did for one of the least of these brothers of mine, you did for me.'"

Today's tithes and offerings look good on the surface, but taking care of the less fortunate looks good in the sight of God - *whatever you did for one of the least of these brothers of mine, you did for me.* Christians need to get to a point where certain 'things' do not mean so much that they have a higher priority than what God actually requires.

The things Christians work for are useless when not sought after with the correct priority in mind and when not in accordance with God's will. Supporting the local church is important, but the priorities of the church need to be in line with the law of Christ. In addition, supporting the local church should *not* have a higher priority than the greatest commandments for Christians. Furthermore, the righteous are *not* those who give monetary tithes and offerings. Instead, the righteous are those who take care of one another - *Then the righteous will answer him, 'Lord, when did we see you hungry and feed you?'*

Not All Will Enter Heaven

According to the Bible, not all will enter into the kingdom of heaven. This includes those who do evil, or those who do not do the will of the Father. Notice in the passage below that there were individuals 'acting right' in the sight of man, but the Lord had nothing to do with them.

Matthew 7:21-23
"Not everyone who says to me, 'Lord, Lord,' will enter the kingdom of heaven, but only he who does the will of my Father who is in heaven.

Many will say to me on that day, 'Lord, Lord, did we not prophesy in your name, and in your name drive out demons and perform many miracles?'

Then I will tell them plainly, 'I never knew you. Away from me, you evildoers!'

Make a special note that even people who prophesied in the name of the Lord, and cast out demons, might not enter into the kingdom of heaven. The acts themselves were good works and not acts of sin or violations of the law. Nevertheless, these particular people were still called *evildoers*. Giving monetary tithes and offerings today is also no guarantee for entry into the kingdom of heaven.

While traveling in towns and villages on His way to Jerusalem (Lk. 13:22-30), Jesus spoke about the 'narrow door.' In one of the towns, someone asked, "Lord, are only a few people going to be saved?" Notice here that even those who ate and drank with the owner were called evildoers.

Luke 13:24-27
"Make every effort to enter through the narrow door, because many, I tell you, will try to enter and will not be able to.

Once the owner of the house gets up and closes the door, you will stand outside knocking and pleading, 'Sir, open the door for us.' "But he will answer, 'I don't know you or where you come from.'

*"Then you will say, 'We ate and drank with you, and
you taught in our streets.'*

*"But he will reply, 'I don't know you or where you
come from. Away from me, all you evildoers!'"*

Is This a Salvation Issue?

Christians should act according to the law of Christ, which
includes meeting the needs of the poor as a top priority. This
is the perfect law that gives freedom from the old law, sin, and
death (Jas. 1:25). Actions must follow faith as explained in
James 2:14-26.

James 2:14
*What good is it, my brothers, if a man claims to have
faith but has no deeds? Can such faith save him?*

Therefore, justification is by works that follow faith. These
works are not those of obeying old covenant law because "the
law is not based on faith" (Gal. 3:12). The righteousness that
comes through faith in Christ Jesus must have accompanying
deeds, as opposed to having no deeds - *Can such faith save
him?* The faith and salvation of Christians should be
manifested by actually doing appropriate works. "Continue to
work out your salvation with fear and trembling" (Phil. 2:12).

James 2:20-22
*You foolish man, do you want evidence that faith
without deeds is useless?*

*Was not our ancestor Abraham considered righteous
for what he did when he offered his son Isaac on the
altar?*

*You see that his faith and his actions were working
together, and his faith was made complete by what he
did.*

Recall in Matthew 25:35-40 that the righteous are the ones
who feed the hungry, clothe the naked, etc. The question is
whether or not taking care of the needs of others is actually a

deed required of people of faith in order for that faith to save them. To determine this, let us look at that passage in context by considering the surrounding verses.

Matthew 25:31-34

"When the Son of Man comes in his glory, and all the angels with him, he will sit on his throne in heavenly glory.

All the nations will be gathered before him, and he will separate the people one from another as a shepherd separates the sheep from the goats.

He will put the sheep on his right and the goats on his left.

"Then the King will say to those on his right, 'Come, you who are blessed by my Father; take your inheritance, the kingdom prepared for you since the creation of the world."

Those on the right are those that took care of the 'least of these' as previously shown in verses 35 through 40. Those on the left, however, are not so fortunate.

Matthew 25:41-46

"Then he will say to those on his left, 'Depart from me, you who are cursed, into the eternal fire prepared for the devil and his angels.

For I was hungry and you gave me nothing to eat, I was thirsty and you gave me nothing to drink,

I was a stranger and you did not invite me in, I needed clothes and you did not clothe me, I was sick and in prison and you did not look after me.'

"They also will answer, 'Lord, when did we see you hungry or thirsty or a stranger or needing clothes or sick or in prison, and did not help you?'

"He will reply, 'I tell you the truth, whatever you did not do for one of the least of these, you did not do for me.'

"Then they will go away to eternal punishment, but the righteous to eternal life."

Christians must do the will of the Father. Notice that those who are cursed did not provide for those in need - *For I was hungry and you gave me nothing to eat.* These people *will go away to eternal punishment.*

The will of the Father is that Christians take care of one another. "And this is his command: to believe in the name of his Son, Jesus Christ, and to love one another as he commanded us. Those who obey his commands live in him, and he in them. And this is how we know that he lives in us: We know it by the Spirit he gave us." (1 Jn. 3:23-24). First John 4:20-21 continues by stating, "For anyone who does not love his brother, whom he has seen, cannot love God, whom he has not seen. And he has given us this command: Whoever loves God must also love his brother."

WALKING BY THE SPIRIT

With new covenant commands available, why do Christians revert to the old law for additional instructions? Of the 613 old covenant commandments, which ones should Christians obey? What happens if one obeys a certain set of them, and another obeys a different set? Is it possible that these two Christians will debate who is really the true follower of Christ?

This is easily resolved by understanding that *none* of the old covenant commands should be obeyed for righteousness, justification, or judgment. Some new covenant commands do overlap with the old covenant law. Nevertheless, this does not deem the remaining laws under the old covenant appropriate for the new covenant believer. When Christians walk in the Spirit according to the new covenant commands, they produce fruit of the Spirit.

Galatians 5:22-23
But the fruit of the Spirit is love, joy, peace, patience, kindness, goodness, faithfulness,
gentleness and self-control. Against such things there is no law.

The *fruit of the Spirit* emanating from within a Christian cannot be regulated since written laws do not govern the work of the Spirit. There is no law, or a set of rules, to regulate love, joy, peace, or any other fruit of the Spirit. The command to love thy neighbor is one that knows no limit in relation to the law. As far as supporting local churches with monetary gifts is concerned, Christians should understand the following in particular: Spirit-led acts cannot be regulated by the rules of tithes and offerings because, *Against such things there is no law.*

If the Bible had instructions telling Christians what to do in every situation, there would be an innumerable amount of commands. Of course, this is not the case. If it was, there would be no need to walk by, or under the influence of, the Holy Spirit. Therefore, Christians should not use the old covenant law to regulate what should be their Spirit-led walk in Christ - especially if the regulation is a grossly mis-interpreted, old covenant ritual like tithing!

The Challenge of Freedom

Some Christians fail to walk by the Spirit, choosing instead a strict set of regulations derived from the old covenant. It may be easier for some to follow the old covenant law rather than the new covenant law. Let us look at an analogy.

A prison inmate has followed all of the rules and regulations of the system, and is scheduled for a parole board hearing. According to prison rules, he has been a model inmate. At the parole hearing, the board judges the inmate fit for society and releases him. Not more than a day later, however, the ex-inmate violates his probation by assaulting someone, resulting in a return trip to prison. What happened? He was a model inmate and judged fit for society by the parole board. How or why did he violate his parole?

What happened here is similar to what is happening in modern day Christianity. While an inmate, this person operated flawlessly within the rules. However, he did not act responsibly while free and under the direction of his own conscience. It was much easier for the inmate when the strict rules were in place, providing justification by the works of them. Similarly, the freedom that is in Christ Jesus may impose too much responsibility on some Christians. Therefore, they turn to old covenant rules and regulations to govern their actions, including their financial giving to the church. It is much easier to give 10 percent of a paycheck than to decide for themselves how much to give (as led by the Spirit). In addition, giving 10 percent is measurable, and therefore, Christians can be justified by meeting the requirements of the rule.

Returning to the analogy, the inmate receives a second chance, and does not violate his probation this time. In addition, the former inmate accepts Jesus into his life and is currently a Christian. Now he has the law of Christ written on his heart. However, he finds this law much harder than any previous law that governed his actions. For instance, someone recently upset him, and although he refrained from assaulting the person, in his heart he had an overwhelming amount of hate.

The law of love, however, says to love thy enemy, so he was very troubled internally by his hate toward the other individual. For the former inmate, it is much easier 'not to hit' someone than it is 'not to hate' someone. He, like some Christians, recently decided to obey the old covenant law instead. For him, it is easier to follow the law and not hit someone than walking freely under the influence of the Spirit and not hate someone. Now his actions are justified by the law since he did not hit the individual. In addition, everyone in the community where he lives is satisfied with his behavior since it appears he is functioning well with those around him.

Similarly for Christians, it is much easier to have someone, or something, govern their giving rather than deciding how much, what, how, when, and to whom to give, as the Spirit leads. Therefore, like the inmate, they also turn to the old covenant regulations of tithes and offerings in an attempt to govern their gifts to the church. Christians, as well as the inmate, appear to be free, but they are actually behind old covenant bars. Furthermore, many Christians are quite comfortable with the old covenant regulations, and seem content to receive justification by them. Unfortunately, this complacency causes many to stray from the will of God by not walking under the influence of the Spirit.

You Foolish Galatians!

A thorough search of the Bible does not reveal any evidence that *monetary* tithes and offerings are biblically based. This may lead some Christians to correct their practice and conform to *biblical* tithes and offerings. However, to obtain justification by the letter of the law is still contrary to the will of God for those who recognize the sacrifice of Jesus. It is simply not good Christian practice to emulate old covenant sacrificial rituals (recall Chapter 6, "Freedom Through Death"). This situation is similar to the one in Galatia. Paul wrote to them concerning their daily walk and the things they were practicing as believers.

Galatians 3:1-5

You foolish Galatians! Who has bewitched you? Before your very eyes Jesus Christ was clearly portrayed as crucified.

I would like to learn just one thing from you: Did you receive the Spirit by observing the law, or by believing what you heard?

Are you so foolish? After beginning with the Spirit, are you now trying to attain your goal by human effort?

Have you suffered so much for nothing - if it really was for nothing?

Does God give you his Spirit and work miracles among you because you observe the law, or because you believe what you heard?

The Galatians were a body of believers seeking justification and righteousness by the law, attempting to attain their goal *by human effort*. Paul explains that to rely on the law now would be to suffer *so much for nothing*. The deception of observing the law was so great that Paul called them *foolish*, and asked them if they received the Spirit *by observing the law* or by believing what they heard. He even felt it necessary to remind them that *before your very eyes Jesus Christ was clearly portrayed as crucified.*

The Galatians received the Spirit by hearing the word. It is not possible to walk in the Spirit and rely on the law for justification from God. In addition, Christians cannot perform communion under the new covenant, recognizing the body of Christ, if they are observing the rules under the old covenant. Therefore, Christians should crucify the regulated monetary tithe and offering and give as the Spirit leads them because "against such things there is no law" (Gal. 5:22-23).

The Work of God

Many individuals may still require some form of step by step instructions, or something very structural, to find approval from God. For those in this position, this is accomplished by doing the work of God, literally. If the following work is done, then pleasing God will be accomplished.

John 6:27-29
"Do not work for food that spoils, but for food that endures to eternal life, which the Son of Man will give you. On him God the Father has placed his seal of approval."

Then they asked him, "What must we do to do the works God requires?"

Jesus answered, "The work of God is this: to believe in the one he has sent."

For those who require work to find favor from God, then be obedient to the word and *believe in the one he has sent.* On the other hand, for those who desire religion, there is a religion God accepts as pure and faultless. This religion is not in conflict with what is stated above, but it is actually one of the goals of obeying new covenant commands.

James 1:26-27
If anyone considers himself religious and yet does not keep a tight rein on his tongue, he deceives himself and his religion is worthless.

Religion that God our Father accepts as pure and faultless is this: to look after orphans and widows in their distress and to keep oneself from being polluted by the world.

The requirements of religion can be satisfied by practicing the religion that God accepts as pure and faultless - *to look after orphans and widows*. In contrast, monetary tithes and offerings, along with old covenant law, are not part of the religion that is pure and faultless.

Christians can do work to find favor with God as long as it is *to believe in the one he has sent*. They can also be religious if they *look after orphans and widows in their distress and to keep oneself from being polluted by the world*. Religion is permissible if it is in accordance with James 1:26-27, or one could simply walk in the Spirit instead. In order to accomplish either of these, however, Christians must listen to the word of God and be doers of his word (Jas. 1:23-25).

Some say Christians should have faith and obedience like Abraham, and therefore, are obligated to tithe money as a means of showing it. To have 'faith like Abraham' does not mean Christians are to 'do exactly what he did' (recall Chapter 7). Faith and actions work together, which is what Abraham demonstrated. Forcing someone to give a certain amount of money to a local church does not stem from faith. In contrast, faith is not required to give this way, just a little fear - the fear of a curse for not tithing money. On the other hand, Christians should honor the requirements as listed above in this chapter and in the following chapter.

———

Tithing does not guarantee a relationship with Jesus or find favor with God. The Pharisees and Sadducees followed as many old covenant regulations as possible, yet they still did not find favor with God. In addition, monetary tithes and offerings today are based on human commands and teaching, only have the appearance of something good, and are destined to perish (see Col. 2:20-23). Christians can tithe money until they go broke, but that will not keep the Lord from saying, "I never knew you."

Are Christians so concerned with rules of old that they forget to love the Lord with all their strength and to love thy neighbor as thyself? The Bible shows that this is, in fact, the will of God and a determining factor in separating the sheep from the goats. Christians ought to examine themselves and ask these questions: "Do I worship the Lord in spirit and truth while helping meet the spiritual and physical needs of others?" Or, "Am I a religious person simply putting one foot in front of the other, hoping one day I will walk right into heaven?"

Compare the commands for today's believers with what Christians are actually doing, or attempting to do, regarding their daily walk. Are they obeying God's instruction for believers or obeying the law of sin and death? Are they obeying the law of Christ written in their hearts or the law written on stone tablets? Are they walking under the influence of the Holy Spirit or living according to human customs and teachings?

It should be clear that Christians never need to refer to old covenant law to determine whether or not they are acting in accordance with God's will. Every Christian conscience has been cleansed by the blood of Jesus (Heb. 9:14). Therefore, they should follow it, becoming one with the Spirit, and continue to grow in the Lord by observing the new covenant commands. These commands are summed up as follows - love the Lord with all thy heart and love thy neighbor as thyself.

Matthew 25:37-40

"Then the righteous will answer him, 'Lord, when did we see you hungry and feed you, or thirsty and give you something to drink?

When did we see you a stranger and invite you in, or needing clothes and clothe you?

When did we see you sick or in prison and go to visit you?'

"The King will reply, 'I tell you the truth, whatever you did for one of the least of these brothers of mine, you did for me.'"

9

Grace Giving

Many Christians are taught to give monetary tithes and to give money 'above and beyond' their monetary tithe (monetary offering) in order to become true givers. This is a clear example of what happens when Christians call their church contributions something other than 'grace giving.' The rules and regulations under the old covenant have nothing to do with free persons in Christ pleasing God.

In addition to individual priorities, the priorities of the church need to change. Giving to the community should be first and foremost, as opposed to being a last minute thought after all else has been accomplished. Then, and only then will the image of the church resemble even more 'the household of God.'

Christians should come to the same conclusion as the teacher of the law in Mark 12:33: "To love him with all your heart, with all your understanding and with all your strength, and to love your neighbor as yourself is more important than all burnt offerings and sacrifices." Only then can Christians, within their freedom, perform corporate level giving that supports the life work of the church in accordance with the will of God.

This chapter brings into focus how, why, and when Christians are to give under the new covenant as Spirit-led believers. This way of giving is called *grace giving* or true Christian giving. It provides the correct approach to giving, showing that generous giving to the church, and to one another, should be exercised within a person's freedom and responsibility. More specifically, this chapter explains the following:

1. The power of grace;
2. Christians reap what they sow;
3. Christians meet the needs of the poor according to their ability;
4. Christians give cheerfully, and in so doing, this will please God;
5. Instructions for the wealthy;
6. How to support instructors of the word; and
7. Christian responsibility.

GRACE

This section focuses briefly on 'grace' since it is by grace that Christians can do anything and by grace all things are possible. It took grace in order for anyone to be saved, for in Titus 2:11 Paul states, "For the grace of God that brings salvation has appeared to all men." In addition, Christians "are justified freely by his grace through the redemption that came by Christ Jesus" (Rom. 3:24), and the gift of reconciliation came by the grace of one man, Jesus Christ (Rom. 5:15).

John 1:17
For the law was given through Moses; grace and truth came through Jesus Christ.

The Word Grace Defined

Translated from the Greek word charis, grace means that which brings pleasure, delight, joy, happiness, good fortune, or causes favorable regard. From the point of view of the one bestowing grace, the gift proceeds out as graciousness, loving–kindness, and goodwill. On the other hand, the receiver has a sense of gratitude or a feeling of thanksgiving. To study the term 'grace' thoroughly involves the additional study of other subjects such as forgiveness, salvation, regeneration, repentance, mercy, and kindness.

Access by Faith Into Grace

In John 1:16 the author writes that, "From the fullness of his grace we have all received one blessing after another." It is through grace that Christians receive blessings, not through obedience to the law or the work of man. In addition, Paul's statements in Romans chapter 9 concerning God's sovereign choice show that even in Old Testament times, favor was not based on the effort of man.

Romans 9:15-16
For he says to Moses, "I will have mercy on whom I have mercy, and I will have compassion on whom I have compassion."
It does not, therefore, depend on man's desire or effort, but on God's mercy.

Furthermore, in Acts chapter 4, verse 33, it is seen that Christians were under this grace. "With great power the apostles continued to testify to the resurrection of the Lord Jesus, and much grace was upon them all." Christians entered into this grace as stated in Romans chapter 5, but this gift is not by works of man as explained in Ephesians chapter 2.

Romans 5:1-2
Therefore, since we have been justified through faith, we have peace with God through our Lord Jesus Christ,
through whom we have gained access by faith into this grace in which we now stand. And we rejoice in the hope of the glory of God.

Ephesians 2:8-10
For it is by grace you have been saved, through faith -
and this not from yourselves, it is the gift of God -
not by works, so that no one can boast.

For we are God's workmanship, created in Christ Jesus to do good works, which God prepared in advance for us to do.

The Enabling Power of Grace

Grace is also the divine power that enables Christians to live a moral life or a life pleasing to God. The dynamic sense of grace results in fearless courage and effective witnessing for believers, as seen with Paul's position as a minister in Ephesus.

Ephesians 3:7-9
I became a servant of this gospel by the gift of God's grace given me through the working of his power.

Although I am less than the least of all God's people, this grace was given me: to preach to the Gentiles the unsearchable riches of Christ,

and to make plain to everyone the administration of this mystery, which for ages past was kept hidden in God, who created all things.

In addition, Paul's mission was to preach about this grace of God. "If only I may finish the race and complete the task the Lord Jesus has given me - the task of testifying to the gospel of God's grace" (Acts 20:22-24). Paul talks again about this enabling power in 1 Corinthians 15:9-10. "For I am the least of the apostles and do not even deserve to be called an apostle, because I persecuted the church of God. But by the grace of God I am what I am, and his grace to me was not without effect. No, I worked harder than all of them - yet not I, but the grace of God that was with me."

When God called each Christian, it was on the basis of unmerited favor - "For it is by grace you have been saved" (Eph. 2:5). In addition, God's grace also means divine empowering, and this grace or empowerment helps Christians keep God's commands. Presently, however, Christian 'giving' is done mostly through personal strength and works, and through the fear of the law and its curse. The new covenant, in contrast, promotes 'giving' that is by the power of grace, within the freedom that is of Christ Jesus, and under the influence of the Holy Spirit. Hence the phrases used in this book, 'grace giving' or 'giving by grace.'

BACK TO BASICS

Have the Love of Christ

Grace giving is centered on the Christian obligation of administering to the needs of others. Therefore, Christians are encouraged to do nothing out of selfish ambition. Instead, they should look into the interest of others, in addition to their own.

Philippians 2:1-4
If you have any encouragement from being united with Christ, if any comfort from his love, if any fellowship with the Spirit, if any tenderness and compassion,

then make my joy complete by being like-minded, having the same love, being one in spirit and purpose.

Do nothing out of selfish ambition or vain conceit, but in humility consider others better than yourselves.

Each of you should look not only to your own interests, but also to the interests of others.

Grace giving focuses primarily on giving to the needy (*having the same love* as Christ). This chapter is full of examples showing why it is important to focus on the needy. Accordingly, the church, and the individuals who make up the church, need to shift their 'priorities' from traditional church expenses to the expense of helping those in need - *being one in spirit and purpose.* This does not imply that Christians should neglect current church expenses, but they should rearrange their priorities to be in line with the will of God. The priorities of Christians should reflect the love of Christ, and in doing so, Christians can begin to fulfill the law of Christ.

Galatians 6:1-2

Brothers, if someone is caught in a sin, you who are spiritual should restore him gently. But watch yourself, or you also may be tempted.

Carry each other's burdens, and in this way you will fulfill the law of Christ.

Reap What You Sow

Before one can enter the arena of giving, some basic principles should be understood. First, a person is not cursed for not doing a particular work (see Gal. 3:13). Secondly, there is no condemnation for those in Christ Jesus (Rom. 8:1). The only thing that can happen when one does not do something, in this case not giving, is that the person simply does not reap the blessing that would have otherwise been made available.

Where one sows does not matter as long as it is according to the will of God. The book of Galatians shows that sowing to please the Spirit will from the Spirit reap eternal life. In contrast, sowing to please the sinful nature will reap destruction.

Galatians 6:7-10

Do not be deceived: God cannot be mocked. A man reaps what he sows.

The one who sows to please his sinful nature, from that nature will reap destruction; the one who sows to please the Spirit, from the Spirit will reap eternal life.

Let us not become weary in doing good, for at the proper time we will reap a harvest if we do not give up.

Therefore, as we have opportunity, let us do good to all people, especially to those who belong to the family of believers.

Regarding true Christian giving, these verses show that Christians *will reap a harvest at the proper time* if they continue in doing good. So Christians are encouraged *not to become weary in doing good*. They should also *do good to all people*, but especially to those who are believers. A specific example of reaping what one sows is found in Luke chapter 6.

Luke 6:37-38

"Do not judge, and you will not be judged. Do not condemn, and you will not be condemned. Forgive, and you will be forgiven.

Give, and it will be given to you. A good measure, pressed down, shaken together and running over, will be poured into your lap. For with the measure you use, it will be measured to you."

Verse 38 is usually misinterpreted by some as referring to money and the four-fold blessing of giving it. This passage is not talking about giving money. These verses actually state that if someone judges, condemns or forgives another, the same things are returned to the giver. If someone forgives his brother of a 'small' sinful act, then this individual may be forgiven by a third person of a much more 'severe act' of sin - *forgive, and you will be forgiven.*

In the case where one shares material blessings with another, however, the return may be received in areas other than where the original seed was sown. For example, someone may give another a pair of shoes, but in return, may receive a pair of pants, two bags of food, and help with a bill.

MEETING THE NEEDS OF THE POOR

Supporting those in need was prevalent during Old Testament times, in that tithes provided support for the Levites, priests, aliens, the fatherless and widows. The concept of supporting one another is also prevalent under the new covenant, as evidenced by the new covenant commands. This section illustrates how one is to support his/her neighbor. Since many people do not understand who their neighbor is, this issue is addressed first.

Who Is My Neighbor?

An expert in the law asked Jesus, "What must I do to inherit eternal life?" (Lk. 10:25-37). Jesus had the expert answer his own question by referring him to the law where it says to, "Love your neighbor as yourself." The expert then asked, "Who is my neighbor?" Jesus followed with the parable of the Good Samaritan, wherein a man was stripped of his clothes at the hand of robbers. In this parable, a *priest* was walking along and moved from one side of the road to the other in order to avoid the man. A *Levite* did the same as the priest.

Luke 10:33-37

But a Samaritan, as he traveled, came where the man was; and when he saw him, he took pity on him.

He went to him and bandaged his wounds, pouring on oil and wine. Then he put the man on his own donkey, took him to an inn and took care of him.

The next day he took out two silver coins and gave them to the innkeeper. 'Look after him,' he said, 'and when I return, I will reimburse you for any extra expense you may have.'

"Which of these three do you think was a neighbor to the man who fell into the hands of robbers?"

The expert in the law replied, "The one who had mercy on him." Jesus told him, "Go and do likewise."

The Samaritan took pity on the man by applying a bandage to his wounds, taking him to an inn, and paying the expenses. Jesus asked the expert, *"Which of the three was a neighbor to the man?"* Notice again that Jesus let the expert answer his own question. As stated earlier, a person knows the difference between right and wrong, and Jesus gave the expert the opportunity to use his own judgment. The expert of the law replied, *"The one who had mercy on him."* Notice that the Samaritan was not portrayed as living next door to this man, but he was still called *a neighbor to the man*.

The Good Samaritan is a familiar parable, and everyone knows the Samaritan acted as the neighbor. However, Christians seem to fall short of being this kind of neighbor. A neighbor in the Bible is not just somebody who lives next door, but a neighbor is one with a need or one who can assist another with a need. Therefore, the term 'neighbor' is used interchangeably with 'someone in need,' and 'to be a neighbor' is used interchangeably with 'someone who can provide for a need.'

At one time or another, everyone has probably felt needy, thinking it would be nice if someone would act neighborly towards them. But which brother or sister will heed the words of Jesus when referring to the Good Samaritan who had mercy and *go and do likewise?*

Communal Giving of the Early Church

As recorded in the Book of Acts, the early church grew rapidly. The believers devoted themselves to the apostles' teachings, to the fellowship, and were on one accord. Acts chapter 2 shows that believers had everything in common, even selling their belongings in fund raisers so they could distribute the money to those who had a need.

Acts 2:41-45

Those who accepted his message were baptized, and about three thousand were added to their number that day.

They devoted themselves to the apostles' teaching and to the fellowship, to the breaking of bread and to prayer.

Everyone was filled with awe, and many wonders and miraculous signs were done by the apostles.

All the believers were together and had everything in common.

Selling their possessions and goods, they gave to anyone as he had need.

Luke continues in Acts chapter 4 by writing that no one claimed any of their possessions as their own, as they were one in heart and mind.

Acts 4:32-35

All the believers were one in heart and mind. No one claimed that any of his possessions was his own, but they shared everything they had.

With great power the apostles continued to testify to the resurrection of the Lord Jesus, and much grace was upon them all.

There were no needy persons among them. For from time to time those who owned lands or houses sold them, brought the money from the sales

and put it at the apostles' feet, and it was distributed to anyone as he had need.

Charity events such as these served to meet the needs of the poor. Since the believers shared everything they had, it is easy to see why *there were no needy persons among them.* However, the *needs* were not the usual load that could be handled by all, since everyone was instructed to carry their own burdens (Gal. 6:5). The needs here were the more heavy or extreme burdens. Nevertheless, when Christians participate in this type of ministry, much grace is upon them (v33). This form of giving, where needs are met, is 'true Christian giving.'

Your Plenty Will Supply Their Need

Christians are instructed to love their neighbor and to help carry each other's burden when necessary. The goal is for equality in sufficiently meeting the needs of others. However, it should be achieved in a way that it does not burden the one doing the giving. Instead, it is a person's plenty that will supply the needs of others.

2 Corinthians 8:13-15

Our desire is not that others might be relieved while you are hard pressed, but that there might be equality.

At the present time your plenty will supply what they need, so that in turn their plenty will supply what you need. Then there will be equality,

as it is written: "He who gathered much did not have too much, and he who gathered little did not have too little."

As stated earlier, there is no penalty - in a negative sense, like a curse - for not doing a particular deed if one is not able.

In this case, one can decide based on the circumstance that he is not going to give. That is acceptable. In contrast, tithers believe that even if they are making very little money, they must tithe from their income anyway. This contradicts the passage in Corinthians. According to the charity work shown above, it is the *plenty* that will supply the needs of the poor so that the giver is not *hard pressed*.

Tithers may claim that tithes are not the same as charity work, and that the charity work here is above and beyond the tithe - that it is an offering. For that reason, they feel no comparison can be made between the charity events and the tenth Christians are required to give. A comparison does exist in that tithes and charity work each govern what people should do with their material or monetary possessions. In contrast, however, tithes are *not* required of Christians, while the work of charity is! In giving charity, whether to the local church or to someone in need, Christians are not to be hard pressed.

Ananias and Sapphira - What Not to Do

When giving gifts under false pretenses, people are really deceiving the Holy Spirit and not one another. In Acts chapter 5, the story of Ananias and his wife, Sapphira, tells of one such couple who tried this. The charity at the time was to sell some land, if someone decided to do so, and place the money at the apostles' feet for distribution to those in need. Ananias and Sapphira sold the land they personally committed, but held back some of the money for themselves.

Acts 5:1-5
Now a man named Ananias, together with his wife Sapphira, also sold a piece of property.

With his wife's full knowledge he kept back part of the money for himself, but brought the rest and put it at the apostles' feet.

Then Peter said, "Ananias, how is it that Satan has so filled your heart that you have lied to the Holy Spirit and have kept for yourself some of the money you received for the land?

> *Didn't it belong to you before it was sold? And after it was sold, wasn't the money at your disposal? What made you think of doing such a thing? You have not lied to men but to God."*
>
> *When Ananias heard this, he fell down and died. And great fear seized all who heard what had happened.*

The point here is that the land belonged to the couple before they committed it to the charity, and that nobody forced them to make that commitment. Once they sold the land and received the money, they were in complete control of the money just as they were with the land. This couple had the opportunity to follow through with this act of charity, but instead, they lied to God by keeping some of the money for themselves. Since they were not under old covenant law, there was no vehicle in place forcing them to complete their initial desire (like a vow). As a result of their selfishness, their initial joy of giving was replaced with that of greed, thus ruining their opportunity to give freely.

The story continues when three hours later Sapphira also said the price given for the land sold was what Ananias told Peter. Peter said to her, "How could you agree to test the Spirit of the Lord?" She also fell down and died. This is a case where the wife should not have supported her husband! The couple did not finish the work they at one point had desired (see 2 Cor. 8:11 in the following section). Christians may have good intentions or desires, but these desires will never feed or clothe anyone. Followers of Christ must act on their desire to actually be neighborly, thus, completing good works that are pleasing to God.

In Keeping With Your Income

When Christians decide to give, their gifts should not be governed with respect to what to give, how to give, when to give, to whom to give, and definitely not how much to give. Christians should especially refuse instructions on giving when under the guise of tithes and offerings. This is when Spirit-led giving becomes hostage to old covenant rules and regulations. Instead, giving should be decided according to each person's own ability and with the help of the Holy Spirit. The initial desire to give should be completed by following through with the charitable act, thereby pleasing God. The Bible shows that individuals ought to give according to their ability, not according to someone else's ability, a previously written rule or regulation, or a man-made tradition or custom.

Paul instructs the Corinthians in the area of giving by telling them to do as he instructed the Galatians to do. As noted earlier, the letter written to the Galatians shows that 'Christians reap what they sow.' Paul must have also told them what he is telling the Corinthians to do here.

1 Corinthians 16:1-2
Now about the collection for God's people: Do what I told the Galatian churches to do.

On the first day of every week, each one of you should set aside a sum of money in keeping with his income, saving it up, so that when I come no collections will have to be made.

Tithing Christians might say that *setting aside a sum of money in keeping with his income* is actually 10 percent of someone's salary because tithing is what Paul is supposedly talking about here. Some go so far as to say it is 10 percent of the gross income, since everyone who pays taxes will reap the benefit of them at some point in their lifetime. However, Christians being told how much to give does not conform to the Bible - *set aside a sum of money in keeping with his income*. The disciples themselves were not instructed to give a certain amount. Instead, when deciding to help a brother or sister, they gave as they were able (Acts 11:27-30).

For clarification, the Corinthian collection was taken up by a body of believers for another body of believers (poor saints in Jerusalem) and was not for local church expenses. In contrast with today's version of tithing, this money set aside weekly was *kept* by each believer and was not actually collected until a later time, as opposed to being collected once a week by a local church organization.

According to Your Means

The idea of giving 'according to your means,' and not a specific amount, is shown below. Paul clarifies what he said earlier by encouraging the believers in Corinth to give according to their means. This clears up any misunderstanding that results from the phrase *in keeping with his income.* He also states that since they have the desire to give, they ought to finish the work.

2 Corinthians 8:8-11

I am not commanding you, but I want to test the sincerity of your love by comparing it with the earnestness of others.

For you know the grace of our Lord Jesus Christ, that though he was rich, yet for your sakes he became poor, so that you through his poverty might become rich.

And here is my advice about what is best for you in this matter: Last year you were the first not only to give but also to have the desire to do so.

Now finish the work, so that your eager willingness to do it may be matched by your completion of it, according to your means.

Notice that Paul is not commanding the Corinthians to give, but is testing the sincerity of their love with the earnestness of others. If the Corinthians were not commanded to give by Paul, why are today's leaders commanding Christians to give 10 percent of their income to the local church?

In the passage above, Paul made reference to Jesus becoming poor so they might become rich. This should have encouraged the Corinthians to give, but would have left the impression they were to become poor in the process. However, God's concern is for the giver as well as the receiver. So Paul compares the love of the Corinthians with that of others, and then asks that they give *according to your means.*

As extreme as the story is in Acts 5, Ananias and Sapphira were probably eager to help at first in the charity for the saints. As noted earlier, they were not commanded to participate, and like everyone else, their involvement probably excited them initially. Unfortunately, no one probably told them what Paul told the Corinthians to do here - *Now finish the work, so that your eager willingness to do it may be matched by your completion of it.* This bit of knowledge might have saved the couple's lives!

GIVE CHEERFULLY

This section covers some of the passages in which Paul explains the mood, or mindset, in which Christians should give. These passages show the joy of the Corinthians in their giving, and also show Paul's eagerness to support the needy.

Paul's Eagerness to Give

Since most Christians look at ministers to see if they practice what they preach, let us take a look at Paul in a similar manner. Although Christians ought to obey what the Bible requires of them, many do tend to emulate the acts they see from their minister.

Galatians 2:9-10
James, Peter and John, those reputed to be pillars, gave me and Barnabas the right hand of fellowship when they recognized the grace given to me. They agreed that we should go to the Gentiles, and they to the Jews.

All they asked was that we should continue to remember the poor, the very thing I was eager to do.

Paul was very eager to minister to the poor through giving. Notice here that when he was given the right hand of fellowship, all he was really asked to do was to remember the poor. This passage shows that Paul, one who had no problem asking people to assist the poor, was one himself who wanted to remember the poor - the very thing I was eager to do.

Corinthian's Act of Grace

In his second letter to the Corinthians, Paul explains that they ought to excel in the grace of giving. He notes the grace of God given to the Macedonian churches as a result of their giving. They actually pleaded for the privilege of giving.

2 Corinthians 8:1-7

And now, brothers, we want you to know about the grace that God has given the Macedonian churches.

Out of the most severe trial, their overflowing joy and their extreme poverty welled up in rich generosity.

For I testify that they gave as much as they were able, and even beyond their ability. Entirely on their own,

they urgently pleaded with us for the privilege of sharing in this service to the saints.

And they did not do as we expected, but they gave themselves first to the Lord and then to us in keeping with God's will.

So we urged Titus, since he had earlier made a beginning, to bring also to completion this act of grace on your part.

But just as you excel in everything - in faith, in speech, in knowledge, in complete earnestness and in your love for us - see that you also excel in this grace of giving.

In this passage, Paul called the contribution by the Corinthians an *act of grace*. This shows that an act of grace can manifest itself through the work of the saints. In contrast, many Christians today do *not* have the freedom to give willingly because they face a tremendous stumbling block - the mandatory collection process of monetary tithes and offerings.

Notice how the Macedonians *gave as much as they were able*, not 10 percent of their money. They also did this *entirely on their own*, not with the help of the pulpit quoting old covenant rules and regulations - such as bringing tithes to the storehouse or else be cursed. Some tithers use 2 Corinthians 8:2-3 to encourage Christians to tithe money - even when they cannot afford it - because the Macedonians gave out of *their extreme poverty*. This passage is not an example of mandatory giving out of poverty, but the *grace of giving* (v7).

The Generous Gift

Paul had been boasting about the Corinthians to the Macedonians because of their eagerness to give, and he did not want to be ashamed of having been so confident. So in Second Corinthians chapter 9, Paul arranged for some brothers to go in advance to Corinth to finish the arrangements of this *generous gift*.

2 Corinthians 9:1-5

There is no need for me to write to you about this service to the saints.

For I know your eagerness to help, and I have been boasting about it to the Macedonians, telling them that since last year you in Achaia were ready to give; and your enthusiasm has stirred most of them to action.

But I am sending the brothers in order that our boasting about you in this matter should not prove hollow, but that you may be ready, as I said you would be.

For if any Macedonians come with me and find you unprepared, we - not to say anything about you - would be ashamed of having been so confident.

So I thought it necessary to urge the brothers to visit you in advance and finish the arrangements for the generous gift you had promised. Then it will be ready as a generous gift, not as one grudgingly given.

Notice that the gift was not required, but instead, it was described by Paul as *the generous gift you had promised*. Paul explained how the Corinthians should set some money aside once a week, so when he comes, no collection will be required (1 Cor. 16:1-2). In the second letter, Paul sent some brothers in advance to help them get ready. Paul did not want anyone to be ashamed of having been so confident in this matter. So he wanted the gift to *be ready as a generous gift, not as one grudgingly given.*

ACCEPTABLE GIFTS

Willingness Required

To further show how old covenant rules are not necessary for Christians, particular in the area of giving, the Bible says that a person's gift is acceptable if the willingness is there. Therefore, giving tithes and offerings, or calling today's church contributions tithes and offerings, is not necessary for the acceptance of monetary gifts.

2 Corinthians 8:12
For if the willingness is there, the gift is acceptable according to what one has, not according to what he does not have.

It is important for the willingness to exist, in order for the gift be a generous gift and not one grudgingly given. A gift offered willingly is one given *according to what one has.* In the Old Testament, one could give tithes and offerings reluctantly, but it was still offered because it was required. Today's monetary tithe is no different. It can be given reluctantly, but since it meets the 10 percent requirement, it is accepted by the church and provides a feeling of justification for the giver. Many pastors will tell their congregation not to give it grudgingly. In other words, one must give 10 percent of their money to the Lord and they better give it cheerfully or else!

Some may read this book and come to the conclusion that they should not give in the name of tithes and offerings. This, of course, is one goal of the book. The downside, however, is that some may feel that without the mandate of tithes and offerings, their giving to the church will be less than before. This is not true for those who possess both the willingness and the means to give. Some individuals may actually give more once the burdens of monetary tithes and offerings are lifted.

Once Christians decide to give freely, fluctuations or reductions in the amount they give to the local church may occur initially. Some reasons include: giving reluctantly and not cheerfully in the past; giving based on a standard approved by men and not based on a willingness approved by God; legitimate financial reasons such as current debt or an unforeseen medical expense; or deciding to take better care of one's family and friends.

All Christian giving should reach the point where it is performed willingly. What happens after that, as well as how much one gives, is between that individual and the Lord, and is nobody else's business. Finally, Christians should not base their level of faith, or commitment to the local church, on the amount of money they are able to give.

Jesus Rebukes the Pharisees

Some may feel they are performing acts pleasing to God by tithing. However, it is possible to tithe and not have the love of God in their hearts, or the willingness required by God. Matthew chapter 23 shows an example of this when Jesus goes through the seven woes. One of the woes happened to include the subject of tithing.

Matthew 23:23-24
"Woe to you, teachers of the law and Pharisees, you hypocrites! You give a tenth of your spices - mint, dill and cummin. But you have neglected the more important matters of the law - justice, mercy and faithfulness. You should have practiced the latter, without neglecting the former.

You blind guides! You strain out a gnat but swallow a camel.

Jesus explains that the Pharisees were indeed giving a tenth of the required items under the law - not money, but food products. Nevertheless, He still called the Pharisees hypocrites because they only performed the letter of the law, not the more important matters such as *justice, mercy and faithfulness.*

Under the old covenant, no one found favor with God by simply obeying the letter of the law. Similarly, a Christian gift is not acceptable simply because it is given, or because it is a tithe of one's possessions - even the Pharisees did that. Instead, a willingness to give and a love for God must accompany the gift. Otherwise, the gift is not acceptable.

As the passage above demonstrates, the Pharisees performed the smallest detail of the law, giving what they should have, but lacked the most important requirements of God - *You strain out a gnat but swallow a camel.* Some Christians today also pay attention to minor details, but forget the major detail of loving their neighbors, which is instructed by the law of Christ under the new covenant.

Tithing Christians say Jesus had the opportunity in this passage to tell the Pharisees not to tithe. Since He did not, Christians are required to tithe money today. Fortunately, there was a good reason Jesus did not tell anyone to stop tithing. Jesus was born under the law in the form of sinful man (Gal. 4:3-5; Rom. 8:3), and therefore, he was under the same law as the Pharisees. The Father's plan of reconciliation required the ultimate sacrifice of Jesus for the remission of sins, thus, redeeming those who believe in Him from the law and its curse.

In the book of Matthew, however, Jesus had not been crucified until late in the book. Therefore, He could not inform people of their freedom from the law as Paul did in later times. Jesus also added, "Anyone who breaks one of the least of these commandments and teaches others to do the same will be called least in the kingdom of heaven, but whoever practices and teaches these commands will be called great in the kingdom of heaven" (Matt. 5:19).

During Jesus' walk in the flesh, he had not redeemed anyone from the law yet. Most Christians do not think about this when reading the four books in the Bible - Matthew, Mark, Luke and John - which tell of Jesus' walk on Earth. This is confusing to some because it may appear to conflict with other New Testament books such as Romans and Galatians, which were written after Christ died. In light of this, Christians should not focus on what Jesus 'did not say.' Instead, Christians should focus on what He 'did say' and within context.

The Widow's Mite

This section has shown that a willingness is necessary for the gift to be acceptable. By showing the Pharisees' lack of justice, mercy and faithfulness, it should be evident that the physical act of giving should not have the importance currently placed on it. Continuing with the theme of acceptable gifts, let us look at the widow's offering.

Mark 12:41-44

Jesus sat down opposite the place where the offerings were put and watched the crowd putting their money into the temple treasury. Many rich people threw in large amounts.

But a poor widow came and put in two very small copper coins, worth only a fraction of a penny.

Calling his disciples to him, Jesus said, "I tell you the truth, this poor widow has put more into the treasury than all the others.

They all gave out of their wealth; but she, out of her poverty, put in everything - all she had to live on."

Many pastors and teachers use this passage, along with 2 Corinthians 8:2-3 discussed earlier, to emphasize that poor individuals today should tithe money. They say that if this poor widow can give all she had, then everyone can give at least 10 percent of their money to the Lord.

Notice that Jesus did not praise anyone for coming to the temple and giving tithes to the temple treasury. However, He focused on what the widow gave. Jesus saw that what she gave were *two very small copper coins.* Jesus called the disciples to Him and pointed out the *good* in the widow's gift, not so much the quantity of her gift. The widow put into the treasury according to the grace given her (Rom. 12:6). As shown in the next section, a person who sows generously will reap generously, and for the widow, this was a generous gift. Jesus then stated, *I tell you the truth, this poor widow has put more into the treasury than all the others.*

How is it possible that this widow gave more than anyone else? Every church member knows that a new sanctuary cannot be built if everyone gave two small copper coins. Her gift was more because it was *out of her poverty*, not out of wealth like the others. She had a willingness to give. Whereas the others, at this particular time, were probably like the Pharisees who gave out of their wealth so others could *see* the good they were doing. As a result, Jesus only made note of her giving.

THE GIFT OF GIVING

Decision of the Heart

God responds to generous giving, as shown above. In the passage below, Paul states that a person reaps in accordance to how much is given - generosity is measured according to what a person owns. Notice that the one offering the gift decides the amount to give, and then reaps accordingly.

2 Corinthians 9:5-8

... Then it will be ready as a generous gift, not as one grudgingly given.

Remember this: Whoever sows sparingly will also reap sparingly, and whoever sows generously will also reap generously.

Each man should give what he has decided in his heart to give, not reluctantly or under compulsion, for God loves a cheerful giver.

And God is able to make all grace abound to you, so that in all things at all times, having all that you need, you will abound in every good work.

In Chapter 8, "New Covenant Commands," several guidelines are listed for believers in Christ. Within the commands, emphasis is placed on how Christians treat their neighbors and fellow believers. In line with these commands, or the law of Christ, notice above that God is pleased with a cheerful giver when supporting those in need - *for God loves a cheerful giver.*

Out of this love (see 1 Cor. 13:3), Christians will reap according to how they sow, and God will make all grace abound to them. In addition, *whoever sows generously will also reap generously.*

Paul also says that a person is to give *what he has decided in his heart to give.* This is the only true requirement of Christian giving, along with a willing heart. However, this is in contrast to what tithing Christians would have people believe. How can it be the 'decision of the individual' and at the same time a 'requirement to give a tenth?' The truth is, Christians are not supposed to give a tenth. Therefore, there is no conflict between what Paul is saying here for the Christian, and what is stated in the old covenant law for Jewish people.

Giving as one decides from the heart follows from the fact that everyone is to give according to his/her individual means. When Christians give according to what they have, they give out of their blessings from God. As a result, the gifts are not reluctantly given but given cheerfully. However, in the case where someone goes above and beyond their means (according to his faith), God is surely to make grace abound to them all the more.

Our Gifts to the Poor

There are some who feel God is only at work when something mystical happens, or if something materializes from out of thin air. Unfortunately, this mentality carries over into the area of assisting the poor. Christians believe the poor will be taken care of, but fail to realize that they are taken care of through those who do the will of God.

There are many passages in the Bible instructing Christians to share their possessions with the poor - to the saints in particular. Examples include the following: The disciples were upset when a woman poured expensive perfume on the head of Jesus, saying the perfume could have been sold and the money given to the poor (Matt. 26:9); Jesus told a rich man, "If you want to be perfect, go, sell your possessions and give to the poor" (Matt. 19:21); Jesus also taught the people to sell their possessions and give to the poor in Luke 12:33, which is what the early church did in Acts 4:34-35; Zacchaeus gave half of his possessions to the poor in Luke 19:8; in

Romans 15:26, a contribution was made by the saints to the poor in Jerusalem; and Cornelius' prayer was answered by an angel who stated,

Acts 10:4
... Your prayers and gifts to the poor have come up as a memorial offering before God.

Many teach that the prayers of Cornelius went up as a memorial offering before God without acknowledging that his gifts to the poor were also seen by God. Prayer is an act of faith and faith without works is dead (Jas. 2:20-22). Therefore, prayer alone is not good enough. There probably would have been no memorial before God had Cornelius not followed his prayers with an action that was pleasing to God. Some Christians tend to pray for those in need of warmth and food without physically helping them. However, the verse above is a clear example of an individual who did more than just pray for those in need. Cornelius actually gave gifts to the poor.

Continuing from earlier verses in Second Corinthians, observe below how God's gifts are scattered abroad to the poor through his saints, because his saints will abound in every good work.

2 Corinthians 9:8-9
And God is able to make all grace abound to you, so that in all things at all times, having all that you need, you will abound in every good work.
As it is written: "He has scattered abroad his gifts to the poor; his righteousness endures forever."

God's Indescribable Gift

God blesses some Christians abundantly for the purpose of supplying the needs of others. In addition, he blesses them for giving to the poor. Second Corinthians chapter 9 completes the explanation of this awesome, never ending, circular, indescribable, gift of God - the *gift of giving.*

2 Corinthians 9:10-15

Now he who supplies seed to the sower and bread for food will also supply and increase your store of seed and will enlarge the harvest of your righteousness.

You will be made rich in every way so that you can be generous on every occasion, and through us your generosity will result in thanksgiving to God.

This service that you perform is not only supplying the needs of God's people but is also overflowing in many expressions of thanks to God.

Because of the service by which you have proved yourselves, men will praise God for the obedience that accompanies your confession of the gospel of Christ, and for your generosity in sharing with them and with everyone else.

And in their prayers for you their hearts will go out to you, because of the surpassing grace God has given you.

Thanks be to God for his indescribable gift!

Observe here that the needs of the recipient are met; God is praised; the receiver's prayers go out to the giver; and God, who supplied the seed to the giver, *will also supply and increase your store of seed and will enlarge the harvest of your righteousness.* It is not 'what a person gives,' but 'that a person gives,' that is important. Then blessings will come. They will likely come through someone else who meets the needs of the giver by *giving* out of his surplus - also supplied by God. This is in effect returning the gift of giving.

It is no wonder, then, that it is more blessed to give than to receive. Maybe this is why Paul never asked for anything, but instead, preferred to work for his keep in addition to helping meet the needs of his companions (Acts 20:34-35).

WEALTHY PEOPLE

Ironically, those who find it hardest to give are sometimes the ones who have the most to give (materially). Understanding the passages in the preceding section, it should be clear that hoarding material goods for oneself is utterly useless.

Building Bigger Barns

Here is a parable from the book of Luke that warns people about gathering too much for themselves (see also Proverbs 11:24-26).

Luke 12:16-21

And he told them this parable: "The ground of a certain rich man produced a good crop.

He thought to himself, 'What shall I do? I have no place to store my crops.'

"Then he said, 'This is what I'll do. I will tear down my barns and build bigger ones, and there I will store all my grain and my goods.

And I'll say to myself, "You have plenty of good things laid up for many years. Take life easy; eat, drink and be merry."'

"But God said to him, 'You fool! This very night your life will be demanded from you. Then who will get what you have prepared for yourself?'

"This is how it will be with anyone who stores up things for himself but is not rich toward God."

Notice the problem had nothing to do with a lack of giving tithes and offerings, since he may have been a tither. Instead, the parable focuses on hoarding for oneself as opposed to not sharing with others. To hoard possessions is not to have at heart the interest others. To be *rich toward God* is to use material blessings for the work of charity. Besides, no one brought anything into the world, and no one will take anything out of it (1 Tim. 6:7). So it makes good sense to share with others what is only had temporarily so true riches in heaven can be obtained.

The second problem is that storing goods up for himself meant less dependence on God. This would allow the rich man to *take life easy; eat, drink and be merry.* Matthew 6:26 states,

"Look at the birds of the air; they do not sow or reap or store away in barns, and yet your heavenly Father feeds them. Are you not much more valuable than they?" God wants his people to put their trust in him, but this rich man put his trust in wealth instead. See also Luke 12:22-31.

<u>Putting Hope in Wealth</u>

In 1 Timothy 6:3-10, the Bible specifically addresses the love of money, and encourages Christians to steer away from its temptation. Some mistakenly think 'money' is the root of all evil, but it can be used for good purposes, such as charity. In fact, it is the 'love of money,' not money itself, that is the root of evil.

1 Timothy 6:9-10
People who want to get rich fall into temptation and a trap and into many foolish and harmful desires that plunge men into ruin and destruction.

For the love of money is a root of all kinds of evil. Some people, eager for money, have wandered from the faith and pierced themselves with many griefs.

This passage continues by informing the rich not to put their hope in wealth, but to put their hope in God who richly provides for his people. The previous section shows that Christians reap generously if they sow generously and that God will continue to provide the seed required for sowing. In addition to this, the Bible instructs Christians how to lay up treasure for themselves for the coming age.

1 Timothy 6:17-19
Command those who are rich in this present world not to be arrogant nor to put their hope in wealth, which is so uncertain, but to put their hope in God, who richly provides us with everything for our enjoyment.

Command them to do good, to be rich in good deeds, and to be generous and willing to share.

In this way they will lay up treasure for themselves as a firm foundation for the coming age, so that they may take hold of the life that is truly life.

God *provides us with everything for our enjoyment.* Once some people obtain a few earthly items, they have a tendency not to let others share in their blessing. In contrast, Christians should *be generous and willing to share.* This benefits those with whom they share, as well as the owner since there is additional joy in the sharing.

The Heart Follows Treasure

Below is a passage concerning 'where a person's heart is' regarding treasures. In these verses, Jesus encourages His followers not to worry because life is more than food and clothes, and that they should work on obtaining a treasure in heaven that will not wear out.

Luke 12:32-34
Do not be afraid, little flock, for your Father has been pleased to give you the kingdom.
Sell your possessions and give to the poor. Provide purses for yourselves that will not wear out, a treasure in heaven that will not be exhausted, where no thief comes near and no moth destroys.
For where your treasure is, there your heart will be also.

Notice the requirement to get *a treasure in heaven that will not be exhausted.* It is not the act of giving monetary tithes and offerings, but instead, the instructions are to *give to the poor.* The theme of giving to the poor is prevalent throughout the whole Bible. However, it does not seem prevalent throughout today's church. Thus, the plea to the church is to adjust its priorities in favor of supporting those in need.

What Do I Still Lack?

Another 'rich man' passage is located in Matthew chapter 19. A man approached Jesus and asked, "Teacher, what good thing must I do to get eternal life?" Jesus responded to this initial question by telling him to obey the commandments - He mentioned some that were a part of the original ten commandments. From Chapter 6, recall that the old covenant law is for the unsaved, and that it helps them to recognize sin in their lives. Therefore, it should not be surprising that Jesus started off His side of the conversation this way, telling the rich man to obey the commandments.

The rich man said he kept all of these commandments, and proceeded to ask a second question, "What do I still lack?" The conversation continues as follows.

Matthew 19:20-24

"All these I have kept," the young man said. "What do I still lack?"

Jesus answered, "If you want to be perfect, go, sell your possessions and give to the poor, and you will have treasure in heaven. Then come, follow me."

When the young man heard this, he went away sad, because he had great wealth.

Then Jesus said to his disciples, "I tell you the truth, it is hard for a rich man to enter the kingdom of heaven.

Again I tell you, it is easier for a camel to go through the eye of a needle than for a rich man to enter the kingdom of God."

The rich man knew what he was doing was not good enough in the sight of God, so he asked the second question, *"What do I still lack?"* Jesus started His second response by stating, *"If you want to be perfect,"* so the question really being answered by Jesus was, "What do I still lack if I want to be perfect?"

Notice that Jesus did not command the individual to give money as a tithe or offering to the local temple or synagogue. Instead, He tells the rich man to *sell your possessions and give to the poor. ... Then come, follow me.* One might argue that

Jesus broke the law by telling this man to give his money to the poor without giving 10 percent to the Lord. Recall earlier that the Pharisees tithed mint, dill, and cummin, all of which are required. Money, on the other hand, is not a required tithing substance. Therefore, Jesus did not violate the law by telling this person to give the money to the poor.

Once again, the importance of giving to the needy resurfaces. In addition, this passage demonstrates an act of love that must come from within. As shown earlier, if Christians give, they will have treasure in heaven. If they want perfection, Jesus states, *then come, follow me.* Giving money to the poor alone would not have made this individual perfect. He also had to follow Jesus. Similarly, people giving 10 percent of their money to the local church will not make them perfect. Everyone must follow Jesus, not the old covenant law.

As the story goes, the rich man's love for his money was stronger than his love for his neighbor. That love must have been awfully strong since he was having a conversation with Jesus in the flesh, face to face! It is not certain, though, that Jesus would have actually had the rich man sell all of his possessions. Recall that God told Abraham to sacrifice his son Isaac as a burnt offering (Gen. 22:1-2). Abraham showed his fear of God by taking Isaac to the designated place for the offering. However, when he was about to go through with it, an angel of the Lord said, "Do not lay a hand on the boy" (Gen. 22:12) and provided an appropriate sacrifice for Abraham to offer.

SUPPORT YOUR INSTRUCTOR OF THE WORD

In the area of giving, the poor have been mentioned to a great extent. The Bible also states that Christians are to support teachers and preachers, as well as others who work in the ministry.

Paul talked plenty about giving and supporting one another during his ministry. Being an expert in old covenant law, he could have quoted Scripture to get people to tithe money in order to cover his expenses, as well as taking care of the needs of the Christian community. Nevertheless, Paul did not do this because he knew the truth behind tithing, and behind old covenant rules and regulations. Tithing never even surfaced as an alternative for supporting the church, nor a modified version of tithing. Instead, Paul only went so far as to compare the love of one with the earnestness of others when encouraging people to give (2 Cor. 8:8).

Profession Deserving of Pay

Paul did not mention (monetary) tithing when talking about support for instructors of the word. Instead, he simply explained that those who sow spiritual seed are entitled to reap a material harvest.

1 Corinthians 9:11-14

If we have sown spiritual seed among you, is it too much if we reap a material harvest from you?

If others have this right of support from you, shouldn't we have it all the more? But we did not use this right. On the contrary, we put up with anything rather than hinder the gospel of Christ.

Don't you know that those who work in the temple get their food from the temple, and those who serve at the altar share in what is offered on the altar?

In the same way, the Lord has commanded that those who preach the gospel should receive their living from the gospel.

The tone here is clear by Paul asking, *is it too much if we reap a material harvest from you?* It seems there existed some tension in the past concerning those in the ministry receiving support. Maybe the ministry was not to the point where it was viewed as a profession deserving of pay. Or maybe it just goes to show what some people actually value, which, unfortunately, may not be the ministry. In any case, Christians are clearly to support those who preach and 'work in the ministry.'

Paul goes on to say that they did *not use this right*, but instead, they *put up with anything rather than hinder the gospel of Christ*. Paul's devotion to the gospel was so great that he waived his rights to a material harvest rather than disrupt the work of God. Nevertheless, this did not stop him from teaching what is correct according to the gospel. Today's church should also proceed forward when people do not give, or cannot give. Spreading the good news should continue regardless of a lack of support. Contrary to what many believe, a shortage of money cannot stop the gospel from going forward.

Compensation Principle

The chapters "Offerings Defined" and "Tithing Defined" show that the Levites, priests and temple overseers shared in all of the offerings as part of the sacrificial rituals. Notice that Paul cites Scripture when he says, *those who work in the temple get their food from the temple, and those who serve at the altar share in what is offered on the altar* (see 1 Cor. 9:13 above). Was Paul talking about some principle of receiving tithes, or about the principle of receiving compensation in general?

1 Corinthians 9:7-9

Who serves as a soldier at his own expense? Who plants a vineyard and does not eat of its grapes? Who tends a flock and does not drink of the milk?

Do I say this merely from a human point of view? Doesn't the Law say the same thing?

For it is written in the Law of Moses: "Do not muzzle an ox while it is treading out the grain." Is it about oxen that God is concerned?

This passage shows that people who work should reap from their labor. Since only Levites collected tithes, Paul could not have been talking about laymen receiving tithes. Instead, he was actually talking about the principle of receiving compensation for work performed. He also claimed this to be true of those that preach the gospel. "Surely he says this for us, doesn't he? Yes, this was written for us, because when the plowman plows and the thresher threshes, they ought to do so in the hope of sharing in the harvest" (1 Cor. 9:10).

In principle, Paul is saying that the Lord commands the same for today - "those who preach the gospel should receive their living from the gospel" (1 Cor. 9:14). Therefore, Christians should support their instructors of the word just as they would consider compensating anyone else for work performed - but not through monetary tithes.

A pastor or someone may ask, "How are Christians to support the church and its preachers if they do not tithe?" When faced with this question, simply point them to 1 Corinthians 9:9-14 and ask them to study how it was done there. Pastors should simply inform their congregations that those who teach and preach deserve compensation. If the people are willing, and they should be willing once they learn about biblical giving, then they will provide the necessary support.

Worthy of Double Honor

The Bible also states in Galatians 6:6, "Anyone who receives instruction in the word must share all good things with his instructor." Here it explains that Christians should support those appointed to teach. Not only should they receive some form of compensation, they deserve double that of what other positions in the church ministry receive.

1 Timothy 5:17
The elders who direct the affairs of the church well are worthy of double honor, especially those whose work is preaching and teaching.

Paul learned to be content with whatever he had and knew he could do anything through God who gave him strength. Although Paul did not use his rights as an apostle to receive support, that does not mean Christians should consider not supporting those who teach and preach.

Church Support for Instructor

The Philippians were a group of believers who supported the ministry of God when they provided aid for Paul - sending him aid on more than one occasion when he was in need. Paul received full payment and even more.

Philippians 4:10
I rejoice greatly in the Lord that at last you have renewed your concern for me. Indeed, you have been concerned, but you had no opportunity to show it.

There was a time the Philippians were not able to share with Paul in his time of need. This shows that not all Christians are in a position to support one another, including those in the ministry. In the passage above, however, the Philippians renewed their concern for Paul.

Christians can only give when they possess what it is they want to give, and as stated earlier, giving according to their ability is perfectly acceptable. Therefore, the local church should not try to squeeze 10 percent of the people's money from them if they are not in a position to give it. In contrast, when Christians give freely, as opposed to operating under the old covenant law of tithing, they will come through in ways the church has not seen lately.

An Old Testament example of a group of people who gave freely is in Exodus 36, where, "the people continued to bring freewill offerings morning after morning." The result is recorded in Exodus 36:6-7. "Then Moses gave an order and they sent this word throughout the camp: 'No man or woman is to make anything else as an offering for the sanctuary.' And so the people were restrained from bringing more, because what they already had was more than enough to do all the work." This is a classic example of people responding to a free will offering, not a mandatory offering. Similarly, when the Philippians could afford to help Paul, they gave freely and the gifts were also overflowing.

Philippians 4:16-19

for even when I was in Thessalonica, you sent me aid again and again when I was in need.

Not that I am looking for a gift, but I am looking for what may be credited to your account.

I have received full payment and even more; I am amply supplied, now that I have received from Epaphroditus the gifts you sent. They are a fragrant offering, an acceptable sacrifice, pleasing to God.

And my God will meet all your needs according to his glorious riches in Christ Jesus.

Notice here that Paul was not *looking for a gift*. On the contrary, Paul was looking to commend them for the gifts previously sent. *They are a fragrant offering, an acceptable sacrifice, pleasing to God.* As revealed from the passages in Galatians and Corinthians above, generous Christians will reap according to how they sow and God will bless them. This is reiterated here when Paul says to the Philippians that his God will meet all their *needs according to his glorious riches in Christ Jesus.*

CHRISTIAN RESPONSIBILITY

Old covenant law allowed God's people to react in situations involving one another, as opposed to responding to them. A reaction to a situation does not require time or thought, whereas a response requires both time and thought. Examination of new covenant law requires Christians to actually respond to the needs of others, with the ultimate law being to love thy neighbor as thyself. Since the church is composed of many Christian individuals, this should be the priority of the local church organization as well. Christians should not form a local church and forget what God instructed them to do individually.

Responding to heavy burdens is a Christian's responsibility. Many people already have in mind the burdens of others, and therefore, should take their time in deciding what and how to give. The gift of giving under the new covenant will guide them to respond appropriately to the needs of others. This type of giving comes before any other, which includes many current functions of the local church. The obvious exception is supporting those in the ministry. Their needs should be considered equally with the poor. Supporting the local church is important, but it is not required above the commandments of God. Therefore, it must only be done out of the desire of each person's heart and should not supersede giving to the needy.

Although the hearts of some Christians are in line with the poor, many sometimes cave into tithing because of outside pressures instead of obeying the law of Christ. Monetary tithing should not be mandated from the pulpit since giving tithes and offerings is not for Christians. The early church had the 'circumcision group,' and today's church has the 'tithing group.' Contrary to what the tithing group requires, the hearts, minds, and inner spirits of many Christians are constantly tugged at by the Holy Spirit to support those in need.

This struggle with the Spirit is partly evident when persons in the pulpit say some Christians are uncomfortable with the concept of tithes and offerings. It should now be clear why. It is *not* because these people are stingy or lovers of money. One reason is that Christians have a conscience bearing witness to the truth and some would rather put their blessings from God to a better use. Another reason is that the method for collecting money today is in conflict with what the Bible teaches concerning Christian giving. Many times people would rather respond to the needs of the poor than construct a new building, add padding to the pews, pay an expensive light or gas bill, pave a parking lot, buy faster computers, etc.

The local church needs to provide an outlet for its members to support the needy at all times. This would give believers the ability to follow through with their responsibility to the community, if they want to do this within the organized church. This is considered helping at the corporate level. When necessary, each person can still respond to the needy at the individual level.

Disregarding unnecessary rules and regulations, and adhering to their call to give, Christians may respond more favorably to the needs of their communities - whether individually or within the function of the local church. The Philippians, Corinthians, and the early church in the Book of Acts, are all good examples of Christian responsibility. These examples can easily be followed today if Christians are allowed to give freely and according to the will of God.

Rightly Divide the Word of Truth

The Bible makes it clear that giving should be Spirit-led. It shows that there is no law governing the grace of giving, not even the law of tithing. Christians may think they understand tithing, but the gift of giving is difficult for many to understand.

1 Corinthians 1:25
'For the foolishness of God is wiser than man's wisdom, and the weakness of God is stronger than man's strength.'

One problem faced when trying to understand Spirit-led giving is the simplicity of the gospel, since it may be confusing to some intellectuals. "Where is the wise man? Where is the scholar? Where is the philosopher ..." (1 Cor. 1:20). Can the wise understand the simple act of giving to support thy neighbor? Probably not since God destroys the wisdom of the wise (1 Cor. 1:19) and reveals it to little children instead (Matt. 11:25).

2 Timothy 2:15 KJV
Study to shew thyself approved unto God, a workman that needeth not to be ashamed, rightly dividing the word of truth.

One of the most important things Christians must do is study the Bible. The reason many Christians lack true knowledge is, in fact, the lack of Bible study. To make up for a lack of time, many Christians blindly believe whatever someone else tells them - especially if those doing the teaching are quoting from the Bible. The problem here is that some who teach are blind themselves in the area of giving. This is the main reason why everyone should read the Bible for themselves - to avoid falling into a ditch (Matt. 15:14) and to avoid following false doctrine (see also Titus 1:9; 2:1).

1 Timothy 4:16
Watch your life and doctrine closely. Persevere in them, because if you do, you will save both yourself and your hearers.

2 Timothy 4:3-4
For the time will come when men will not put up with sound doctrine. Instead, to suit their own desires, they will gather around them a great number of teachers to say what their itching ears want to hear.
They will turn their ears away from the truth and turn aside to myths.

Today's doctrine includes giving 10 percent of a person's income to a local church. This raises the following questions regarding Christian responsibility. Is the church or the Christian really using the money to do the will of God or the will of man? Are their plans in line with what God has for them, or are their plans in line with false doctrines created by men? Christians must examine themselves to see if their giving is led by the Spirit or governed by rules and regulations. Studying the Bible helps to determine if today's practices line up with sound doctrine.

Who Are the Children of God?

The most important - and sometimes the most em-barrassing - question someone could ask is, "How do non-Christians know who the Christians are?" Or "How do people really know who the Children of God are?" The Bible provides an answer in First John.

1 John 3:10-11

This is how we know who the children of God are and who the children of the devil are: Anyone who does not do what is right is not a child of God; nor is anyone who does not love his brother.

This is the message you heard from the beginning: We should love one another.

According to this passage, the children of God are those who love their brother. Over and over again the Bible shows that the main responsibility Christians have is to love their neighbor and the passage above is repeating it - *This is the message you heard from the beginning.*

In light of the responsibility of the children of God, people should be able to receive financial support from the local church as they did in the early church. In today's church, however, people attend and are required to give the church money or they are declared disobedient unto the Lord.

People cannot be children of God nor have biblical principles manifest in their lives if they are not obeying the will of God. For instance, if Christians disregard what Paul said to the Corinthians *(Each man should give what he has decided in his heart to give)* and decide to obey the rules of tithing instead, they will not reap the benefits of grace *(And God is able to make all grace abound to you).* This is similar to God's people in the book of Samuel when they wanted a king instead of obeying the old covenant law of the Lord.

God Has Called You

Christians are good at praying for others. However, they should not let their prayers replace actually helping someone or allowing God to work through them. Some Christians actually pray for God to handle something he has already given them the ability to accomplish. In addition, it is the responsibility of Christians to meet the needs of others when they can, as often as they can, according to each person's ability. However, some people fail to assist the needy thinking they are not qualified or capable.

Exodus 3:11
But Moses said to God, "Who am I, that I should go to Pharaoh and bring the Israelites out of Egypt?"

Many may ask God the same question, "*Who am I,*" when it comes to doing the will of God. Everyone has shortcomings in their lives, and Moses was no exception in that he was not eloquent in speech (Ex. 4:10). Moses may have even lacked leadership skills, but he was chosen by God to lead his people out of Egypt. Furthermore, God calls people today who may not be considered wise by human standards.

1 Corinthians 1:26-29
Brothers, think of what you were when you were called. Not many of you were wise by human standards; not many were influential; not many were of noble birth.
But God chose the foolish things of the world to shame the wise; God chose the weak things of the world to shame the strong.
He chose the lowly things of this world and the despised things - and the things that are not - to nullify the things that are,
so that no one may boast before him.

What Is Love?

1 John 3:16-18
This is how we know what love is: Jesus Christ laid down his life for us. And we ought to lay down our lives for our brothers.
If anyone has material possessions and sees his brother in need but has no pity on him, how can the love of God be in him?
Dear children, let us not love with words or tongue but with actions and in truth.

How much more straight forward can the Bible get? True Christian love is that *we ought to lay down our lives for our brothers.* How many people would see someone in need and pass right on by - like the priest and Levite did in the Good

Samaritan parable - even though they had what the person required? In order to be children of God, Christians must first obey what God commands them to do.

First John 4 sums it up completely and leaves no doubt as to what love is. It says love comes from God and that God loves his children. Therefore, Christians also should love one another.

1 John 4:7-12

Dear friends, let us love one another, for love comes from God. Everyone who loves has been born of God and knows God.

Whoever does not love does not know God, because God is love.

This is how God showed his love among us: He sent his one and only Son into the world that we might live through him.

This is love: not that we loved God, but that he loved us and sent his Son as an atoning sacrifice for our sins.

Dear friends, since God so loved us, we also ought to love one another.

No one has ever seen God; but if we love one another, God lives in us and his love is made complete in us.

God is love, and whoever lives in love lives in God and God in him (1 Jn. 4:16). Christians cannot love God and not love their brother. "And he has given us this command: Whoever loves God must also love his brother" (1 Jn. 4:21).

Responsible Giving

There are many inappropriate reasons for giving. These include: Old covenant legalism; fear of a curse; standard based giving; and expectation of money in return. As far as expecting money in return, the book of Luke states that Christians should expect nothing in return for giving.

Luke 6:32-36

"If you love those who love you, what credit is that to you? Even 'sinners' love those who love them.

And if you do good to those who are good to you, what credit is that to you? Even 'sinners' do that.

And if you lend to those from whom you expect repayment, what credit is that to you? Even 'sinners' lend to 'sinners,' expecting to be repaid in full.

But love your enemies, do good to them, and lend to them without expecting to get anything back. Then your reward will be great, and you will be sons of the Most High, because he is kind to the ungrateful and wicked.

Be merciful, just as your Father is merciful."

Christians should not give to see if God will reward them liberally, or allow the hope of a material reward to motivate them to give. In addition, Christians should not give as a means to find favor with God (see also Lk. 17:7-10). Instead, Christians should imitate Christ by, "being like-minded, having the same love, being one in spirit and purpose" (Phil. 2:2).

Acceptable reasons for giving, within the freedom provided through Jesus, include giving proportionately, voluntarily, spontaneously, generously, and humbly. Each Christian should give according to his/her means, as he decides in his heart to give, and in proportion to his own faith. This model of giving is useful for every Christian and does not burden those who do not have a lot to offer. All Christians should manage their finances so that they can give as their hearts lead them, which begins with eliminating as much debt as possible. If people are burdened with excessive debt, they will find it difficult to contribute financially to one another and to the ministries of the local church.

In addition, Christians are to first take care of their immediate family.

1 Timothy 5:8
If anyone does not provide for his relatives, and especially for his immediate family, he has denied the faith and is worse than an unbeliever.

Responsible giving provides support for those in need. In addition, congregations blessed with money should provide assistance to poorer congregations similar to the Jerusalem offering in the second book of Corinthians (2 Cor. 9).

Finally, Christians ought to take seriously the work of those who teach and preach, as well as the work of the other church ministries. The lack of support puts preachers and teachers in the position of 'begging' for money, when their material and monetary support should be overflowing. The calling of one to teach the word is worthy of support that would alleviate the struggle of daily living. Christians should get their ministers out of 'survivor' mode, with concerns about paying bills, so that they can effectively handle the ministries of the church.

A New Benevolence Organization

The Salvation Army, United Way, Habitat For Humanity, Red Cross, and the like, have good intentions concerning those in need. However, organizations such as these lead to a problem when trying to understand the principle of giving. This problem is the belief that God will use 'somebody else' to carry out his will. Therefore, some believe that helping the masses should be handled by entities that can manage the needs of many. This may seem appropriate for those who have many resources, but everyone can still participate in some way.

The less fortunate must usually wait until some pre-determined day to receive help, such as a holiday. People, including Christians, come out in groves to participate in helping the needy and the homeless, all in the spirit of a particular holiday. Unfortunately, some Christians are programmed to wait until they are moved into action by the holiday spirit. Consequently, they are not moved into action by the Holy Spirit. Christians should allow the Spirit to lead them to give according to their means. Then they will perform the level of holiday giving every day of the year. The world would then finally get a glimpse of true Christian giving and the kingdom of God on Earth.

There are a great number of people in need, and the handful of organizations that exist today cannot meet the needs of everyone. In fact, today's approach requires a few to do the work of many. A better method is to have many Christians supporting those in need according to their individual abilities. If all Christians honor their calling to love their neighbor, then more needs can be met. Why not form one more charitable organization composed of Christians? The top priority of this organization would be meeting the needs of people. It sounds like a good idea. A good and appropriate name for this organization would be, "Christianity."

Christians are not under the old covenant law, but are under a new law, the law of Christ, which makes them slaves to righteousness. Christians should not ignore any part of their requirements from God, which includes their duty to share in the burdens of others, and to support the ministries of the church. Since Christians are to carry their own burdens as well, they should not give to the point that they overextend themselves, but should give according to their means.

The Bible instructs Christians to give as each decides in his heart to give. Also, they should not grow weary of doing good to others, for in due season they shall reap a harvest. The law of love requires compassion towards one another in the area of giving, and it in no way implies that this gift of giving, or grace giving, can be measured or regulated by old covenant laws - such as tithes and offerings.

Christians should not let anyone judge them, or compare what they are doing with anyone else. If people compare their actions with others, they may think they are something, when they may be nothing (Gal. 6:3-4). Each person is blessed in different ways and in different amounts according to faith. How much one gives may not be how much another gives, but they both will be blessed.

Romans 12:4-8
Just as each of us has one body with many members,
and these members do not all have the same function,

so in Christ we who are many form one body, and each member belongs to all the others.

We have different gifts, according to the grace given us. If a man's gift is prophesying, let him use it in proportion to his faith.

If it is serving, let him serve; if it is teaching, let him teach;

if it is encouraging, let him encourage; if it is contributing to the needs of others, let him give generously; if it is leadership, let him govern diligently; if it is showing mercy, let him do it cheerfully.

Christians have different gifts, according to the grace given to each of them. One function, or gift, within the body of Christ is contributing to the needs of others. For these individuals, they should do so generously according to their means. Christians should not let anyone else compare what they have done with the works that follow their faith. Instead, each person should use individual gifts in proportion to his own faith - *let him use it in proportion to his faith.*

Realizing that giving is a gift, some may think that they do not have this gift, or the calling to support the needy. This is simply not true or it would conflict with the fact that all Christians are called to love their neighbor. Luke 3:11, however, provides a simple example of giving that demonstrates that some form of giving can be performed by all. "The man with two tunics should share with him who has none, and the one who has food should do the same." The principle here is that anyone can share, but they ought to share out of what they have, not out of what they do not have.

Recall that the one who gives is not to be hard pressed as a result of helping others (2 Cor. 8:13). As noted above, Jesus says, "The man with two coats (tunics) ..." If the man only had one coat, Jesus may not have suggested that this man give up his coat, since then he would be in need of one. Likewise, if a person only has enough money for rent, he should not be coerced into giving 10 percent of his money to the local church. Contrary to what some teach, this is not considered an act of faith; believing God will pay the rest of his rent if he pays his tithe. Certain situations simply require good old-fashioned common sense. Adhering to the teaching of monetary tithes would cause this individual to be a burden to someone else, which is contrary to the teachings of the Bible.

Hopefully, the beliefs around monetary tithes and offerings have been replaced with the simple truths found in the Bible. Now that these truths are known, all the needs of the Christian community can be met by its members. Armed with an accurate principle of giving, Christians can move forward in relation to God's will - furthering the kingdom of God on Earth.

1 John 3:16-18

This is how we know what love is: Jesus Christ laid down his life for us. And we ought to lay down our lives for our brothers.

If anyone has material possessions and sees his brother in need but has no pity on him, how can the love of God be in him?

Dear children, let us not love with words or tongue but with actions and in truth.

10

The Church Collection

Supporting the local church is good when it is done in the name of the Lord and with the correct priorities in place. However, this support should not be in the form of a mandatory monetary tithe followed by subsequent voluntary offerings - supposedly above and beyond the tithe. Many Christians typically give monetary tithes and offerings to the church, while simultaneously ignoring the will of God - the main priority of which is meeting the needs of the poor.

Besides spreading the gospel, Christians are obligated to carry the burdens of others. However, the priority of today's giving is in funding the needs of the local church facility, including building funds, electric bills, phone bills, sports teams, ministry and staff payroll, etc. Unfortunately, many focus on what the hands of man can build and forget about the less fortunate. Whatever is done, it is done in vain when Christians 'first' do not obey the will of God and their number one calling - to love thy neighbor.

Some churches have implemented benevolence programs, but not many are beneficial to the poor in their local congregation - simply ask those who need help financially. Given the priorities of many Christians, churches usually focus on church expenses and rarely on giving to those in need. This is how Christians 'rob their neighbors.' Instead of redistributing their blessings to the needy, most give it to something else through monetary tithes and offerings.

Non-tithing believers are usually the subject of sermons and teachings, simply for holding on to gospel truths. Whether or not they know they are holding on to gospel truths, the conscience directed by the Spirit bears witness to what is right, and most Christians know when something is not in line with the will of God. Nevertheless, they are told they are disobedient, and will be cursed for not giving the Lord the required tenth of their incomes. As a result of this pressure, they give monetary tithes anyway. Some Christians do recognize their freedom in Christ apart from the rules and regulations of old covenant law. Some tithing Christians, however, may not realize their total freedom in the area of giving, and, thus, have unfairly thrown accusations at others over the issue of tithing.

This chapter presents an uncommon view of the collection of money in the church. It shows the ill effect of monetary tithing on Christianity. First, this chapter depicts a day in the life of a Christian family in order to set the tone for the rest of the chapter. Following this are the concepts of certain kinds of giving - especially public giving and its downside. Next, the root of all kinds of evil and how it may be present in some believers is addressed. Finally, a scenario is given that paints a picture of how tithing churches are viewed in the absence of a ministry for the poor, and how such churches might have ended up this way.

Please keep in mind that this chapter is not meant to generalize. It only expresses worst case scenarios when rules prevent Christians from Spirit-led giving.

A DAY IN THE LIFE

Introducing Mr. & Mrs. Burden

Mr. and Mrs. Burden, along with their children, Faith, Love, and Hope, belong to a local church. They are experiencing problems in several areas of their lives. Part of their difficulties includes the following: currently behind on rent; automobile problems; expectation of another child; no pay raises in sight; utilities being cut off in three days; two of the children are sick; and their dog, Scruffy, is on medication.

They pray every morning and night for God to deliver them from their current troubles. The Burdens, strong in faith, are expecting the mighty hand of God to intervene.

Mr. and Mrs. Burden are faithful tithers, and have been for years. They believe that the Lord requires the first 10 percent of their income, even before the bills are paid. They are also taught to tithe even when they cannot afford it. Fearing that bad things will start to happen, this practice continues in spite of collection agencies threatening them for immediate payment.

The Burdens cannot understand how financial problems can happen to them. They tithe faithfully, but the windows of Heaven seem to be slammed shut. Facing the possibility of their utilities being cut off, the Burdens decide to use their tithing money to ease the problem. Instead of giving it to the church, they use it for the utility bill in order to keep heat in their home. Fearing the curse for not tithing that week, they decide to ask their pastor for assistance.

Burdens Seek Church Support

Sunday is upon them, so the Burdens prepare themselves for church service. They cannot wait to get there because their church is on fire for the Lord! Their church is the way one should be, a church that is obedient to the word of God, and one whose members are not *stuck* on money. Yes, their church is one that believes in the rules and regulations of monetary tithes and offerings!

The church that the Burdens are members of is called Tither's Temple, and it is conveniently located on the corner of Tenth and Firstfruit. The name of their pastor should ring a bell since he is featured in the first chapter of this book. That's right! None other than the Rev. Dr. Pastor Tithe!

After service, Mr. Burden approaches Pastor Tithe to explain to him their current situation, and to seek some form of financial assistance from the church. Pastor Tithe explains that he recently had a budget committee meeting and that church funds are limited due to the current ministries - building fund, missions, parking lot, staff, phone bill, padded pews, computer needs, etc. Therefore, the church cannot make any financial contributions of this nature since it is not factored into the budget. So they pray instead. As the meeting continues, Pastor Tithe asks Mr. Burden, "Are you still tithing?"

Wow! What a heavy burden to place on someone when they are in financial need! Mr. Burden, a child of God, went to the church seeking help, but the church instead asks him for money! According to Pastor Tithe, those who tithe will receive a four-fold blessing. This is how Christians get out of the troubles they face.

Road to Recovery Without the Church

Four years have elapsed since the Burdens were in need of help. Since then, they have gone to a consolidation agency to receive help with their financial crisis. They also received some money here and there from a couple of friends, but after missing three months rent, they were eventually evicted.

Although the Burdens received no church support outside of a prayer, God was still working behind the scene on their behalf. God worked through a Christian couple that operates a nonprofit organization. Not confined by traditional practices, this organization helped the Burdens by paying a month's rent for an apartment, along with the initial utility bill. Soon afterwards, Mrs. Burden found a higher paying job. In addition, their second youngest child is now in an all day first grade class, which means less day care costs. Furthermore, Mr. Burden finally received a modest cost of living increase for the first time in six years.

The Burdens rarely went to church during the past four years. They were turned off by the church they had been faithful members of for the previous nine years - due to the lack of support in their time of need. Since the current situation is looking up for them, they return to Tither's Temple and even start tithing once again from their income as they are taught. They saved up money for a down payment on a home, and have purchased a new car. With this new outlook on life, they, like Abram (Abraham) and Jacob (Israel), received new names. They are now known as Mr. and Mrs. Blessed because they are now truly blessed by the Lord.

Blinded by Wealth

This story continues with Mr. Blessed driving his nice car to the store before church one Sunday morning - to buy the items he wants for the big house he and his family have, with the money he earned from the job he has, while looking good with the nice clothes he has, bought by his wife with money from the job she has, sitting at home enjoying the vacation she has, worry free because of the healthy children they have, while playing with the newborn puppies they have. (What a long sentence!)

As Mr. Blessed leaves the store, a needy person approaches and asks Mr. Blessed to buy him a sandwich from the local deli. Mr. Blessed thinks to himself, "Man, get a job. After all, my wife and I have jobs and work hard everyday. I am not going to just buy you some food with my hard earned money. I have a wife, four children, and several dogs to care for." (Pray that a needy person does not ask him for some money!)

In his new found wealth, Mr. Blessed forgot he was once in need himself. As he walks by the needy person, he does not really say anything, barely acknowledging that this individual even exists. Since he is a 'godly' person, though, he ends up praying instead, that this person might get out of his current predicament. Of course, he is going to wait until he returns home so he can pray with his godly wife. After all, Pastor Tithe prayed for him when he was in need, and this is much more convenient than actually helping the needy person himself! If one prays for something and believes God will meet the need, then God will do it, will he not? Therefore, let God take care of it!

Mr. Blessed returns home from the store, gathering the troops for the trip to church. He drives their nice car through town along the way. As they drive along Benevolence Boulevard, they sometimes pass needy people, including the homeless. His heart is torn at what he sees, thinking to himself that someone from the church ought to go down there and share the word of God with them. Oh well, he cannot wait to arrive at church and be with God's people!

After the family leaves church service, they go to the store where a Christian group is outside soliciting money to support the homeless in the area. These are volunteers from the same nonprofit organization that helped the Blessed family in their time of troubles (a.k.a., the Burdens). The Christian couple that runs the organization, and friends of the Blesseds, were also there. The Spirit tugs at Mr. Blessed's conscience to give to this organization. Ironically, he tells them, "Sorry, we already gave our tithes and offerings to the church."

Obviously, not all Christians are like this when it comes to those in need. However, from the viewpoint of people in need, they cannot tell the difference between Christians who are like the Blesseds and those Christians that want to help but cannot. In the end, the less fortunate simply are not relieved of their burdens.

Unfortunately, Christians are bombarded with scriptures and personal stories about how giving tithes and offerings can help one's position in life. These testimonies show that tithing helps one to maintain good health, financial prosperity, well behaved children, etc. These arguments lead Christians to believe that life's problems are resolved, and happiness attained, by giving money to the local church.

Stories like the one facing the Burdens earlier never seem to make it to the pulpit and into a sermon. There are Christians who tithe money, but are in desperate need of help financially. Furthermore, individuals in need such as these are accused of having a lack of faith in some other area of their lives, or a lack of budgeting skills.

The Blessed family, on the other hand, is an example of how traditional teachings on tithes can prevent someone from being led by the Spirit. Instead, some follow rules that govern their giving, and consequently, believe they are justified by these works. In the Book of Acts, Christians did not behave this way toward those in need - not giving to the living church made up of God's people. Christians today, therefore, do have good examples of how to prioritize their giving by observing the behavior of Christians in the Bible.

ACTS OF GIVING

This book has shown several times, and with much biblical support, that followers of Christ are not required to give tithes and offerings. On the other hand, Christians should give some financial support to those in need, and in this way they will be giving to God. "Whatever you did for one of the least of these brothers of mine, you did for me" (Matt. 25:35-40). Furthermore, the gifts to the 'least of these brothers' is not only supplying the needs of God's people, but those in need will praise God for the generosity of sharing with them (2 Cor. 9:12-13). Nevertheless, some Christians settle for giving monetary tithes and offerings instead of truly experiencing grace giving.

Collecting Tithes & Offerings Today

One problem with the local church collection is the way in which it is conducted. First of all, tithes and offerings are included in the worship service as a means of supposedly give something back to God. More times than not, tithes and offerings are sectioned out from the rest of the praise and worship service as if it is 'now time to do what is right, obedient, and pleasing to the Lord.'

This part of the service usually has several phases. The first phase consists of an offertory statement, usually said while the congregation stands. By the way, the offertory statement usually has nothing to do with tithes and offerings (for example, when referring to passages in Corinthians). Even if it did, it is misleading to recite them during a time to 'give' since Christians should not tithe anyway.

The second phase usually includes an offertory prayer, which is given with the people still standing. The third phase is the collection of the money itself, sometimes with a song in the background, followed by symbolically taking it to an altar. In the final phase, the doxology is given. Whew! 'Loving thy neighbor and meeting the needs of the poor' never receive this much actual attention in many church services! On the other hand, monetary tithes and offerings receive plenty of attention during each and every service - and sometimes more than once!

Acts of Righteousness Before Men

One of the issues addressed by Jesus was giving to be seen by men, or letting other individuals know what one is doing in the area of giving.

Matthew 6:1
"Be careful not to do your 'acts of righteousness' before men, to be seen by them. If you do, you will have no reward from your Father in heaven."

In spite of passages such as this one, monetary tithing is highly esteemed among many Christians today. Some attend a church where they are asked to stand up if they are a tither, or where tithe records are printed out on a monthly basis for everyone to see. Others have their tithing record mailed to their house reminding them of how much they gave that month. Still, other churches require their members to walk to the front of the church and place their monetary tithe in a basket. But unfortunately, some Christians cannot afford to tithe, so they do not participate in this event. Some churches, however, let their members walk to the front and touch the baskets as some kind of act of faith.

How should people feel about these type of collections? Should non-tithers feel like they are less of a Christian or less of a human being? Should Christians feel condemned or proud? Maybe tithing makes some people think they have done their good deed for the week, as if they are good Christians, or maybe better Christians than those who do not tithe.

Non-tithing Christians should not feel distressed because of these practices. Christians are asked to give according to their means, and to do so cheerfully (2 Cor. 8:12; 9:7). If, however, someone feels good about the kind of public tithing practices mentioned above, then they should reread Matthew 6:1, where it says *not to do your 'acts of righteousness' before men.*

For those who enjoy giving to the needy, or to the local church, without tooting their own horn, they are more in line with the law of Christ.

Matthew 6:2-4

"So when you give to the needy, do not announce it with trumpets, as the hypocrites do in the synagogues and on the streets, to be honored by men. I tell you the truth, they have received their reward in full.

But when you give to the needy, do not let your left hand know what your right hand is doing,

so that your giving may be in secret. Then your Father, who sees what is done in secret, will reward you.

The Bible states that Christians are not to let anyone know what they are doing in the area of giving. Especially when the purpose for doing so is solely to show acts of righteousness before others - *Do not announce it with trumpets to be honored by men.* Instead, everyone ought to be thankful they are in a position to give, and that they are willing to give for the benefit of someone else - as well as the local church.

Believers in the Book of Acts

Despite the manner in which the money is collected, there is some good coming from the traditional collection of money. Some people are giving their money and do actually want to assist in any way they can. Let us return to the Book of Acts and the collection of money.

Acts 4:32-35

All the believers were one in heart and mind. No one claimed that any of his possessions was his own, but they shared everything they had.

With great power the apostles continued to testify to the resurrection of the Lord Jesus, and much grace was upon them all.

There were no needy persons among them. For from time to time those who owned lands or houses sold them, brought the money from the sales and put it at the apostles' feet, and it was distributed to anyone as he had need.

Notice here that besides taking care of the ministers of the gospel, the collection of money *was distributed to anyone as he had need.* People bring tithes and offerings to the Lord's house in accordance with old covenant law, which consists of crops and livestock of their increase. This passage, however, shows an example of *believers bringing the money from the sales of their possessions* unto the apostles for those in need. This money did not come directly from their jobs, nor was it mandatory, as demanded from the pulpit. Instead, these believers sold some of their possessions *from time to time* and gave the money to help the needy. As the early church did this from time to time, they accomplished what many churches fail to accomplish today - *there were no needy persons among them.* See also Acts 2:44-45.

The Prayer of a Pharisee

The Pharisees were much different from the followers of Christ in the area of giving. The believers in the early church were interested in the welfare of others, while the Pharisees were interested in their own righteousness.

Luke 18:10-14
"Two men went up to the temple to pray, one a Pharisee and the other a tax collector.
The Pharisee stood up and prayed about himself: 'God, I thank you that I am not like other men - robbers, evildoers, adulterers - or even like this tax collector.
I fast twice a week and give a tenth of all I get.'
"But the tax collector stood at a distance. He would not even look up to heaven, but beat his breast and said, 'God, have mercy on me, a sinner.'
"I tell you that this man, rather than the other, went home justified before God. For everyone who exalts himself will be humbled, and he who humbles himself will be exalted."

The Pharisees were confident of their own righteousness and looked down on everyone else (Lk. 18:9). This is evident by the difference between the prayers of the Pharisee and the tax collector. The Pharisee prays about the good he thinks he is doing - *I fast twice a week and give a tenth of all I get.* The tax collector, on the other hand, prays, *'God, have mercy on me, a sinner.'* Nobody should have confidence in monetary tithing because, *everyone who exalts himself will be humbled.*

Be Like a Samaritan

Recall the parable of the Good Samaritan in Luke 10:31-37. Jesus tells the story of a priest and a Levite who walked past a person who needed help. However, the Samaritan stopped to help this person, bound up his wounds, and paid for his expenses at an inn. This type of giving was both public and private. Public in that it was performed in a public place. Private in that there was no 'church record' of the help provided, nor was the intention of the Samaritan to be recognized for the good work.

In one respect, some Christians want to follow in the steps of the Samaritan, but not actually be a Samaritan because they were looked down upon in biblical times. Many tithers and non-tithers do what the Samaritan did once in a while, which is to help someone. However, non-tithers are treated no better than Samaritans were treated in biblical times. The frustration mounts when this mistreatment comes from those in the pulpit and from the elders in the church. Nevertheless, the Good Samaritan is an example of giving that was not preceded by a monetary tithe, as well as an example of spontaneous Spirit-led giving.

Looking through the eyes of a person in need, many pastors and elders are viewed as the equivalent of the priest and Levite. That is, when someone has a legitimate burden, many times pastors and elders pass them right on by. Not only that, many tithe-believing pastors pour salt on the wound instead of addressing the need. They require people to tithe money even in their time of need. Does this seem like true Spirit-led giving on behalf of church leaders? Is this the meaning of being a neighbor?

Is There a Lack of Deeds?

Are Christians today following rules taught by men? Do there exist local church congregations with a lot of faith, yet fail to take care of the people's physical needs? Are Christians so spiritual that they forget they live in a physical world?

James 2:14-17
What good is it, my brothers, if a man claims to have faith but has no deeds? Can such faith save him?

Suppose a brother or sister is without clothes and daily food.

If one of you says to him, "Go, I wish you well; keep warm and well fed," but does nothing about his physical needs, what good is it?

In the same way, faith by itself, if it is not accompanied by action, is dead.

Christians claim to have faith, for, "We live by faith, not by sight" (2 Cor. 5:7). But are local church bodies so heavenly minded that they are no earthly good? Do local churches ask for the congregation's money through tithes and offerings, and then say to them, *Go, I wish you well; keep warm and well fed?* Many Christians have been deceived into giving monetary tithes and offerings to the four walled church. Moreover, they sometimes fail to give benevolently to the living church - their brothers and sisters in need.

There are probably several reasons people do not help their neighbor financially. One is the burden of the church collection centered on monetary tithes and offerings. In addition, by giving tithes and offerings, many feel as if they are already doing the will of God. Therefore, they do not bother doing any more, including helping others. Instead, many who think they are already justified by the works of tithing only pray for those in need, believing God will answer their prayers. The problem with this form of Christianity is that believers, who make up the kingdom of God on Earth, are the answers to many prayers. They simply need to obey the gospel and love their neighbor - not only in word, but in deed. God works through those who allow themselves to be used (Phil. 2:13).

ROOT OF ALL KINDS OF EVIL

As noted earlier, the church needs money to fund its ministries. Also, people called to the ministry are entitled to compensation for their work. But when does the right for reaping a material harvest go beyond what is really meant? This section covers the love of money and how it requires a collection *at* the *physical* church instead of a collection *for* the *living* church, which are the members of God's family.

Judas, Mary, and the Perfume

The worst case concerning money, and even greed, could easily be that of Judas. In John chapter 12 (Mk. 14:3-9; Lk. 21:1-4), Mary poured expensive perfume on Jesus. This upset those who were present, and they even called it a waste.

John 12:5-8
"Why wasn't this perfume sold and the money given to the poor? It was worth a year's wages."

He did not say this because he cared about the poor but because he was a thief; as keeper of the money bag, he used to help himself to what was put into it.

"Leave her alone," Jesus replied. "It was intended that she should save this perfume for the day of my burial.

You will always have the poor among you, but you will not always have me."

At first glance it seems as if the disciples had in mind the needs of the poor - *Why wasn't this perfume sold and the money given to the poor.* However, Jesus knew the hearts of those present and the greed of Judas. Judas was not really interested in the welfare of the poor, but pretended to do what was right for his own interest, which was *greed.*

Christians add to the collection plate at church and sincerely think they are doing the will of God. Tithers give tithes (or so they think) because they are doing what is good and required by God (or so they think). The sad truth is that many times the money collected is not used to help the poor, or even to help the members of the local congregation - this should be a priority. The Bible explains how and why collections were taken. They were mainly to help the needy among them (see Acts chapter 2 and 4 and also Chapter 9 of this book), and to support the teachers of the word.

In an extreme sense, some local church bodies are helping themselves *to what was put into it* (the money bag) when they do not have the needs of the poor on their agendas, much like Judas. There are many like Judas in the world who really *love* money and not their neighbors. Is it any wonder that the average church member in need might perceive a church leader as a Judas? Yes, this may seem harsh. But tell that to faithful tithers in their time of need, such as the Burdens. After asking their church for help, they received nothing but an empty prayer.

Dishonest With Little, Dishonest With Much

As seen above, Judas was responsible for the treasury and used the concept of providing for the poor as a cover for his greed. The Bible also shows that people like this, if they cannot be responsible with a little, will not be responsible with much.

Luke 16:10-12
Whoever can be trusted with very little can also be trusted with much, and whoever is dishonest with very little will also be dishonest with much.
So if you have not been trustworthy in handling worldly wealth, who will trust you with true riches?
And if you have not been trustworthy with someone else's property, who will give you property of your own?

Here is another example of the love for money, in this case, that of the Pharisees. If those in charge of handling money are not trustworthy in handling worldly wealth, they will not be trusted to handle true riches. There is also concern for the local church. It is made up of individuals who take up collections and handle money. When people handle money and do not take care of the needy, are they considered trustworthy?

Cannot Serve Both God and Money

Continuing the thought above, the next verse in the book of Luke states that no one can serve two masters.

Luke 16:13
"No servant can serve two masters. Either he will hate the one and love the other, or he will be devoted to the one and despise the other. You cannot serve both God and Money."

This passage raises the following questions. Is the church working hard for money, or working hard for God? What is the real reason for giving in the first place? Is it to get something in return from God, like an investment? Do some people think God is running some kind of heavenly mutual fund?

Giving money to get more money means actually getting less of God - since what is sought after is more money. When people are wealthy, they tend to be less dependent on God, hence, wealth cannot be the only reward for faithfulness. God does not give rewards that take away from a relationship with him. Therefore, monetary gifts should be given with the intent that a person will get more of God, not more money.

There are plenty of sincere people who 'want' to do the will of God. The point here is to get Christians to focus on what God actually wants, and what he considers acts of righteousness. The reason for giving is to help one another, and in so doing, furthering the kingdom of God. Nevertheless, it is evident that some are more interested in money than in ministering to the poor.

Luke 16:14-15
The Pharisees, who loved money, heard all this and were sneering at Jesus.

He said to them, "You are the ones who justify
yourselves in the eyes of men, but God knows your
hearts. What is highly valued among men is detestable in
God's sight."

THE COLLECTION AGENCY

The early chapters of this book show that tithes and
offerings are taken to the place where the Lord put his name.
They also show that only consumable items, such as produce
or animals, are either burnt or prepared for consumption as
part of the sacrificial rituals.

There are provisions in Scripture that allow for the
redemption (purchase) of tithes, dedicated persons, and
property, by the person who possesses them (Lev. 27). This
purchase is with money and requires adding a fifth part to its
value. Along with the ram for a trespass offering, the offender
also compensates for the trespass with shekels of silver, adds
20 percent interest, and gives it to the priest. The priest then
compensates the wronged individual (Lev. 5:15-16).

When it is impractical to carry a tithe to the designated
place, one could sell it for its cash value and buy replacement
food once they reached their destination (Deut. 14:24-26). In
conclusion, it is fair to say that the Levites and priests (or
temple overseers) collected a large sum of money from all of the
above transactions.

Handling this much money can be overwhelming, and
overseers during Jesus day who were once upright and law-
abiding became corrupt. This level of corruption reached the
point where the function of the temple overseers was in fact
the 'collection of money,' as opposed to carrying out the
sacrificial ritual of tithes and offerings themselves. In this
case, the temple turned into a monetary collection agency, and
continued in this manner for years. Operating the temple
courts in a manner contrary to its purpose opened the door for
the overseers to add more rules. The amount and extent of
additional regulations led to the extortion of God's people. This
is what occurred prior to Jesus entering into the temple area.

A Den of Robbers

During His ministry, Jesus saw what was happening in the temple areas and said to those selling doves, "Get these out of here! How dare you turn my Father's house into a market!" This cleansing of the temple by Jesus did not keep the teachers of the law from continuing in their ways. In Matthew 21 it states the following (see also Mk. 11:15 and Lk. 19:47).

Matthew 21:12-13
Jesus entered the temple area and drove out all who were buying and selling there. He overturned the tables of the money changers and the benches of those selling doves.

"It is written," he said to them, "'My house will be called a house of prayer,' but you are making it a 'den of robbers.'"

Jesus accused those selling in the temple area of *making it a den of robbers*. He prevented everyone from carrying merchandise through the temple courts. The teachers of the law feared Jesus because He had the attention of the whole crowd. In addition, His words were contrary to what the teachers allowed to go on in the temple areas. So when they heard what Jesus was saying, they began looking for a way to kill Him.

Some local church bodies require Christians to give money in the name of tithes and offerings. Are these churches concerned with providing their members a place where they can share in the sacrificial nature of tithes and offerings? Do they provide a place where the giver can literally share in the tithes and offerings? Or, do they provide a place where the Lord has designated for the people to 'eat' in His presence?

Some local church bodies, in contrast, have created another meaning for tithes and offerings, converting the substance of the tithe into money. In effect, they, similar to the temple overseers, have formed collection agencies. These agencies add rules to the word of God in an attempt to extract money from God's people. When Jesus returns, will He have to overturn the tables of the money changers at the local church? It seems as if Jesus will go through this all over again! The Spirit today, however, is already reminding God's people that his house is called a house of prayer.

Building on a Foundation With Gold

Local church congregations were established on the foundation of Jesus Christ. The concern here is that some are using 'monetary tithes and offerings' to build something that is *not* contributing to the welfare of God's people or that is not in line with the gospel. When preaching or teaching, someone may say 'Jesus' or 'Lord' when promoting a different version of tithing. However, using the name of Jesus when discussing anything does not mean the person is building something biblical. In addition, simply quoting Scripture is not enough either, for even Satan said in Luke 4:10, "For it is written ..." There must be truth behind what is taught, which is proven by actually 'studying' the Bible. Monetary tithes and offerings are, in fact, commandments of men.

1 Corinthians 3:10-15
By the grace God has given me, I laid a foundation as an expert builder, and someone else is building on it. But each one should be careful how he builds.

For no one can lay any foundation other than the one already laid, which is Jesus Christ.

If any man builds on this foundation using gold, silver, costly stones, wood, hay or straw,

his work will be shown for what it is, because the Day will bring it to light. It will be revealed with fire, and the fire will test the quality of each man's work.

If what he has built survives, he will receive his reward.

If it is burned up, he will suffer loss; he himself will be saved, but only as one escaping through the flames.

Well-intentioned Christians can take something as beautiful as the gift of giving and turn it into a religious fiasco - monetary tithes and offerings. Recall that the love of money is the root of all evil. This love of money within the church causes non-Christians to look at the church today and think it is a scheme for making money - as if preaching the gospel is a means to financial gain. How many times has someone visited a church and asked, "How many collections do you have?" The collection of money is sometimes the only thing remembered about a church service - "Man, they had five collections!"

Preachers and teachers today should be more like Paul. He did not preach tithes as a means for financial gain, or as a means to support the church. Paul taught according to the will of God based on the new covenant, not the old covenant. Paul never deceived God's people with his knowledge of the old covenant law in order to get money from them.

The *Day* will come, however, when the modern day work of tithes and offerings will come to light. It will be revealed by fire, and the fire will test the quality of man's work - this new way of giving tithes and offerings. So be careful when building *on this foundation using gold, silver, costly stones, wood, hay or straw,* since that *work will be shown for what it is.*

Scare Tactics

How many times has Malachi 3:8-10 been used to instill fear in Christians? This message of extortion emerges from the pulpit insisting that Christians contribute 10 percent of their monetary blessings or they will be cursed. On the contrary, when the book of Malachi says to bring the *tithe* into the *storehouse*, it did not mean for someone to put money into a church bank account.

Some distort Scripture concerning tithes in order to acquire the congregation's money through a message of fear. The money is then used for purposes outside of the original intention of tithing. Chapter 4 shows that tithing is for the person who brought it forward, his family, the Levite (and the priests), the fatherless, etc. Today, however, the twisted monetary version of tithes is used to buy bigger buildings, parking lots, choir robes, etc. Biblical tithes do not support these kinds of things.

In addition to instilling fear in a person, some in the ministry use this tactic at the worst possible time. For instance, some members go into church counseling seeking true help for financial problems. However, one of the first things the counselor asks is whether or not the person is tithing (recall Mr. & Mrs. Burden). Sometimes the counselor even tells the person that not contributing the whole 10 percent of their income is the reason they are having problems.

Counselors and ministers such as these pull out all the stops when it comes to getting a hold of money! When Jesus died on the cross, He did away with all old covenant sacrificial rituals for the believer, including tithes and offerings (Chapter 6). Any reference to Bible passages in an attempt to justify monetary tithing is clearly in the interest of collecting money, and not in the interest of serving the Lord or obeying God's commands for Christians. Moreover, the early church in the Bible did not blame financial woes on Christians because they did not tithe. Instead, the early church provided for everyone who had a need. What a concept!

Distorting the Word of God

In order for this collection agency to survive, some in today's ministry twist the word of God around. They do this because they love money, and therefore, they read the Bible looking for ways to acquire it. Sometimes Christians are told the following by pastors: "I don't need the money. Tithing is for your benefit so you can receive a blessing." These pastors rely on their own clever manipulations to provide for their personal comforts, rather than relying on God's ability to provide for them. Some even teach others to think and do the same. In Matthew 23:15, Jesus says, "Woe to you, teachers of the law and Pharisees, you hypocrites! You travel over land and sea to win a single convert, and when he becomes one, you make him twice as much a son of hell as you are."

If Christians do not give in the name of tithes and offerings, and obey new covenant commands instead, they can take away the power the pulpit has over them concerning their financial gifts. For instance, many pastors today have no problem telling Christians that not giving monetary tithes and offerings will result in a curse. For the Christian who understands his freedom in Christ, this threat of a curse has no effect. Free Christians can rest assured that the Spirit of God will lead them in what to give.

Some churches have put their hope in wealth, and as a result, they will do what ever they can to obtain money. They even collect monetary tithes and offerings as often as they can, and by any means necessary. However, the Bible says not to put hope in wealth which is so uncertain. Instead, Christians and the church should put their hope in God. Therefore, everyone should stop searching the Bible for ways to deceive people into parting with their money. Teachers and preachers, and anyone for that matter, should search the Bible for the truths that help everyone understand God's good and perfect will. The Bible has shown time and time again that God's will is centered on supporting one another. When people search the Bible with correct motives, and hold onto correct teachings, they will find the truth and the truth will set them free (Jn. 8:31-32).

Rules Taught by Men

In First Timothy, the Bible covers the love of money, and states that those who think godliness is a means to financial gain are the ones *robbed*, because they are robbed of the truth. God is *not robbed* because Christians do not give tithes and offerings, as is the case for the Jewish community under the law (recall Chapter 4 and Mal. 3).

1 Timothy 6:3-7
If anyone teaches false doctrines and does not agree to the sound instruction of our Lord Jesus Christ and to godly teaching,

he is conceited and understands nothing. He has an unhealthy interest in controversies and quarrels about words that result in envy, strife, malicious talk, evil suspicions

and constant friction between men of corrupt mind, who have been robbed of the truth and who think that godliness is a means to financial gain.

But godliness with contentment is great gain.

For we brought nothing into the world, and we can take nothing out of it.

Many believers are simply caught up in the commandments of men and tradition. The people doing the teaching will be held accountable. James 3:1 states, "Not many of you should presume to be teachers, my brothers, because you know that we who teach will be judged more strictly." Please refrain from teaching monetary tithes and offerings from within the local church. This teaching has turned local churches into collection agencies as opposed to households of prayer.

Unfortunately, some people may appear to be doing what is right by giving monetary tithes and offerings, but in reality, their hearts may truly be far from Jesus. Sadly enough, some of these people do not even realize it (for the Deceiver is hard at work).

Matthew 15:8-9
" 'These people honor me with their lips, but their hearts are far from me.*
They worship me in vain; their teachings are but rules taught by men.' "

There may also be some who lead the church and are very well aware of what they are doing. Manipulation, in such cases, is usually where they are most experienced. Some know the church is supposed to take care of the poor, but they want and use the money for themselves. These people have everybody's attention. All of the people look up to them, and everything they do is done for people to see. Some love the place of honor at banquets and the most important seats in the church. They love to be greeted in the marketplaces and have people call them Reverend, Pastor or Father. On the other hand, Jesus would refer to those whose hearts are far from Him as follows, "You snakes! You brood of vipers! How will you escape being condemned to hell?" (Matt. 23:33).

Matthew 23:27-28
"Woe to you, teachers of the law and Pharisees, you hypocrites! You are like whitewashed tombs, which look beautiful on the outside but on the inside are full of dead men's bones and everything unclean.

In the same way, on the outside you appear to people as righteous but on the inside you are full of hypocrisy and wickedness."

Christians should exercise caution when hearing messages on collecting their money. In addition, they should not let old covenant law govern what should be Spirit-led acts, especially in the area of giving. This causes misplaced self-confidence, complacency or even unnecessary burdens. This chapter shows that preaching monetary tithes and offerings is not 'ministering to society,' but is instead a 'menace to society.' Forcing a Christian congregation to obey old covenant law, or tradition, is a hindrance to the kingdom of God on Earth.

Matthew 15:6 KJV
... Thus have ye made the commandment of God of none effect by your tradition.

Support for monetary tithing comes primarily from old covenant law, and the money is often used for something other than truly loving thy neighbor. Therefore, giving in the name of tithing, is in fact today's 'lawful way to rob thy neighbor.'

Webb 3:8-9
Will a man rob his neighbor? Yet you rob him. But you ask, "How do we rob our neighbor?" By giving tithes and offerings.

You don't have the love of God in you - the whole nation of you - because you are robbing your neighbor.

Christians are urged to start loving their neighbor and to flee from the deception of monetary tithing.

Webb 7:21-23

"Not everyone who says to me, 'Lord, Lord,' will enter the kingdom of heaven, but only he who does the will of my Father who is in heaven.

Many will say to me on that day, 'Lord, Lord, did we not pay our monetary tithes and offerings, and did we not teach others to do the same?'

Then I will tell them plainly, 'I never knew you. Away from me, you evildoers!' "

Drugs, guns, lack of jobs, etc., seem like the main problems facing the world today. Monetary tithing, however, is public enemy number one as far as the needy are concerned! The less fortunate require some form of assistance, but many times the church neglects their needs while searching out new ways of collecting money for any purpose other than loving thy neighbor.

In many churches there is an over appropriation of money applied to traditional programs, and a small portion, if any, appropriated for those in need. The programs that are funded seem to be a financial strain on some churches. This debt causes some local churches to lose the focus of their calling or obligation, which is to love the Lord *and* thy neighbor. As a result, many local churches place little focus on helping the less fortunate. Instead, they concentrate on collecting money, even from the needy, to fund traditional church activities.

Christians should financially support the local church. However, the method used to obtain money in many churches lacks biblical support - that of monetary tithes and offerings. Christians must realize that the method of today's collection process is a waste of money. This waste results from giving under false pretenses and the misconception that Christians will receive monetary blessings in return - then your barns will be filled to overflowing. Christians cannot buy their way into a right relationship with God, and giving money to get something in return is not an act of faith.

The unfortunate reality is that the Church has fallen victim to the onslaught of capitalism. The yeast of profit has spread throughout the church. The result is the evolution of the never changing word of God - converting tithes, offerings, and firstfruit, into money. In a manner similar to God's people under the old covenant, Christians have developed their own righteousness based off the rules of monetary tithes. Many do this as opposed to understanding God's righteousness.

In addition, the misuse of the law of tithing has many Christians using it as a comfort device. This falsely assures many that they are doing what pleases God, when in fact, they are actually measuring up to the standards of men. For many Christians, the monetary tithe and offering seem to have replaced all other activities they should be doing today. In reality, tithing is really a stumbling block that prevents the will of God from going forth in the area of Christian giving.

Christians should not worry about rules taught by men by trying to meet their expectations. They are ultimately accountable to God, not to other people or other Christians. "Who are you to judge someone else's servant? To his own master he stands or falls. And he will stand, for the Lord is able to make him stand" (Rom. 14:4).

Romans 14:12-13

So then, each of us will give an account of himself to God.

Therefore let us stop passing judgment on one another. Instead, make up your mind not to put any stumbling block or obstacle in your brother's way.

These stumbling blocks include those items that interfere with appropriate Christian giving and include: giving in the name of tithes and offerings; giving performed under legalism; fear of a curse as motivation for giving; and standard based giving (based on a 10 percent minimum).

Christian responsibility is typically centered on the financial concerns of the local church. The problem of focusing mainly on the economic side of responsibility is the selective use of Bible passages read out of context - usually reading something into what is not necessarily there. This kind of teaching leads to a form of legalism when based on the old covenant law. This turns a group of Christians into an organization without regard to individualism and freedom.

The local church can take away a Christian's freedom in Christ when it controls any aspect of a person, especially in the area of giving. No organization, or local church, should regulate their members' thinking or actions to the point that the Spirit has little or no control.

Christians must advance beyond monetary tithes and offerings, which is nothing more than a fraudulent form of old covenant practices. The charitable heart, on the other hand, is led by the Spirit of Christ. Furthermore, Christians must rid themselves of false doctrine, and overcome the influence of money, if the 'poor among us' are to have a fighting chance.

Philippians 2:12-13
Therefore, my dear friends, as you have always obeyed - not only in my presence, but now much more in my absence - continue to work out your salvation with fear and trembling,

for it is God who works in you to will and to act according to his good purpose.

As believers, Christians must realize who is serving whom. Christians do not serve organizations, but instead, they serve God by serving others - *for it is God who works in you to will and to act according to his good purpose.* Organizations, on the other hand, serve the needs of its members, including the local church. Therefore, the local church should meet both the spiritual needs and the physical needs of its members.

1 Corinthians 3:10-15

By the grace God has given me, I laid a foundation as an expert builder, and someone else is building on it. But each one should be careful how he builds.

For no one can lay any foundation other than the one already laid, which is Jesus Christ.

If any man builds on this foundation using gold, silver, costly stones, wood, hay or straw,

his work will be shown for what it is, because the Day will bring it to light. It will be revealed with fire, and the fire will test the quality of each man's work.

If what he has built survives, he will receive his reward.

If it is burned up, he will suffer loss; he himself will be saved, but only as one escaping through the flames.

11

What Christians Should Be Taught

During the last four years, Pastor Tithe continued his traditional teachings on the monetary tithe and offering. However, his spirit became troubled by the departure of Mr. and Mrs. Burden from his church - most likely prompted by his teachings and by some of the decisions he made. After much prayer, Bible study and yielding to the Holy Spirit, Pastor Tithe realized his mistakes. In a sincere effort to right all of his wrongs, he began teaching a new message, starting at his own church, Tither's Temple.

A NEW MESSAGE: BEYOND TITHES AND OFFERINGS

"Good morning, Saints. How are all of you doing this beautiful Sunday morning? Blessed, I hope. I would like to start off by saying that today's message will challenge each of you to examine how you give, what you give, why you give, and to whom you give. Today's message will take a closer look at traditional giving and its impact on Christian responsibility. This message is a far cry from the one I preached years ago titled, 'A Return to Tithing.' Today's focus on the less fortunate will cause many of you to question what you may have been taught since childhood, not to mention what you have previously been taught here at Tither's Temple.

"This Sunday is going to be a special Sunday. Today's message is about meeting the needs of others. To that end, it focuses on a collection *for* God's people, not *from* God's people. This day is so dear to my heart that I am giving it a special name so that we may always remember it - Benevolence Sunday. The message for today is titled, 'Beyond Tithes and Offerings.' Let us pray.

"Father, first of all I ask that you forgive me for leading your people astray. I also pray that your people will forgive me for the error in my teaching and any undue stress or harm it may have caused them. Please open their hearts and minds to receive what you have for them on this day. I am praying that despite me, they will trust you, as they listen to you through this message. And Father, I pray that when everyone leaves here today, they will leave as changed individuals who truly understand the Christian responsibility of meeting the needs of others. Use me to teach thy people. In the name of Jesus Christ, I pray. Amen.

"Well, my Christian brothers and sisters, I have a lot of territory to cover today, so I will get right to it. A couple of months ago I had a dream about a character called Tithing Hood. Somewhat like Robin Hood who took from the rich and gave to the poor, Tithing Hood took from the poor and gave to earthly kingdoms. He took 10 percent of everyone's monetary income, claiming that according to the Scriptures, it was holy to the Lord. Once the money was collected, he took it to the local church, or what he told the people was God's storehouse.

"In this dream, Tithing Hood carried a shield, but it was not the shield of faith that extinguishes all of the flaming arrows of the evil one. This shield actually prevented the pain of the silent sufferers from penetrating Tithing Hood's heart! Not only that, but the shield had the image of a cross, symbolizing the church, overlaid with an 'S', creating the image of a dollar sign. This image was indicative of Tithing Hood's true character - one whose focus was placed on collecting money from Christians instead of meeting the needs of Christians.

"The Holy Spirit revealed to me that in the dream, I was the one called Tithing Hood! The Lord showed me that I was not a pastor, but a monetary tither in shepherd's clothing. He made me wonder if the people actually visualize a dollar sign on the top of our church building as opposed to a cross; as if Tither's Temple is just another capitalistic, money making business.

"The dream prompted me to seek the truth about Christian giving through intense prayer and studying. I asked God to lead me to a better understanding of what Christian giving is all about. Of course, my biggest source of guidance came from the Bible. But the Lord also led me to a book titled 'Beyond Tithes & Offerings.' I thought to myself, 'I do not need to read such a book because I know everything there is to know about the subject. Besides that, it was written by two unknown authors. What could they possibly have to tell me that I do not already know?' Well, the Spirit within me would not let me rest, so I read the book. As a result, I was astonished by my lack of knowledge in the area of tithing versus Spirit-led giving.

"Now that the Lord has revealed the truth to me, I must teach the truth about traditional giving and its impact on true Christian responsibility - not only for myself personally, but for the good of this local body. Based on what the Spirit has taught me through God's word and through this book, I would like to share three basic truths regarding Christian giving: 1) the freedom Christians have from the old covenant laws, 2) the true definition of tithes and offerings, and most importantly, 3) Christian responsibility.

"Some of us are bound by tradition and old covenant law despite the existence of a new covenant. This is largely based on my teachings. I am the reason many of you are performing old covenant rituals in new covenant times! My traditional teaching has made the word of God of none effect in many of your lives! Since I have done these things in the past, let me be the first to tell you what freedom is all about; freedom from the law, freedom from tradition, freedom from bondage, freedom from peer pressure, and yes, freedom from mis-interpreted teachings from pastors like me!

"The law, with all of its rules and regulations, was given because of sin. It was only to be followed until Jesus came, as explained in Galatians 3:19. First Timothy 1:9-10 also states that the 'law is not for the righteous, but for the lawbreakers and rebels, the ungodly and sinful, the unholy and irreligious; for those who kill their fathers and mothers, for murderers, for adulterers and perverts, for slave traders, and liars and perjurers, and for whatever else is contrary to the sound doctrine.' Wow! How many of you want to be in the same classification as adulterers and perverts? Well, this is for whom the law is made.

"As Jesus says in Matthew 5:17, He did not come to abolish the law, but He did come to fulfill it. He did this when He was sacrificed for us. In doing so, He released us from the old law so that we can do as Paul instructs us to do in Romans 7:6, and that is to live by the Spirit. Christ is the mediator of the new covenant. When you accepted Jesus as Lord and Savior, you became free. It is that simple! Once you grasp the true meaning of Jesus' death on the cross, you will understand that your freedom from old covenant rules came when you asked Jesus to be your Lord and Savior!

"Hebrews chapter 8 addresses the issue of a new covenant by explaining that a time was coming when the Lord would make a new covenant with the house of Israel. It would not be like the covenant He made with their forefathers when He took them by the hand to lead them out of Egypt. In other words, there will not be hundreds of laws written down on stone, scrolls, paper, or even computers, for the people to follow. This is because the Lord has promised to put His laws in their minds and write them on their hearts.

"This, along with the Comforter, is what guides Christians today. We cannot live by faith and follow parts of the old covenant law for righteousness and justification. As Christians, we have the Spirit, or Comforter, to guide us in our daily walk - not old covenant law. How can we fully walk in the Spirit while obeying the written law? Doing so defeats the whole purpose of the new covenant.

"Now that we know the freedom we have from the old covenant law, let us look at the rules that still have some of us bound - the laws of tithes and offerings that regulate our giving. Not only do I want to share with you that tithing is not for Christians today, but I am here to let you know what a true tithe is - and what it is not.

"The true tithe is holy unto the Lord. The monetary tithe is not.

"The true tithe is an edible substance that consists of food products that feed the one giving the tithe, his family and servants, the Levite and the priest, the stranger, widow, and fatherless. Today's monetary tithe does not feed anyone because the monetary tithe is not edible!

. "The true tithe always meets the needs of people. The monetary tithe does not. Instead, many churches collect additional money to meet the needs of others and call this a benevolence offering - above and beyond the tithe.

"The true tithe has not evolved into money. In fact, money, as well as a money standard, were evident in both the Old and New Testaments. Throughout biblical times, money was also used to purchase products, compensate people for work performed, used to pay taxes; but never was it used as a tithing substance unto the Lord!

"The true tithe and the true firstfruit are not equivalent, nor are they 10 percent of the money we earn from our occupations.

"And while we are at it, biblical offerings are sacrificial offerings, and we all know that the sacrifice of Jesus ended all sacrifices. The two monetary offerings mentioned in the Old Testament were collected to restore tabernacles and temples, which do not have any place within Christianity. And most of all, an offering is not something that is bestowed after a monetary tithe has been given.

"Tithes and offerings are a part of the old covenant law. Jesus freed all Christians from all of the rules and regulations under the old covenant so that we can live under the influence of the Spirit! We need to rid ourselves of those things which hinder our walk in the Spirit - including giving in the name of tithes. It is time to take off those 10 percent shackles from around our feet so that we can walk freely in the Spirit!

"I realize that one of my biggest mistakes as a pastor was teaching thousands of Christians how and why they should give tithes and offerings from their income to the local church.

"I taught the rich to tithe money; telling them not to build bigger barns for themselves because God may literally take their lives as stated in Luke 12:16-21!

"I taught the middle class to tithe money; telling them the windows of heaven only open up for those who tithe as found in Malachi 3:10!

"I taught the poor to tithe money; telling them they will always be poor until they learn to tithe!

"I indirectly taught children to tithe money; telling their parents to teach them to tithe at a young age so that they will not stray from giving tithes when they grow up!

"I taught the sick to tithe money; telling them that God will bless them with good health if they tithe!

"I taught the elderly to tithe money; telling them to tithe from their retirement income if they want to continue living a long and prosperous life!

"I even taught that people will be cursed for not tithing, but now I know better. Not only did Jesus become sin for us, according to Galatians 3:13, He also became a curse for us. Therefore, we can no longer be cursed for not obeying the law!

"It is sad to say, but I must admit that some of the people I encouraged to give 10 percent of their income to the local church, were the very ones who should have received money from the local church. A case in point is the Blessed family. A few years ago, when they were known as the Burdens, they were in need of financial assistance. Instead of helping them, which both I and the church were fully capable of doing, I prayed for them, insisted that they continue to tithe, and then I sent them on their way. I saw a need, but because I was blinded by contemporary tithing practices based on one way giving, I did not fulfill the need. As a result, they experienced financial hardship.

"As you can see, focusing on monetary tithes and offerings day in and day out has caused us to forget the weightier matters of our Christian calling as found in Matthew 22:37-40 - to love your neighbor as yourself. Perhaps the biggest lesson I have learned during the past two months of praying and studying is that we have forgotten the poor among us. That brings me to the final point of the day, which is Christian responsibility.

"What I have been teaching about tithing actually prevents true Christian giving. True Christian giving is not centered on a regulated amount of money each of you must give to the local church. True Christian giving is Spirit-led giving. Spirit-led giving will ensure that the needs of others are met. In addition, Spirit-led giving will not allow the needs of the church to be neglected. We are charged to do as Paul commands in Romans 12:2, which is to be transformed by the renewing of our minds according to the gospel of Christ; that is, if we are to truly give in the name of Jesus.

"Have you ever wondered why Jesus said the second greatest commandment is to love thy neighbor as thyself? Have you ever wondered why He said that the second command is like the first - to love the Lord with all your heart? The reality is, in order to show true love for the Lord, you must actually take care of your neighbor. Just as the writer wanted to know in 1 John 3:17, I want to know how the love of God can be in you if when you see your brother in need and you have what he needs, you do nothing to help him? In order to truly love thy neighbor, the new covenant makes it clear in the book of James that one must do so with deeds, not only with words. Do not pray for your brother, like I did, and tell him to 'go, I wish you well, and keep warm and well fed' when you have what he needs. This is a clear example of what not to do.

"We also need to stop looking for a blessing when we give. In fact, we need to look for the opportunity to *be* a blessing to others. This is accomplished when we are willing to give freely from what we have to those who need it. When you decide to be a blessing to someone else, do not limit yourself as to what, how, how much, when, and to whom you bestow this charitable act.

"This may be a revelation to some, but let me be the first to tell you that giving is not limited to just money! The Bible instructs us to give from what we have, not from what we do not have. As stated in 2 Corinthians 8:14, it is from our plenty that we are to supply what others need! If you have plenty of food, then supply the one who is hungry with some of your food. Jesus said Himself that if you have two coats and your brother has none, give him one. This is true giving because it is focused on the needs of others. By the way, if you give money to this church, do not expect your bank account to soon be overflowing. If you do, then you are giving with the wrong motivation. Christians should give because they have already been blessed or want to simply be a blessing to someone else.

"Furthermore, do not limit how much you give out of your material or monetary possessions based on some rule.

Determine for yourself, through the inspiration of the Holy Spirit, what you can give and then it will not be given grudgingly. The Bible teaches us to decide from the heart what to give, not grudgingly, nor because we are told to, for as we see in 2 Corinthians 9:7, God loves a cheerful giver. If your giving is based on rules, then you are no better off than the Pharisees, whom Jesus in the book of Matthew called hypocrites, snakes, and vipers. True blessings only come when you give freely.

"Christian giving should be performed out of love. God teaches us in 1 John 4:21 that whoever loves him must also love his brother. We show our love by giving to our brother in need. It follows, then, that the love of Christ and giving to one another go hand in hand. This giving out of love does not include counterfeit tithes and offerings, i.e., tithes, offerings, and firstfruits that are converted into money and subsequently given to the local church. We need to realize that the biblical tithes and offerings never evolved into a monetary tithe and one combined monetary offering, nor did the storehouse evolve into the local church.

"In order for our priorities to be in line with the gospel of Christ, we must plot a course beyond tithes and offerings.

"In order for Christians to *walk* by faith, we must *travel* beyond tithes and offerings!

"In order for Christians to *have faith* greater than a mustard seed, or even like that of Abraham, we must *demonstrate faith* beyond tithes and offerings!

"In order for Christians to *run* the race for Christ, we must *dash* beyond tithes and offerings!

"In order to *see* blessings materialize in our lives, we must *look* beyond tithes and offerings!

"In order for our giving to truly *surpass* that of the Pharisees, we must *progress* beyond tithes and offerings!

"In order for Christian giving to *ascend* to a higher level, we must *rise* beyond tithes and offerings!

"In order for Christians to *mature* in the grace of giving, we must *advance* beyond tithes and offerings!

"In order for Christians to meet the needs of the poor among us, we must be delivered from tithes and offerings and thus, begin to further the kingdom of God on Earth through Spirit-led giving!

"Once we, as Christians, realize that we are under a new covenant, and therefore, beyond tithes and offerings, we can then call our giving what it really is - an act of grace! Telling ourselves the truth about giving is the beginning of the end of confusion. To grow in the Lord, Christians must free their acts of grace from the rules under the old covenant. If they do not, they are actually trying to describe in detail the gift of giving through these rituals. However, in 2 Corinthians 9:15, Paul called it an indescribable gift.

"My prayer is for all of us to be one in heart and mind just like the early church believers. In Acts 4:32-35 we see how they shared everything they had and no needy persons were among them! In order for today's church to return to the giving ways of the early church, where giving was alive and well, we must call Christian giving what it is - an act of grace!

"If you want to be free from old covenant rules and regulations, and live in the new way of grace, then call your giving what it is!

"If you are tired of performing modified old covenant rituals, and want to live in the new way of the Spirit, then call your giving what it is!

"If you believe righteousness is for those who believe in Christ, and is not attainable for those who obey the law, then call your giving what it is!

"If you are tired of being told you owe tithes and offerings as if they were taxes, then call your giving what it is!

"If you are tired of being told to bring your tithe into the storehouse, then call your giving what it is!

"If you are tired of threats of a curse for not giving monetary tithes and offerings, then call your giving what it is!

"If you want to give out of the desire of your heart, and according to your ability, then call your giving what it is!

"If you believe your plenty should supply the needs of others, then call your giving what it is!

"If you want to test your own actions without comparing them to others, then call your giving what it is!

"If you were called to be free and want to use your freedom to serve, then call your giving what it is!

"If your giving is a result of the surpassing grace God has given you, then call your giving what it is!

"If you want to excel in the grace of giving, then you must call your giving what it is!

"We must perform true acts of grace in order to support our neighbor and the church. In order to support one another according to God's will, we must first stop disguising our giving and start calling it what it is - an act of grace!

"I was sorely lacking in regard to grace giving, and at this point, I must apologize.

"I must apologize for countless 'Tithing Hoods' I have created; teaching them about the traditional monetary tithe.

"I must apologize for my teachings that resulted in many being neglected during their time of need.

"I must apologize for all the time I spent praying instead of actually meeting people's needs.

"I must apologize to those who I deemed disobedient for not tithing.

"I must apologize for creating a new righteousness based on the monetary tithe.

"I must apologize for creating a new faith based on dollars and cents and not the Gospel of Christ.

"I must apologize for letting the love of money spread throughout this church.

"I must apologize for not responding to the important calling to love thy neighbor. A pastor is like a shepherd - he should take care of his flock. I did not take care of my flock and therefore, I was not the pastor I should have been. I truly pray that you all will accept my heartfelt apology.

"It is time for me to bring this message to a close. You have been told plenty of things today, and I am sure I have used up my time. Bear with me for a couple of more moments, please. I am almost finished.

"Many of you here know that what was said today is true. According to Romans 9:1, your conscience confirms the truth in the Holy Spirit, and the truth has been revealed today. Let God be true and every man a liar! Some of you will undoubtedly leave here the same as when you arrived. Some of you will probably leave here and not return. Some of you will still insist that a curse will come on me even though the curse of the law does not apply to free persons in Christ. For those people, all I can do is pray that you do what is right. For the rest of us, however, let us remember the words of 1 John 3:14: 'We know that we have passed from death to life, because we love our brothers. Anyone who does not love remains in death.'

"Christians should never be concerned about what others think - as long as what they are doing is in line with the will of God. We should not come together as believers and then let organizational rules prevent us from performing true Christian giving. So let us begin loving and helping our neighbors today! I truly believe that is what many of you really want to do!

"The good news is that we can rely on grace to perform the will of God in meeting the needs of our neighbors. Philippians 4:13 says, 'I can do everything through him who gives me strength.' Christians are required to be strong in the Lord, and in the power of His might and to be strong in the grace which is in Christ Jesus! In addition, Ephesians 3:16 says we are 'strengthened with might by his Spirit in the inner man!'

"As it says in 1 Corinthians 15:57, God has already given us the victory through our Lord, Jesus Christ, so we need to start acting like it! We need to pick up our weapon - the weapon of giving. Satan has no defense against this! Let us make it a personal goal of ours, as believers, to help as many as we can. For in Galatians 6:9-10 Paul instructs us 'to not become weary in doing good, for at the proper time we will reap a harvest if we do not give up. Therefore as we have opportunity, let us do good to all people, especially to those who belong to the family of believers.' And in doing so, we can begin to 'praise' our way out of the terrible situations we are in! We can praise our way out of the drug use situation! We can praise our way out of the hunger situation! We can praise our way out of the homeless situation! You can say amen if you want to! As Matthew 5:13-16 says, let us be the salt of the earth and the light of the world by letting our light shine before men! Let us show every one the love of God Almighty!

"Allowing the Spirit of God to move through us, we can collectively say from the innermost part of our hearts, 'Your

kingdom come, your will be done! On earth as it is in heaven!'
For we know it is not about what we can do, but it is about
what God can do through us! Amen! Then and only then can
we truly lift up holy hands, magnify His name, and worship
Christ the Lord! Then all of us - whether we were once hungry,
desperate, naked, homeless, blind, without hope, having little,
or having much - can sing on one accord:

"To God be the glory,
To God be the glory,
To God be the glory
For the things he has done!"

A NEW CHURCH: THE GOOD SAMARITAN CHURCH

Soon after Pastor Tithe preached the message, "Beyond
Tithes and Offerings," he conducted a two-month series on
Christian responsibility. The classes were appropriately
named, "Tither's Anonymous," because the pastor felt he had
produced many tithaholics under his old teachings. In fact, he
was the first one to stand up and jokingly admit, "My name is
Rev. Dr. Pastor Tithe, and I am a tithaholic!" In these classes,
he explained that he wanted to change the present church
doctrine on tithing to reflect what Jesus had intended for his
new bride, the church. During this two month period, he
focused on the indescribable gift of grace giving and how it
promotes taking care of the needy.

As a result of the classes, a drastic change overcomes
Tither's Temple. Now the number one priority of the church is
to meet the needs of others. Consequently, Tither's Temple is
now known as The Good Samaritan Church and Pastor Tithe
is now known as Pastor Benevolence. Not only that, but the
church moved from Tenth and Firstfruit to a new location at
the heart of Benevolence Boulevard, near the intersection of
Burden Avenue.

Many changes are taking place inside the church as well.
First and foremost, tithing envelopes are no longer handed out
since the true tithe cannot fit in one! The new envelopes are

simply labeled, "Donations." Also, offering plates cease to be passed around the church. Instead, members of the congregation place their donations in a basket at the beginning or end of each service. No stipulations are put on when or how much to give. The parishioners are simply encouraged to let the Spirit guide their giving.

Many benevolence programs are now in effect at The Good Samaritan Church. Members are now able to donate money for the needy on a weekly basis. They are instructed to give only what they are able to give - out of their abundance. A food and clothing program also exist. This makes it possible for those who do not have extra money to donate something else, such as any extra clothing or food they may have. In addition, a hospitality program is included as a part of the benevolence ministry. For this program, those who have extra space in their houses are asked to open their doors as a temporary shelter for those in need of such assistance. Pastor Benevolence explained to his congregation that all of these programs are necessary if their church plans to tear down any strongholds that deprive the poor, and thus, give the poor a fighting chance to live a decent life.

During the classes, the pastor taught that in the Bible, when material blessings were given away, including money, it was no secret as to whom received the blessings. Therefore, the members of The Good Samaritan Church no longer simply give in faith and wonder where their donations are going. Contrary to the ways of old, the church's financial dealings are now a matter of public record.

The nature of the changes taking place at what is now called The Good Samaritan Church are only possible due to the studying of God's word. Because Pastor Benevolence heeds the words of the Bible, he is able to bring about a change not only in himself, but in the local church as well. He now teaches sound doctrine, especially as it relates to Christian responsibility.

As a result of the congregation's response to God's word, the needs of the church members, the needs of the local church organization, and the needs of the community at large, are starting to be met - all because they were able to get beyond tithes and offerings.

The 10 Commandments of
The Good Samaritan Church

✝ *Love the Lord your God with all your heart and with all your soul and with all your mind and with all your strength. In addition, Love your neighbor as yourself. There is no commandment greater than these.* (Mk. 12:30-31)

✝ *Provide for your relatives, and especially for your immediate family. If anyone does not do this he has denied the faith and is worse than an unbeliever.* (1 Tim. 5:8)

✝ *Therefore, as we have opportunity, let us do good to all people, especially to those who belong to the family of believers.* (Gal. 6:10)

✝ *Everyone should give what they have decided in their heart to give, not reluctantly or under compulsion, for God loves a cheerful giver. For if the willingness is there, the gift is acceptable according to what one has, not according to what one does not have.* (1 Cor. 9:7; 2 Cor. 8:12)

✝ *Therefore, he that has two coats, let him impart to him that has none; and he that has meat, let him do likewise. Faith without works is dead.* (Lk. 3:11; Jas. 2:15-17)

The 10 Commandments of The Good Samaritan Church
(continued)

✟ *When you see a person hungry, give him food: when you see him thirsty, give him something to drink: when you see a stranger, provide him hospitality: when you see someone naked, clothe him: when someone is sick or in prison, go visit him. Whatever you do for one of the least of these in Christ, you do as unto the Lord. This is the work of the righteous.* (Matt. 25:35-40)

✟ *Do not be hard pressed while helping one another. At the present time your plenty will supply what they need, so that in turn their plenty will supply what you need.* (2 Cor. 8:13-14)

✟ *Let us not become weary in doing good, for at the proper time we will reap a harvest if we do not give up.* (Gal. 6:9)

✟ *Let no debt remain outstanding, except the continuing debt to love one another, for he who loves his fellowman has fulfilled the law.* (Rom. 13:8)

✟ *You are not under the law, but under grace. Therefore, do not set aside the grace of God by obeying old covenant law, for if righteousness could be gained through the law, Christ died for nothing!* (Rom. 6:14; Gal. 2:21)

Personal Notes

Personal Notes

Personal Notes

Personal Notes

Personal Notes

Personal Notes

Personal Notes

Personal Notes

Personal Notes

Personal Notes

Personal Notes

Personal Notes

Bibliography: Sources Consulted

Achtemier, Paul J., Th.D., *Harper's Bible Dictionary*, (San Francisco: Harper and Row, Publishers, Inc.) 1985.

Avanzini, John, *John Avanzini Answers Your Questions About Biblical Economics*, (Tulsa, OK: Harrison House) 1992.

Burkett, Larry, *Giving & Tithing*, (Chicago, Illinois: Moody) 1991.

Burkett, Larry, *How to Manage Your Money*, (Chicago, Illinois: Moody) 1975.

Chayim, Chafetz, *The Concise Book of Mitzvoth*, (Spring Valley, NY: Feldheim Publishers) 1990.

Cunningham, Richard B., *Creative Stewardship*, (Nashville, Tennessee: Abingdon Press) 1984.

Enhanced Strong's Lexicon, (Oak Harbor, WA: Logos Research Systems, Inc.) 1995.

Good, Joseph, 4 tape series, *Tithes, Concepts of Biblical Giving*, (Port Arthur, TX: Hatikva Ministries) 1993.

Hastings, Robert J., *My Money and God*, (Nashville, Tennessee: Broadman Press) 1961.

Henry, Matthew, *Matthew Henry's Commentary on the Bible*, (Peabody, MA: Hendrickson Publishers) 1991.

Hopkins, John F., *Christian Giving*, (Hazelwood, MO: Word Aflame Press) 1992.

Jakes, Sr., Bishop T.D., *Tithing is a Matter of Love... not Law*, (Dallas, Texas: T.D. Jakes Enterprises) 1997.

Jordan, Dr. E. Bernard, *The Power of Money*, (Brooklyn, NY: Zoe Ministries) 1992.

Kendall, R.T., *Tithing, A Call to Serious, Biblical Giving*, (Grand Rapids, MI: Zondervan Publishing House) 1982.

The King James Version, (Cambridge: Cambridge) 1769.

Mays, James Luther, Ph.D., Editor, *Harper's Bible Commentary*, (New York: Harper and Row, Publishers, Inc.) 1988.

Moss, Roy L., The Lord's Portion, (Hazelwood, MO: Word Aflame Press) 1996.

The New Bible Dictionary, (Wheaton, Illinois: Tyndale House Publishers, Inc.) 1962.

The New International Version, (Grand Rapids, MI: Zondervan Publishing House) 1984.

Swanson, James, Editor, *New Nave's Topical Bible*, (Oak Harbor, Washington: Logos Research Systems, Inc.) 1994.

Vine, W. E., *Vine's Expository Dictionary of Old and New Testament Words*, (Grand Rapids, MI: Fleming H. Revell) 1981.

Walvoord, John F., and Zuck, Roy B., *The Bible Knowledge Commentary*, (Wheaton, Illinois: Scripture Press Publications, Inc.) 1983, 1985.

Wolfson, William, 17 tape series, *Giving, Receiving, and Prospering*, (Tacoma, WA: Bethel Christian Assembly) 1996.

Bible Verse Index

Note: Bold page numbers - key verse(s) in a separate paragraph.
Non-bold numbers - supporting verse(s) and/or reference(s).

13:14-15	**176**	37:29	51
13:15	128	38:1	**62**
17:14-15	173	38:1-7	62
20:24, 25	63	38:24-26	37, 47
21:10-11	161	38:24, 28	70
21:15-17	191	38:24-31	39
21-23	192	**Leviticus**	
23:16	**118**, 121	1	67
23:16, 19	125, 129	1:3	**64**, 66
23:19	118, **119**	1:16	67
25	60	2	67, 68
26:1, 7, 14	60	2:1-3	67
26:33-34	60	2:4	67
27:1-8	62	2:5-6	67
28:3	51	2:7-9	67
29	72	2:12, 14-16	67
29:10-14	69	2:14	118, 120
29:22-28	70	3	68
29:27	70	3:1	**64**
29:38-42	65, 67	4	69
29:40	69	4:7	73
30:1-6	72	5	69, 97
30:1-10	62	5:7, 11	**64**
30:7-9	72	5:11-12	68
30:11-16	47, 73, 97, 102	5:15	37, 40
30:13	36, 37	5:15-16	274
30:14-16	39, **46**	6:1-7	69, 97
30:24	37	6:8-13	67
30:25, 33, 35	51	6:10-12	**66**, 67
30:34-38	72	6:14-23	68
31:3-5	51	6:19-23	65, 72
32:15-16	187	6:24-30	69
34:19-20	128, 176	7:1-7	69
34:26	118	7:8	67
35:5	124	7:11-13, 15	72
35:5, 21-22	**40**	7:11-18	70, 71
35:20-29	73	7:11-21	68
35:21	70	7:12-14	70
35:25-26	51	7:22-27	65
35:31-35	51	7:29-34	70
36:6-7	244	7:32	70
37:25	**62**	8	72
37:25-28	62, 72	8:18-21	67

Note: Bold page numbers - key verse(s) in a separate paragraph.
Non-bold numbers - supporting verse(s) and/or reference(s).

Note: Bold page numbers - key verse(s) in a separate paragraph.
Non-bold numbers - supporting verse(s) and/or reference(s).

12:32	113
13:1-3	51
14:22-23	80, 81, 90, 120
14:24-26	90, **98**, 274
14:27-29	**85**
14:28-29	82, 86
15:1	89
15:11	1
15:19	128
15:19-22	**127**, 176
15:21	91
16:10	69
18:4	118, 120
21:16-17	128
22:28-29	40
23:23	69, 71
24:1-4	161
24:19-21	**87**
25:13-15	36
26:1-4	**122**
26:1-10	**17**
26:2	125, 129
26:10	118
26:12-13	85, 86, 87
26:12-14	**82**
26:14	**18**, 86
27:26	144
28:8	91
28:38, 42	95
33:17	128

Joshua

3:13, 16	91
6:17, 25	51
8:1, 27	163
11:14	163

Judges

6:19-23	62, 63
9:3-5	54
11:1	51
13:19-20	62, 63
16:1	51

16:4-6	54
17:4	51

Ruth

2:5-6	51

1 Samuel

8:7-8	104
8:13	51
8:14-17	**103**
8:18	108
8:20	104
9:23-24	51
13:19-21	**53**
14:31-35	63
14:49	128
15:22	**18**

2 Samuel

5:11	51
10:6	54
14:26	37
24:24	**40**

1 Kings

5:15	51
5:16	51
7:9-11	**61**
7:48	62
8:5-11	61
8:13	**61**
8:22, 54	62
8:64	**62**
9:25	62
10:12	51
10:15	51
10:28-29	41
16:24	41

2 Kings

7:1	41
12:1-8	73
12:11	51
12:12	51
12:13-15	53
16:10	51

Note: Bold page numbers - key verse(s) in a separate paragraph.
Non-bold numbers - supporting verse(s) and/or reference(s).

20:13	90, 91
22:4	51
22:4-7	**53**
22:6	51
23:7	51
23:33, 35	**47**
25:8-17	61
25:18	51

1 Chronicles

1:32	161
2:55	51
6:33	51
9:33	51
15:23-24	51
21:25	41
22:15	51
24:6	51
27:32	51
29:7	38

2 Chronicles

1:16-17	41
2:2, 18	51
5:12	51
7:13	95
24:6-9	46
24:12	51
31:5	118, 120
31:13	52
32:28	92
34:8-13	53
34:17	52
36:3	47

Ezra

3:6-7	53
3:7	51
3:10	51
4:12-13	47
7:24	47
8:27	38

Nehemiah

3:8	51
3:8, 31-32	51
5:4	47
8:1	51
10:35	118
10:35-37	**120**
10:37	122, 125
12:44	**119**, 125
13:10-12	13, **18**, 97
13:13	51
13:20	51

Job

6:2-3	36
31:6	36
38:22	91
41:6	34, 40

Psalms

15:5	41
33:6-7	91
62:9	36
135:7	91

Proverbs

3:1-2	13, **18**
3:5-6	13, **19**
3:9	133
3:9 KJV	49
3:9-10	**19**, 118, **124**
3:9-10 KJV	10, **124**
3:10	**125**
3:13-14	41
11:1	36
11:24	**19**
11:24-26	236
16:11	36
19:17	196
20:10, 23	36
25:4	51
30:6	113
31:19	51

Note: Bold page numbers - key verse(s) in a separate paragraph.
Non-bold numbers - supporting verse(s) and/or reference(s).

Note: Bold page numbers - key verse(s) in a separate paragraph.
Non-bold numbers - supporting verse(s) and/or reference(s).

Note: Bold page numbers - key verse(s) in a separate paragraph.
Non-bold numbers - supporting verse(s) and/or reference(s).

10:35	51
12:16-21	199, **236**, 291
12:22-31	237
12:32-34	**238**
12:33	233
13:22-30	200
13:24-27	**200**
15:30	51
16:10-12	**22, 272**
16:13	**273**
16:14-15	**273**
16:19-31	150
17:7-10	252
18:9	269
18:10-14	47, **268**
19:8	233
19:47	275
21:1-4	271
21:33	**23**

John

1:12-13	148
1:14, 18	105
1:16	213
1:17	**212**
2:21	106
2:22	106
3:3-8	147
3:16-17	144
3:16-18	105
3:18	144, 147
3:36	147
4:24-25	194
6:27-29	**207**
7:37-38	188
8:6-9	**186**
8:31-32	279
8:39 KJV	**158**
10:27	189
12:5-8	**271**
13:29	43
13:34-35	193
14:16	189

15:12-13, 17	193
16:7	189
16:12-15	**189**

Acts

2:1-4	189
2:14-18	189
2:41-45	3, **219**
2:44-45	**23**, 268
3:1-6	45
4:5	51
4:32-35	3, **23**, **219**, **267**, 295
4:33	213
4:34-35	45, 233
5:1-5	**23, 221**
8:17-20	**45**
9:39	51
9:43	52
10:4	**234**
10:6, 32	52
11:27-30	223
15:1-21	149
16:16	51, **55**
19:24	51
20:22-24	214
20:24	191
20:27	13, **24**, 191
20:34-35	235
20:35	**24**
24:16	190
24:17	195

Romans

2:14-16	**187**
2:25	159
2:28-29	**160**
3:19-24	**146**
3:22-25	136
3:24	212
4:23-25	**183**
5:1-2	**213**
5:15	212
5:18-21	139

Note: Bold page numbers - key verse(s) in a separate paragraph.
Non-bold numbers - supporting verse(s) and/or reference(s).

Note: Bold page numbers - key verse(s) in a separate paragraph.
Non-bold numbers - supporting verse(s) and/or reference(s).

Note: Bold page numbers - key verse(s) in a separate paragraph.
Non-bold numbers - supporting verse(s) and/or reference(s).

Note: Bold page numbers - key verse(s) in a separate paragraph.
Non-bold numbers - supporting verse(s) and/or reference(s).

Note: Bold page numbers - key verse(s) in a separate paragraph.
Non-bold numbers - supporting verse(s) and/or reference(s).